SHAREPOINT® 2010 BUSINESS INT
24-HOUR TRAINER

INTRODUCTION xxix

▶ **SECTION I   GETTING STARTED WITH SHAREPOINT 2010**

LESSON 1   Why SharePoint for Business Intelligence? 3

LESSON 2   SharePoint 2010 Technical Overview 13

LESSON 3   SharePoint Central Administration Overview 23

LESSON 4   Data Security Overview in SharePoint 2010 29

▶ **SECTION II   CONFIGURING SHAREPOINT FOR BUSINESS INTELLIGENCE**

LESSON 5   Creating and Configuring Excel Services Applications 41

LESSON 6   Creating and Configuring PerformancePoint Services
Applications 51

LESSON 7   Creating and Configuring Visio Services Applications 61

LESSON 8   Creating and Configuring PowerPivot for SharePoint Services
Applications 69

LESSON 9   Creating Your First SharePoint Site for Business Intelligence 87

LESSON 10   Configuring Reporting Services for SharePoint Integration 99

LESSON 11   Implementing Business Connectivity Services in SharePoint . . . 107

▶ **SECTION III   APPLYING SHAREPOINT 2010 BUSINESS INTELLIGENCE IN OFFICE**

LESSON 12   Developing and Deploying Excel Services
Analytics Applications 127

LESSON 13   Developing and Deploying PowerPivot
Analytics Applications 139

LESSON 14   Developing and Deploying Visio Services
Analytics Applications 153

Continues

▶ **SECTION IV   CREATING ADVANCED ANALYTICS IN SHAREPOINT**

LESSON 15   Implementing Data Refresh in Excel Services and PowerPivot . . 167

LESSON 16   Developing and Deploying PerformancePoint Analytic
Reports 177

LESSON 17   Developing and Deploying PerformancePoint Scorecards 189

LESSON 18   Creating and Deploying PerformancePoint Dashboards 205

LESSON 19   Developing and Deploying PerformancePoint
and SharePoint Filters 223

LESSON 20   Strategy Mapping with Visio and PerformancePoint 241

LESSON 21   Developing and Deploying Reporting Services Reports to
SharePoint 251

▶ **SECTION V   BRANDING AND MANAGING ORGANIZATIONAL
BUSINESS INTELLIGENCE**

LESSON 22   Theming and Personalizing Your Business Intelligence Site 265

LESSON 23   Using SharePoint Designer to Customize Master Pages 279

LESSON 24   Controlling Your Reporting with Versioning, Auditing, and
Content Expiration 299

LESSON 25   Managing Report Approval with SharePoint Workflow 309

LESSON 26   Setting Up SharePoint Search to Catalog
Analytics and Reports 319

▶ **SECTION VI   SCALING SHAREPOINT 2010 BUSINESS INTELLIGENCE**

LESSON 27   Managing and Optimizing SharePoint SQL Server Databases . . 331

LESSON 28   Tuning and Scaling SharePoint Service Applications 337

▶ **SECTION VII   IMPLEMENTING SHAREPOINT BUSINESS
INTELLIGENCE IN YOUR ORGANIZATION**

LESSON 29   Planning Your SharePoint Business Intelligence Project. 347

LESSON 30   Preparing Your Business Intelligence Implementation 355

LESSON 31   Creating Your SharePoint Project Checklist and Kickoff Plan . . .365

APPENDIX   What's on the DVD? 371

INDEX 375

SharePoint® 2010 Business Intelligence

24-HOUR TRAINER

SharePoint® 2010 Business Intelligence

24-HOUR TRAINER

Adam Jorgensen

Mark Stacey

Devin Knight

Patrick LeBlanc

Brad Schacht

WILEY

Wiley Publishing, Inc.

SharePoint® 2010 Business Intelligence 24-Hour Trainer

Published by
Wiley Publishing, Inc.
10475 Crosspoint Boulevard
Indianapolis, IN 46256
www.wiley.com

Copyright © 2011 by Wiley Publishing, Inc., Indianapolis, Indiana

Published simultaneously in Canada

ISBN: 978-1-118-02642-7

Manufactured in the United States of America

10 9 8 7 6 5 4 3 2 1

For general information on our other products and services please contact our Customer Care Department within the United States at (877) 762-2974, outside the United States at (317) 572-3993 or fax (317) 572-4002.

Wiley also publishes its books in a variety of electronic formats. Some content that appears in print may not be available in electronic books.

Library of Congress Control Number: 2011926194

ABOUT THE AUTHORS

 ADAM JORGENSEN, MBA, is an SQL Server MVP and the President of Pragmatic Works. He focuses on mentoring senior executives and technical teams, helping them realize the potential in their organizational data and improve operational execution. Adam is also a regional mentor for the Greater Southeast chapter of SQLPASS and the co-founder and editor of BIDN.com (Business Intelligence Developer Network). Adam co-hosts SQL Lunch, a weekly live presentation series on SQL Server technology, with co-author Patrick LeBlanc. He co-chairs the SQLPASS Virtual Chapter for Business Intelligence and serves on other industry groups and boards. Adam has authored several books, whitepapers, and publications on business intelligence, management, and successful program implementation.

 MARK STACEY has 10 years in data management and another 5 years in visualisation and information management. Mark has a vision for the enterprise - integrated information and data flow, collaborative and intelligent tools, and above all, productive people. He brings this vision about by using SharePoint, and he took one of the very first SharePoint 2010 for BI implementations in the world live.

 DEVIN KNIGHT is a Senior BI consultant at Pragmatic Works Consulting. Previously, he has tech edited the book *Professional Microsoft SQL Server 2008 Integration Services* and was an author on the books *Knight's 24-Hour Trainer: Microsoft SQL Server 2008 Integration Services* and *Knight's Microsoft Business Intelligence 24-Hour Trainer*. Devin has spoken at past conferences like PASS, SQL Saturdays, and Code Camps. He is a contributing member to the Business Intelligence Special Interest Group (SIG) for PASS as a leader in the SSIS Focus Group. Making his home in Jacksonville, Florida, Devin is the Vice President of the local users' group (JSSUG).

 PATRICK LEBLANC, SQL Server MVP and author, is currently a Business Intelligence Architect, trainer, and consultant for Pragmatic Works. He has worked as an SQL Server DBA for the past 11 years. His experience includes working in the Educational, Advertising, Mortgage, Medical, and Financial Industries. He is also the founder of TSQLScripts.com, SQLLunch.com, and the President of the Baton Rouge Area SQL Server User Group. Patrick is a regular speaker at various SQL Server community events, including SQL Saturday's, PASS, SQL Rally, User Groups, and the SQL Lunch.

 BRAD SCHACHT is currently a Business Intelligence consultant and trainer with Pragmatic Works Consulting in Jacksonville, Florida. He has helped numerous customers in successfully developing and implementing new business intelligence solutions into their organizations. He has presented at events, including SQL Saturdays, Code Camps, SQL Lunch, and SQL Server User Groups. Brad is an active member of his local SQL Server user group in Jacksonville, Florida (JSSUG). He is also a contributor on the community site BIDN.com.

ABOUT THE TECHNICAL EDITOR

 THOMAS LANNEN has successfully made the transition from a 2nd class Petty Officer in the US Navy (AM2) to Business Intelligence consultant at Pragmatic Works. He is a member of the Jacksonville SQL Server Users Group and blogger and forum poster on BIDN.com. Tom now claims Jacksonville, Florida as his home town but will be a NY Giants fan for life.

CREDITS

EXECUTIVE EDITOR
Robert Elliott

PROJECT EDITOR
Ed Connor

TECHNICAL EDITOR
Thomas Lannen

PRODUCTION EDITOR
Rebecca Anderson

COPY EDITOR
Kim Cofer

EDITORIAL DIRECTOR
Robyn B. Siesky

EDITORIAL MANAGER
Mary Beth Wakefield

FREELANCER EDITORIAL MANAGER
Rosemarie Graham

MARKETING MANAGER
Ashley Zurcher

PRODUCTION MANAGER
Tim Tate

VICE PRESIDENT AND EXECUTIVE GROUP PUBLISHER
Richard Swadley

VICE PRESIDENT AND EXECUTIVE PUBLISHER
Barry Pruett

ASSOCIATE PUBLISHER
Jim Minatel

PROJECT COORDINATOR, COVER
Katie Crocker

PROOFREADERS
Nancy Carrasco
Kyle Schlesinger, Word One New York

INDEXER
Johnna VanHoose Dinse

COVER DESIGNER
Ryan Sneed

COVER IMAGE
© Joseph C. Justice Jr. / iStockPhoto

ACKNOWLEDGMENTS

THIS BOOK WAS A LABOR OF LOVE. Mostly love but a lot of labor too. I want to thank the love of my life, Cristina, and my family for their never ending support (It's finally time for shushy). I also want to thank those on the Microsoft SharePoint team who helped us out with guidance and content reviews. I want to thank Robert Elliott, Ed Connor, and the whole team at Wiley for their support and guidance as usual on this title. I want to thank my author team for getting this title done even with the holidays, work, and family commitments. Writing a book is a process and usually involves begging a lot of forgiveness from those you would normally spend time with. I want to thank Brian Knight for his advice on any book I'm working on since it always helps. A special thanks to our technical editor for the long hours put in making sure we know what we're talking about and that we've communicated it effectively for the readers.

— Adam Jorgensen

I'D LIKE TO THANK ALL OF MY CO-AUTHORS FROM PRAGMATIC WORKS — it's been great working with you guys for my first book, an awesome experience.

— Mark Stacey

I MUST GIVE THANKS TO GOD, who without in my life I would not have such blessings. Thanks to my wife Erin who has had amazing patience during the late nights of writing, editing, and video recording. To our wonderful son Collin (aka Boy King) who will finally get his daddy back at night. Thanks to the group of writers — Adam, Mark, Brad, and Patrick — who all worked very hard, while missing time with their families too. Lastly, I would like to thank my coach, Phill Drobnick, for always backing me in my quest to be on the next US Olympic Curling team. Being a fifteen alternate is great, and I hope to break into the top five alternates before the next winter Olympics.

— Devin Knight

FIRST I WANT TO THANK GOD for giving me the abilities and knowledge to contribute all that I have to the book. Then I would like to thank my wife and kids. Life can get hectic sometimes and I really appreciate all the support that you all provided while I was writing the book. Thank you family for all your sacrifices. Next, I would to thank my parents for everything that they instilled in me that has attributed to a large part of my success. I would also like to thank my co-authors Adam, Devin, Marc, and Brad, who all worked hard to make this book possible.

— Patrick LeBlanc

I GIVE THANKS TO GOD, who has blessed me with so many wonderful things in life and who I would be lost without. Thanks to my grandparents, Donna and Edward, who have been such a great influence in my life. I would not be who or where I am today without their presence along the way. Thanks to my family and friends for all the support. Thanks to the co-authors for all the hard work and time away from your families. Thanks to Brian Knight for taking a chance on me and for all the opportunities I have been given. Thanks to Devin Knight for all the mentor time you have put in with me over the past couple of years. Finally, the makers of the cola beverage Mountain Dew for not allowing me to sleep until the job was done, and then for a while after that even.

— Brad Schacht

CONTENTS

INTRODUCTION   *xxix*

SECTION I: GETTING STARTED WITH SHAREPOINT 2010

LESSON 1: WHY SHAREPOINT FOR BUSINESS INTELLIGENCE?   3

  Kick Start Your Business Intelligence   4
    Financial   4
    Retail   5
    Manufacturing   5
    Healthcare   5
    Government   6
  SharePoint Features That Enhance Your Business   6
  Extending Office into SharePoint   7
  Customizing SharePoint 2010 to Match Your Company   9
    Security and Service Model   10
      New Architecture   10
  Try It   11
    Lesson Requirements   11
    Hints   11
    Step-by-Step   11

LESSON 2: SHAREPOINT 2010 TECHNICAL OVERVIEW   13

  A New SharePoint Experience   13
    System Requirements   13
    Key Servers and Server Roles   14
    Central Administration   15
  Say Goodbye to Shared Service Providers   16
  Improved Authentication Control   18
    Claims Based Authentication   18
    SharePoint Authentication   19
  Additional SharePoint Features   20
  Try It   20
    Lesson Requirements   20
    Hints   20
    Step-by-Step   20

LESSON 3: SHAREPOINT CENTRAL ADMINISTRATION OVERVIEW — 23

What Is Central Administration? — 23
BI Service Applications — 24
Basics of Site Management — 25
Try It — 26
    Lesson Requirements — 26
    Hints — 26
    Step-by-Step — 26

LESSON 4: DATA SECURITY OVERVIEW IN SHAREPOINT 2010 — 29

Managed Accounts — 29
Unattended Service Account — 31
Office Authentication Options — 31
Best Practices — 34
Try It — 35
    Lesson Requirements — 35
    Hints — 35
    Step-by-Step — 35

SECTION II: CONFIGURING SHAREPOINT FOR BUSINESS INTELLIGENCE

LESSON 5: CREATING AND CONFIGURING EXCEL SERVICES APPLICATIONS — 41

Creating an Excel Services Application — 41
Enabling Excel Services — 42
Configuring Excel Services Security and Authentication — 43
Reporting and Caching Options — 46
Try It — 47
    Lesson Requirements — 47
    Hints — 47
    Step-by-Step — 47

LESSON 6: CREATING AND CONFIGURING PERFORMANCEPOINT SERVICES APPLICATIONS — 51

Enabling PerformancePoint Services — 51
Configuring PerformancePoint Services Security and Authentication — 52
    Kerberos, Per-User, Unattended Service Account — 53
Reporting and Caching Options — 55

Try It   **56**
    Lesson Requirements   56
    Hints   56
    Step-by-Step   56

LESSON 7: CREATING AND CONFIGURING VISIO SERVICES
APPLICATIONS   **61**

Creating a Visio Services Application   **61**
Enabling Visio Services   **62**
Configuring Visio Services Security and Authentication   **63**
Reporting and Caching Options   **64**
Other Considerations   **65**
Try It   **65**
    Lesson Requirements   65
    Hints   66
    Step-by-Step   66

LESSON 8: CREATING AND CONFIGURING POWERPIVOT FOR
SHAREPOINT SERVICES APPLICATIONS   **69**

SQL Server and SharePoint Installations   **69**
    Standalone vs. Existing Farm   70
        Installing SQL Server PowerPivot for SharePoint   70
        Deploying the PowerPivot Solution to SharePoint   72
        Creating the PowerPivot Service Application   72
        Activating the PowerPivot Feature on Site Collections   73
PowerPivot Authentication   **74**
Testing Your Configuration   **76**
Try It   **78**
    Lesson Requirements   78
    Hints   78
    Step-by-Step   79

LESSON 9: CREATING YOUR FIRST SHAREPOINT SITE FOR BUSINESS
INTELLIGENCE   **87**

Understanding Web Applications, Site Collections, and Sites   **87**
Creating a Site in SharePoint 2010   **89**
Site Options and Templates   **91**
Business Intelligence Sites   **92**
Try It   **93**

Lesson Requirements 93
Hints 94
Step-by-Step 94

LESSON 10: CONFIGURING REPORTING SERVICES FOR SHAREPOINT INTEGRATION 99

Configuring Reporting Services for SharePoint Integrated Mode 99
Configuring the SharePoint 2010 Reporting Services Add-In 102
Testing the Reporting Services Configuration 103
Try It 103
Lesson Requirements 104
Hints 104
Step-by-Step 104

LESSON 11: IMPLEMENTING BUSINESS CONNECTIVITY SERVICES IN SHAREPOINT 107

What Is BCS? 107
Business Connectivity Services vs. BDC 107
Design Principles in BCS 108
Installing and Configuring BCS 108
Creating a New BCS List in SharePoint 2010 111
Try It 115
Lesson Requirements 115
Hints 116
Step-by-Step 116

SECTION III: APPLYING SHAREPOINT 2010 BUSINESS INTELLIGENCE IN OFFICE

LESSON 12: DEVELOPING AND DEPLOYING EXCEL SERVICES ANALYTICS APPLICATIONS 127

Developing an Excel Services Report 127
Data Sources 127
Creating a Data Source 128
Displaying Data 130
Table 130
PivotTable 130
Graphically 131
Deploying and Managing Excel Services Reports 132

Deployment Options 132
    Upload 132
    From Excel 132
Try It **133**
    Lesson Requirements 133
    Hints 133
    Step-by-Step 134

LESSON 13: DEVELOPING AND DEPLOYING POWERPIVOT ANALYTICS APPLICATIONS **139**

Choosing the Right Tool for the Job **139**
Developing a PowerPivot Report **140**
Introduction to Data Analysis Expressions (DAX) **143**
Creating and Deploying Reports to a PowerPivot Gallery **145**
Try It **148**
    Lesson Requirements 148
    Hints 148
    Step-by-Step 148

LESSON 14: DEVELOPING AND DEPLOYING VISIO SERVICES ANALYTICS APPLICATIONS **153**

Creating a Diagram with Data Connectivity **153**
Developing an Interactive Visio Diagram for SharePoint **156**
Deploying a Visio Diagram **157**
Try It **159**
    Lesson Requirements 159
    Hints 159
    Step-by-Step 159

SECTION IV: CREATING ADVANCED ANALYTICS IN SHAREPOINT

LESSON 15: IMPLEMENTING DATA REFRESH IN EXCEL SERVICES AND POWERPIVOT **167**

Implementing an Excel Services Data Refresh **168**
Scheduling a PowerPivot Data Refresh **170**
Monitoring Data Refresh Failures **172**
Try It **173**
    Lesson Requirements 173
    Hints 174
    Step-by-Step 174

LESSON 16: DEVELOPING AND DEPLOYING PERFORMANCEPOINT ANALYTIC REPORTS 177

Types of Reports 177
    Analytic Charts 177
    Analytic Grid 177
    Decomposition Tree 178
    Show Details 178
    Excel Services 179
    KPI Details 180
    ProClarity Analytics Server Page 180
    Reporting Services 180
    Strategy Map 180
    Web Page 180
Creating Your First Report 180
Extending the Report 183
Try It 186
    Lesson Requirements 186
    Hints 187
    Step-by-Step 187

LESSON 17: DEVELOPING AND DEPLOYING PERFORMANCEPOINT SCORECARDS 189

Terminology 189
Creating KPIs 190
    Filtering KPIs 192
Using Different Sources for Scorecards 193
Creating and Formatting a Scorecard 194
Try It 197
    Lesson Requirements 198
    Hints 199
    Step-by-Step 199

LESSON 18: CREATING AND DEPLOYING PERFORMANCEPOINT DASHBOARDS 205

Dashboards vs. Web Part Pages 205
Building a PerformancePoint Dashboard 205
Adding Interactivity to Your Dashboard 209
Try It 213

Lesson Requirements 214
Hints 214
Step-by-Step 214

LESSON 19: DEVELOPING AND DEPLOYING PERFORMANCEPOINT AND SHAREPOINT FILTERS 223

PerformancePoint Filters vs. SharePoint Filters 223
Common Filters 224
Time Intelligence Filters 225
Member Selection Filter 228
Named Set Filter 230
Custom MDX Filter 230
SQL Server Analysis Services Filter 232
Try It 234
Lesson Requirements 235
Hints 235
Step-by-Step 235

LESSON 20: STRATEGY MAPPING WITH VISIO AND PERFORMANCEPOINT 241

Why Do We Map Strategy? 241
Creating a Strategy Map 242
Deploying and Testing a Strategy Map 244
Try It 245
Lesson Requirements 245
Hints 245
Step-by-Step 245

LESSON 21: DEVELOPING AND DEPLOYING REPORTING SERVICES REPORTS TO SHAREPOINT 251

Creating a Report Using BIDS 251
Configuring BIDS for SharePoint Deployment 256
Deploying a Report from BIDS to SharePoint 257
Try It 258
Lesson Requirements 258
Hints 258
Step-by-Step 258

SECTION V: BRANDING AND MANAGING ORGANIZATIONAL BUSINESS INTELLIGENCE

LESSON 22: THEMING AND PERSONALIZING YOUR BUSINESS INTELLIGENCE SITE — 265

Themes in SharePoint: An Introduction — 265
Using PowerPoint to Create SharePoint Themes — 265
Navigating a SharePoint Site — 270
Try It — 274
    Lesson Requirements — 274
    Hints — 274
    Step-by-Step — 274

LESSON 23: USING SHAREPOINT DESIGNER TO CUSTOMIZE MASTER PAGES — 279

Introduction to SharePoint Designer — 279
Master Page Concepts — 281
Master Pages in SharePoint — 282
CSS in Master Pages — 291
Try It — 293
    Lesson Requirements — 294
    Hints — 294
    Step-by-Step — 294

LESSON 24: CONTROLLING YOUR REPORTING WITH VERSIONING, AUDITING, AND CONTENT EXPIRATION — 299

SharePoint Governance as Applied to Business Intelligence — 299
Reporting Lifecycle for Self-Service BI Environment — 300
Using Analytics and Content Expiration — 301
Try It — 304
    Lesson Requirements — 304
    Hints — 304
    Step-by-Step — 305

LESSON 25: MANAGING REPORT APPROVAL WITH SHAREPOINT WORKFLOW — 309

Introduction to SharePoint Workflow — 309
Building Simple Workflows for Report Approval — 311

Using Visio to Build Workflows   **313**
Try It   **315**
Lesson Requirements   315
Hints   315
Step-by-Step   315

LESSON 26: SETTING UP SHAREPOINT SEARCH TO CATALOG ANALYTICS AND REPORTS   **319**

Why Do You Need Search?   **319**
SharePoint Search Options   320
SharePoint Foundation Search   320
Search Server   320
SharePoint Search 2010   320
Fast Search Server 2010 for SharePoint and FAST Search Server 2010 for Internet Sites   321
SharePoint Foundation Search   321
Configuring Foundation Search in SharePoint 2010   322
Basic Search Administration   326
Security Trimming   326
Site Search Administration   326
Extending Your Search Configuration   327
What Do You Need from Search?   327
Try It   **327**
Lesson Requirements   327
Hints   327
Step-by-Step   327

SECTION VI: SCALING SHAREPOINT 2010 BUSINESS INTELLIGENCE

LESSON 27: MANAGING AND OPTIMIZING SHAREPOINT SQL SERVER DATABASES   **331**

Overview of SharePoint 2010 Databases   **331**
Types of Content in the SharePoint 2010 Databases   **332**
Optimization Techniques for Each Content Type   **334**
Try It   **335**
Lesson Requirements   335
Hints   335
Step-by-Step   336

LESSON 28: TUNING AND SCALING SHAREPOINT SERVICE APPLICATIONS   337

Tuning and Scaling PerformancePoint   **338**
Tuning and Scaling Excel Services   **339**
Tuning and Scaling PowerPivot   **339**
Try It   **340**
    Lesson Requirements   340
    Hints   341
    Step-by-Step   341

SECTION VII: IMPLEMENTING SHAREPOINT BUSINESS INTELLIGENCE IN YOUR ORGANIZATION

LESSON 29: PLANNING YOUR SHAREPOINT BUSINESS INTELLIGENCE PROJECT   347

Priority Drivers   **347**
    Why Are You Doing This?   347
    End Users Are Important   348
      Getting Stakeholder Buy In   348
      Where Is Your Data?   348
      What Is Your Budget?   349
      When Do You Need It Online?   350
    Systems and People   350
      Security   350
      Requirements   351
      Stakeholders   351
      Hosting and Infrastructure   352
      Integrated Systems   352
Try It   **353**
    Lesson Requirements   353
    Hints   353
    Step-by-Step   354

LESSON 30: PREPARING YOUR BUSINESS INTELLIGENCE IMPLEMENTATION   355

Infrastructure Concerns   **355**
Storage and SQL Concerns   **360**
Licensing Concerns   **361**
End-User Technology   **361**

Try It 363
Lesson Requirements 363
Hints 363
Step-by-Step 364

LESSON 31: CREATING YOUR SHAREPOINT PROJECT CHECKLIST AND KICKOFF PLAN 365

Round Up the Troops 365
Plan the Schedule 366
Checklist Creation 101 367
Putting Things in Motion 367
Try It 368
Lesson Requirements 369
Hints 369
Step-by-Step 369

APPENDIX: WHAT'S ON THE DVD? 371

System Requirements 371
Using the DVD 372
What's on the DVD 372
Troubleshooting 373
Customer Care 373

INDEX 375

INTRODUCTION

IF YOU'VE PICKED UP THIS BOOK, *SharePoint 2010 Business Intelligence 24-Hour Trainer*, you've decided to jump into one of the most dynamic areas of Business Intelligence: the exciting visualizations, collaboration, and data service capabilities built into SharePoint 2010 through its new service application architecture.

This book, then, is your chance to start delving into this powerful and marketable application. And what's more, this is not just a book you're holding right now. It's a video learning tool as well. We became passionate about video training a number of years ago when we realized that in our own learning we required exposure to multiple teaching techniques to truly understand a topic — a fact that is especially true with tutorial books like this one. So, you'll find hours of videos on the DVD in this book to help you learn how to configure, develop, and deploy solutions for solving Business Intelligence problems within SharePoint 2010. These videos are even better than reading about the topic alone and help demonstrate to you the various tutorials in the book.

WHO THIS BOOK IS FOR

This is a beginner book and focuses on covering enough administration to help you through the configuration steps, and leaves the heavy lifting to the other great heavy-duty administration books on the market like *Professional SharePoint 2010 Administration*. It focuses on introducing the large number of accidental SharePoint developers and administrators to the most common and exciting portions of SharePoint Business Intelligence. It also pulls out best practices and lessons from the field to help you make the most of your learning, prototyping, and project planning.

HOW THIS BOOK IS STRUCTURED

Our main principle in this book is to teach you only what we think you need to perform your job task. Because of that, it's not a comprehensive reference book but should blend the best of the basics with some great from the field style tips and tricks with real work best practices and proven techniques to help you deliver value quickly. The book blends small amounts of description, a tutorial, and videos to enhance your experience. Each lesson walks you through how to use a particular area of the new SharePoint platform and contains a tutorial. In this tutorial, called "Try It," you can choose to read the requirements to complete the lesson, the hints of how to go about it, and begin building, or you can read the step-by-step instructions if you learn better that way. Either way if you get stuck or want to see how one of us does the solution, watch the video on the DVD to receive further instruction.

WHAT THIS BOOK COVERS

This book covers SharePoint 2010 Business Intelligence and the setup, configuration, and planning that should go into a project focused on these topics. It covers Excel Services, PerformancePoint Services, Visio Services, and Business Connectivity Services, as well as Reporting Services development and integration into SharePoint.

By the end of this book, you will be able to take the hard work you've put in on the data model and ETL and turn it into dramatic visualizations and support tremendous ad hoc analysis for your power users. This is the type of deliverable that gets projects approved in our experience.

This book contains 31 lessons, which are broken into 7 sections. The lessons are usually only a few pages long and focus on the smallest unit of work in SharePoint 2010 Business Intelligence that we could work on. Each section has a large theme around a given section in SharePoint Business Intelligence:

- ➤ **Section I: Getting Started with SharePoint 2010** — This section covers what's new in SharePoint 2010, how to use the administration tools, and how basic security works.

- ➤ **Section II: Configuring SharePoint for Business Intelligence** — This section walks the reader through configuring the major service applications required for the cool projects you'll be building soon.

- ➤ **Section III: Applying SharePoint 2010 Business Intelligence in Office** — This section introduces how to begin developing SharePoint analysis solutions right from within Office 2010.

- ➤ **Section IV: Creating Advanced Analytics in SharePoint** — This section covers more advanced things like data refresh and extending the analysis to include PerformancePoint analytics.

- ➤ **Section V: Branding and Managing Organizational Business Intelligence** — This section introduces you to theming and customizing your SharePoint sites to match the look of your internal applications and environment.

- ➤ **Section VI: Scaling SharePoint 2010 Business Intelligence** — This section introduces you to scaling out these applications as your new solutions take off and grow.

- ➤ **Section VII: Implementing SharePoint Business Intelligence i n Your Organization** — This section helps you work through the process and mechanics of getting a project going on this new technology to show off your new skills.

INSTRUCTIONAL VIDEOS ON DVD

As mentioned earlier in this Introduction, because we believe strongly in the value of video training, this book has an accompanying DVD containing hours of instructional video. At the end of each lesson in the book, you will find a reference to an instructional video on the DVD that accompanies that lesson. In that video, one of us will walk you through the content and examples contained in that lesson. So, if seeing something done and hearing it explained helps you understand a subject better than just reading about it does, this book and DVD combination is just the thing for you to get started with this technology.

CONVENTIONS

To help you get the most from the text and keep track of what's happening, we've used a number of conventions throughout the book.

> *Notes, tips, hints, tricks, and asides to the current discussion are offset and placed in italics like this.*

> *References like this one point you to the DVD to watch the instructional video that accompanies a given lesson.*

As for styles in the text:

➤ We *highlight* new terms and important words when we introduce them.

➤ We show URLs and code within the text like so: `persistence.properties`.

➤ We present code in the following way:

```
We use a monofont type for code examples.
```

SUPPORTING EXAMPLES AND CODE

As you work through the lessons in this book, you may choose either to type in all the code and create all the examples manually or to use the supporting files that accompany the book. All the support files used in this book are available for download at `www.wrox.com`. Once at the site, simply locate the book's title (either by using the Search box or by using one of the title lists) and click the Download Code link on the book's detail page to obtain all the source code for the book.

> *Because many books have similar titles, you may find it easiest to search by ISBN; this book's ISBN is 978-1-118-02642-7.*

Once you download the code, just decompress it with your favorite compression tool. Alternatively, you can go to the main Wrox code download page at `www.wrox.com/dynamic/books/download .aspx` to see the code available for this book and all other Wrox books.

ERRATA

We make every effort to ensure that there are no errors in the text or in the code. However, no one is perfect, and mistakes do occur. If you find an error in one of our books, like a spelling mistake or faulty piece of code, we would be very grateful for your feedback. By sending in errata you may save another reader hours of frustration and at the same time you will be helping us provide even higher quality information.

To find the errata page for this book, go to www.wrox.com and locate the title using the Search box or one of the title lists. Then, on the Book Search Results page, click the Errata link. On this page, you can view all errata that has been submitted for this book and posted by Wrox editors.

 A complete book list including links to errata is also available at www.wrox.com/misc-pages/booklist.shtml.

If you don't spot "your" error on the Errata page, click the Errata Form link and complete the form to send us the error you have found. We'll check the information and, if appropriate, post a message to the book's errata page and fix the problem in subsequent editions of the book.

P2P.WROX.COM

For author and peer discussion, join the P2P forums at p2p.wrox.com. The forums are a web-based system for you to post messages relating to Wrox books and related technologies and interact with other readers and technology users. The forums offer a subscription feature to e-mail you topics of interest of your choosing when new posts are made to the forums. Wrox authors, editors, other industry experts, and your fellow readers are present on these forums.

At p2p.wrox.com you will find a number of different forums that will help you not only as you read this book, but also as you develop your own applications. To join the forums, just follow these steps:

1. Go to p2p.wrox.com and click the Register link.

2. Read the terms of use and click Agree.

3. Complete the required information to join as well as any optional information you wish to provide and click Submit.

4. You will receive an e-mail with information describing how to verify your account and complete the joining process.

You can read messages in the forums without joining P2P but in order to post your own messages, you must join.

Once you join, you can post new messages and respond to messages other users post. You can read messages at any time on the Web. If you would like to have new messages from a particular forum e-mailed to you, click the Subscribe to this Forum icon by the forum name in the forum listing.

For more information about how to use the Wrox P2P, be sure to read the P2P FAQs for answers to questions about how the forum software works as well as many common questions specific to P2P and Wrox books. To read the FAQs, click the FAQ link on any P2P page.

SharePoint® 2010 Business Intelligence

24-HOUR TRAINER

SECTION I
Getting Started with SharePoint 2010

▶ **LESSON 1:** Why SharePoint for Business Intelligence?

▶ **LESSON 2:** SharePoint 2010 Technical Overview

▶ **LESSON 3:** SharePoint Central Administration Overview

▶ **LESSON 4:** Data Security Overview in SharePoint 2010

Why SharePoint for Business Intelligence?

The question you might be asking yourself is "What can SharePoint do for my Business Intelligence efforts?" In reality you should be asking "How does the new feature set in SharePoint 2010 mesh with the ways my users want to analyze data and improve their understanding of their business operations?"

Let's examine that second question. SharePoint 2010 has a plethora of new features, as shown in Figure 1-1. The goal of this lesson is to introduce you to the areas of SharePoint that will catapult your Business Intelligence (BI) capabilities and give you a number of new ways for your users to analyze data, manage that analysis, and customize the delivery to internal and external customers. By helping you identify the questions to ask, and how best to think through the answers, this first lesson will help you recognize how SharePoint will complete your Business Intelligence solution.

Business Intelligence in an organization should be focused on the following:

➤ Increased insight into business processes

➤ Presenting data in a form the business users will understand and be able to apply

➤ Understanding of business performance based on consistent metrics

➤ Better communication between teams due to a single version of the truth

➤ Improved meeting efficiency because strong reporting and actionable intelligence drives better organizational focus

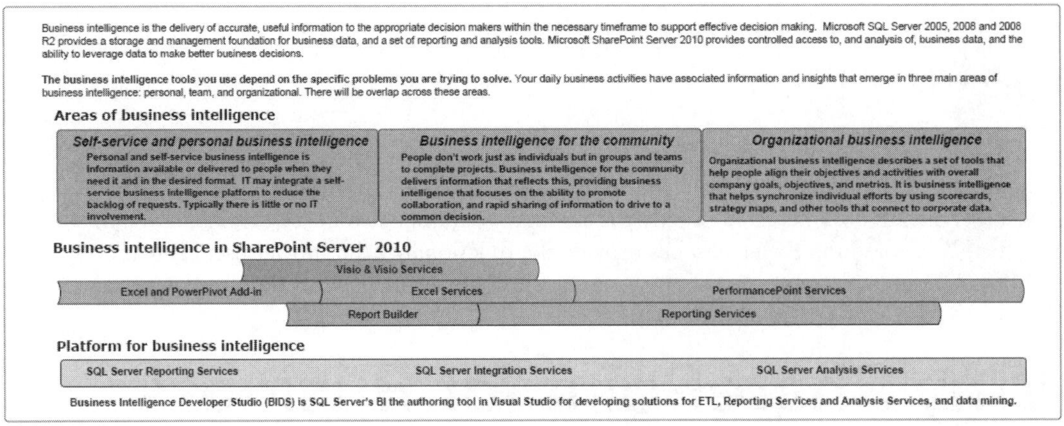

Business intelligence is the delivery of accurate, useful information to the appropriate decision makers within the necessary timeframe to support effective decision making. Microsoft SQL Server 2005, 2008 and 2008 R2 provides a storage and management foundation for business data, and a set of reporting and analysis tools. Microsoft SharePoint Server 2010 provides controlled access to, and analysis of, business data, and the ability to leverage data to make better business decisions.

The business intelligence tools you use depend on the specific problems you are trying to solve. Your daily business activities have associated information and insights that emerge in three main areas of business intelligence: personal, team, and organizational. There will be overlap across these areas.

Areas of business intelligence

Self-service and personal business intelligence	*Business intelligence for the community*	*Organizational business intelligence*
Personal and self-service business intelligence is information available or delivered to people when they need it and in the desired format. IT may integrate a self-service business intelligence platform to reduce the backlog of requests. Typically there is little or no IT involvement.	People don't work just as individuals but in groups and teams to complete projects. Business intelligence for the community delivers information that reflects this, providing business intelligence that focuses on the ability to promote collaboration, and rapid sharing of information to drive to a common decision.	Organizational business intelligence describes a set of tools that help people align their objectives and activities with overall company goals, objectives, and metrics. It is business intelligence that helps synchronize individual efforts by using scorecards, strategy maps, and other tools that connect to corporate data.

Business intelligence in SharePoint Server 2010

Visio & Visio Services

Excel and PowerPivot Add-in | Excel Services | PerformancePoint Services

Report Builder | Reporting Services

Platform for business intelligence

SQL Server Reporting Services | SQL Server Integration Services | SQL Server Analysis Services

Business Intelligence Developer Studio (BIDS) is SQL Server's BI the authoring tool in Visual Studio for developing solutions for ETL, Reporting Services and Analysis Services, and data mining.

FIGURE 1-1

KICK START YOUR BUSINESS INTELLIGENCE

To deliver on these objectives you need to examine your organization and your environment and decide where a product like SharePoint would be a good fit. Then identify what area would be the best fit for a prototype. When evaluating a new BI (Business Intelligence) solution or component, it's best to develop a prototype based on a set of data and reports that the business can use to validate and see the improved functionality over what it already has.

If an internal solution is not a good fit, you can consider implementing a solution that solves an existing problem. Since your prototype is using new technology and new processes you want to make sure you assess the risk appropriately. That way you can maximize your ability to impress management and gain adoption of your ideas.

Begin this process by reviewing a list of questions to help you plan your next steps. Important questions to ask include:

➤ Why types of information do you need to analyze?

➤ What types of analysis would you like to perform that may be difficult to perform now?

➤ Are you stuck in summary land without the ability to get the detail data?

➤ Where does Business Intelligence fit in your industry?

Some good examples of types of analysis depend on the type of industry. Some key industries are analyzed here.

Financial

Financial data is often very structured and comes from a variety of homegrown and industry-leading systems. Much of this analysis is snapshot and transactional, meaning that both point-in-time situations and real-time trends in business demand are important. Many firms need internal financial analysis to tell them how different account bases and books of business are doing. PerformancePoint is great for this because it can provide functionality for the users to go get the information they want and to go in depth and look at the underlying detail.

This capability is really useful to financial staff because they often need to analyze detailed data and look at trends over time. This applies for internal financial staff as well as investment or bank staff. People are not interested in only the summary data but also in the details that make it up. PerformancePoint and Excel Services provide the functionality that power users demand in order to see both summary-level data and provide important powerful visualizations to the customers and internal users.

Retail

Retail data is both significant at summary level and detail level. This is even more so during seasonal fluctuations when detail data is not as important and major decisions can be made with summary level data alone due to volume.

Most retail analysts benefit not only from detailed reporting but also from quick and concise ways to summarize it for presentation and external consumption. This data is often targeted at demographics, product analysis, market basket combinations (who purchased what combinations of items), and sales performance.

This data drives support for hiring, expansion, and stock performance decisions. It also drives product placement and store layout features. Visio Services is a terrific feature to employ to be able to tie data to a floor plan and show success or improvement needed based on estimated goal numbers in the form of a Key Performance Indicator (KPI).

Manufacturing

Manufacturing data is often about performance of a process, down to the individual steps of the process, the outputs of those steps, and the quality of the artifacts being manufactured or produced. Sometimes the waste products of any manufacturing process are more important to analyze than the products themselves. Consumption rates and percentages are common metrics as well. These items all play nicely into both an Excel Services and PowerPivot Analysis because they are usually very detailed and contain large numbers of rows.

PowerPivot for SharePoint 2010 allows you to access and analyze large amounts of data (in the millions of rows), which was previously impossible due to limitations in Excel. You also get to do this right through Excel Services because the Excel Services engine is what renders the PowerPivot workbook in SharePoint. You still get the power of Analysis Services behind the scenes and the exciting new features in Excel 2010, such as slicers and spark lines.

Healthcare

Healthcare data is some of the most disorganized data because it is largely dependent on manual entry from providers' locations. These providers are often paying entry-level workers to enter the data or it is scanned in and given a cursory check. Much of this data is massaged significantly to get it to align and provide value and needs to be handled carefully.

The new security model in SharePoint 2010 and its service applications will deliver a new level of Claims Based Authentication securing data in the most flexible and powerful way yet.

Government

Government data is often very denormalized and comes from a variety of systems. This is largely due to the serious lack of standardization between government organizations. Many government entities spend a significant amount of time just processing the data from other agencies to make sure it is in a form that is useful. Then many of the agencies need to turn around and output it for public consumption. Check out www.data.gov for all the free government data you could wish for. This is a great site for beginning to prototype your own solutions after this book.

Many organizations struggle with analysis in several common areas:

➤ **Be careful about getting stuck in the summary world** — Many organizations struggle with being able to drill down into the detail data because they report primarily at the summary or aggregated level.

➤ **Data from different systems does not match up** — Many firms store data needed for analysis of a single process across multiple systems in different formats. Business intelligence architecture should bring this data together and set it up for the types of analyses you can do in SharePoint.

➤ **Different groups writing their own versions of the same report** — This is the most prolific issue seen out in the world of reporting and Business Intelligence today. Many groups are looking at the same data and calculating things like profitability, turnover, inventory, and other metrics based on their interpretation, leading to inaccurate analysis.

SHAREPOINT FEATURES THAT ENHANCE YOUR BUSINESS

The process of making your business intelligent is not always easy but it starts with a combination of tools and techniques. Some other great texts are available that focus on the techniques for building, loading, and analyzing your data warehouse, so this lesson focuses on how SharePoint 2010 will help you get from just accessing your data to taking action based on what you see.

There are lots of features to highlight but before that, take a look at the characteristics of SharePoint 2010's features that help make your analysis actionable:

➤ Change analysis on the fly.

➤ Switch chart types and report formatting in real time.

➤ Drill though and Decomposition tools.

➤ Extensive customization capabilities, and many more.

PerformancePoint Services provides much of this functionality through some great features. Some of the features in Figure 1-2 are described in the following list.

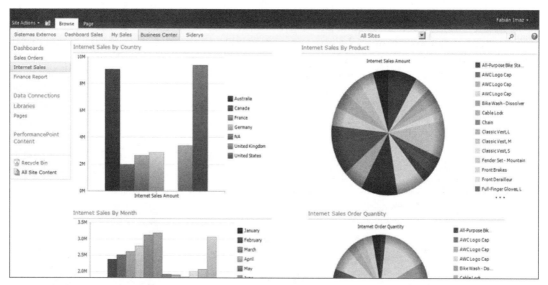

FIGURE 1-2

➤ **Analytic charts and reports** — PerformancePoint Charts and Reports are dynamic and designed to enable the users to change what data points they are analyzing in real time and remove the restriction of typical reports that tie the users to whatever the developer had originally placed in the report.

➤ **Drill-through capabilities** — Many BI suites struggle with drilling though to the underlying data. PerformancePoint Services in SharePoint 2010 simplifies this process by enabling this on all analytic content including charts and reports, and so on.

➤ **Analysis Services actions support** — Actions in SQL Server Analysis Services are a very powerful way to expand the functionality of analysis provided by a cube in Analysis Services. Many action types are supported in SharePoint 2010 through PerformancePoint and Excel Services.

➤ **Extensive filters** — PerformancePoint Dashboards cannot only be changed by contextual filters, but they themselves can be used as filters to drive changes to other items on a page. For example, if you have built a scorecard that trends sales by state and you click on Florida, the rest of the items on the page will now be filtered to show Florida, if you choose.

EXTENDING OFFICE INTO SHAREPOINT

SharePoint 2010 provides a new unparalleled set of methods to integrate Office into your analysis and Business Intelligence. Many of the reports created in a corporation are done in a reporting tool and then immediately exported to Excel. This can lead to delays and folks waiting on data because it needs to be in report format, when all they are going to do is export it directly to Excel.

To combat these delays, many organizations have moved to using Analysis Services to drive data analysis directly through Excel. SharePoint gives us the capability to extend that even further and share those workbooks through the browser with Excel Services. Excel Services is covered in depth later in the book, but this feature has been improved and extended in SharePoint 2010 to provide a new and greater user experience for working with and collaborating on Excel documents and reports. This functionality can be seen in Figure 1-3.

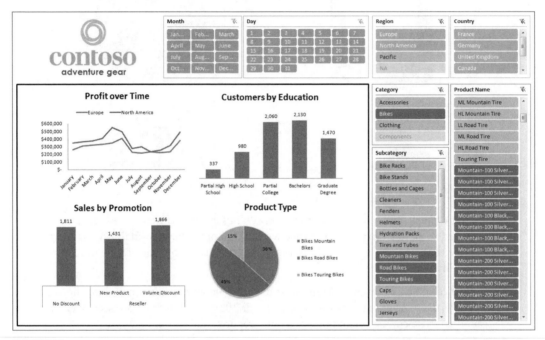

FIGURE 1-3

Visio Services is another exciting improvement in this new release of SharePoint. With this comes the ability to create strategy maps and data drive diagrams that combine visually impressive layouts along with KPIs and other performance indicators. These are created with Visio and PerformancePoint Services and can be deployed alone or in a dashboard. These maps can be quite powerful and used for process mapping to data center management, as shown in Figure 1-4.

FIGURE 1-4

CUSTOMIZING SHAREPOINT 2010 TO MATCH YOUR COMPANY

Customization options abound in SharePoint 2010 from the extensive options in PerformancePoint to customizing master pages and using CSS to standardize your portal to look just like the rest of an organization's portal. With new features such as improved Web Part pages and cascading style sheet (CSS) support, these environments are now customizable to the point of any other web intranet. The SharePoint pieces really plug in where you want them.

Security and Service Model

The new service model and the security changes to go with it can be a source of confusion for new SharePoint developers. This section will guide you through the ins and outs of how and why this architecture is in place and point you in the right direction to get acquainted with these new features.

New Architecture

SharePoint 2010 has some incredible new architectural features, which are discussed in administrative-level detail in *Professional SharePoint 2010 Administration* by Todd Klindt, et al (Wiley, 2010). This lesson focuses on the security aspects that will most affect your SharePoint BI experience. The new Secure Store Service is covered in this book along with the Unattended Service Account, but for this intro their primary purpose is to provide encrypted proxy account data access to your data sources without the need to create and manage many accounts for many users.

This new model provides the end users the ability to leverage one of these accounts or to use their own account if different permissions are needed. This works hand-in-hand with the new services architecture that provides for different accounts and application IDs (secured logins) to be used for each service or instance of a particular service. This is very powerful and replaces the less flexible Shared Service Provider functionality in SharePoint 2007. These new services are outlined in Figure 1-5.

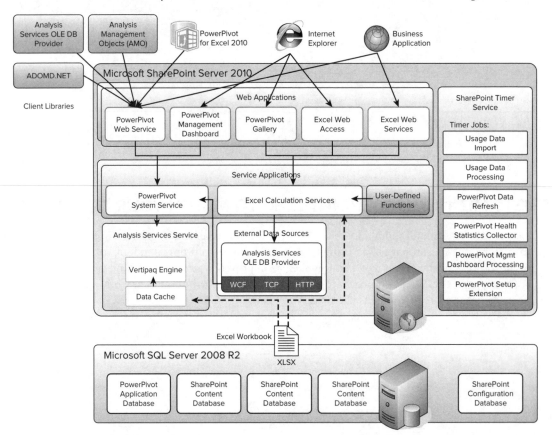

FIGURE 1-5

TRY IT

In this Try It you review the new features in SharePoint Business Intelligence that were discussed and explore where they might be a great fit for your organization. When you finish this lesson, you should have a good understanding of what areas of your organization would benefit from which features in SharePoint 2010 Business Intelligence. This will put you on your way to delivering the most value in the shortest amount of time.

Lesson Requirements

In this lesson you will be going through the sections and making a list of what features will be the best fit for your organization. You will then list out which areas of your organization are the best fit for which features so you can begin targeting them for prototyping. You will need an installation of SharePoint to review. This could be either in a server environment or locally on a development machine. All the features required will be present in either solution.

Hints

➤   Focus on your business and how your users look at data. This will drive how you begin to design your environment.

➤   Review the questions posed earlier in the lesson. These are common starting grounds for this type of analysis.

Step-by-Step

1.   Think about the different user groups in your organization.

2.   Put their names in the header columns in an Excel worksheet.

3.   Make a list of each type of analysis they do underneath their names. Examples would be

    a.   Detailed, Summary, Static Reports, Chart Heavy

4.   In the adjoining cells, place some notes about the current reports and analysis they are doing and any roadblocks that are slowing them down or causing this process not to work as desired.

5.   Underneath each analysis type list specific reports that would be good potential candidates for improving with SharePoint BI.

Select a report from your list to begin prototyping in SharePoint and make a list of where the data is. For this example selecting a report with a mature data source would be the best place to start. This would include an Analysis Services cube or data warehouse. These are typically the most straightforward to analyze for new users.

 Please select Lesson 1 on the DVD to view the video that accompanies this lesson.

SharePoint 2010 Technical Overview

This lesson is focused on updating you on the new and improved architecture in SharePoint 2010. These changes are the foundation for many of the features and functionality you will be configuring and developing later on in the book. This will not provide an exhaustive discussion, but only touch on the major points and try to clarify where the new architecture will affect your development process when working with SharePoint Business Intelligence solutions. For an in-depth administrative look at SharePoint 2010 check out *Professional SharePoint 2010 Administration*.

A NEW SHAREPOINT EXPERIENCE

The new SharePoint experience starts with the improved installation process. You will want to come up with a "Farm PassPhrase," which is required to add or remove servers from the SharePoint farm. This is a new requirement in SharePoint 2010. It is primarily used for basic encryption between member servers in the farm. In SharePoint 2007 this was done using the install account, but could be problematic if that user was not available later.

Additionally the new installer will verify that there are no GPO (Group Policy Objects) set ups in domain services to block SharePoint installations, or assign it to a predetermined OU (Organizational Unit in Active Directory).

System Requirements

It's important to remember there is no 32-bit version of SharePoint 2010 so the installation is available only in 64 bit. The server will need at least 4GB of RAM for development or 8GB of RAM for production, although more is recommended for optimal performance; 16GB is a better starting place for most organizations. Eight or more cores are also recommended although the minimum of four will work in isolated development environments. A total of 80GB is recommended for hard disk space, but this will vary widely based on your storage needs, service applications in use, and document and collaboration volume.

For the servers in the farm you will need to meet the following requirements:

➤ Database Server (one of the following):

  ➤ SQL Server 2008 R2 64-bit (recommended and required for Analysis Services integration with SharePoint, or PowerPivot in SharePoint)

  ➤ SQL Server 2008 (SP1) with Cumulative Update 2

  ➤ SQL Server 2005 (SP3)

➤ Front-End Web Servers and Application Servers:

  ➤ Windows Server 2008 (Enterprise, Data Center, Web Server with SP2) 64-bit

  ➤ Windows Server 2008 R2 (Enterprise, Data Center, Web Server) 64-bit

These are the basic requirements and need to be evaluated in the context of your environment. For full official requirements including hotfixes, feature packs, and more optional software, please visit Microsoft's TechNet site at `http://technet.microsoft.com/en-us/library/cc262485.aspx`.

Key Servers and Server Roles

In the previous section several types of servers were mentioned. These are shown in Figure 2-1 laid out in a typical enterprise deployment of SharePoint 2010.

Exhaustive descriptions of these servers are out of scope for this book, but here's a review of the important ones for introducing Business Intelligence to your SharePoint 2010 farm:

➤ **Web front-end servers** — Web front-end, or WFE, servers are commonly one of the first scaled out from a single server, or standalone, SharePoint 2010 installation. Many firms will see increased utilization around the rendering of SharePoint's web pages and this can be offloaded to WFE servers for processing. These servers can also sit outside of a corporate firewall to help deliver an extranet or public-facing solution for customer data or Business Intelligence.

➤ **Application servers** — With the new service application architecture, these applications can be scaled out like never before. Many applications within SharePoint, such as PerformancePoint, Excel Services, and Search can be used quite heavily in an enterprise deployment and may require scaling out.

➤ **FAST Search servers** — FAST Search is a technology acquired by Microsoft and integrated into SharePoint for enterprise search functionality. This integrates well into the SharePoint Business Intelligence stack and is explored later in the book. A full-featured search implementation may also require additional scale out including Crawl servers that walk the network identifying files in places that were chosen for indexing, and index and application servers. This is a significant feature and performs well if scaled appropriately.

➤ **SQL servers** — These are some of the most important servers because this is where all the content and configuration data is stored for all service applications and Central Administration.

➤ **E-mail servers** — These can be used for SMTP and e-mail processing when integrated with SharePoint. Many don't know that SharePoint can send and receive e-mail with the use of an

SMTP server. This is very useful functionality and enables features like being able to e-mail fields to a document library.

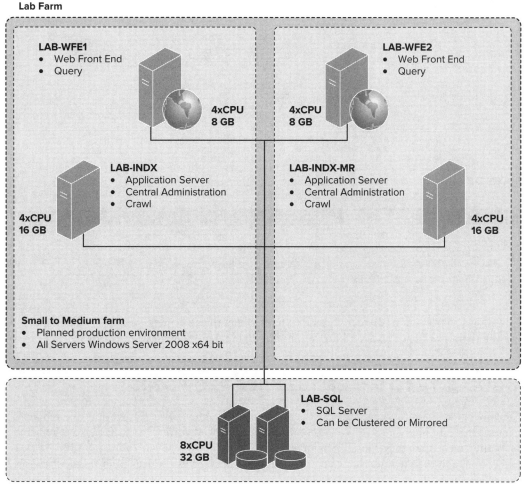

Lab Farm

LAB-WFE1
- Web Front End
- Query

4xCPU
8 GB

LAB-WFE2
- Web Front End
- Query

4xCPU
8 GB

LAB-INDX
- Application Server
- Central Administration
- Crawl

4xCPU
16 GB

LAB-INDX-MR
- Application Server
- Central Administration
- Crawl

4xCPU
16 GB

Small to Medium farm
- Planned production environment
- All Servers Windows Server 2008 x64 bit

LAB-SQL
- SQL Server
- Can be Clustered or Mirrored

8xCPU
32 GB

FIGURE 2-1

Central Administration

Because there were so many improvements in SharePoint 2010 it was time to revamp SharePoint 2010 Central Administration. Central Administration is organized more efficiently on the page, making the page wider but requiring less scrolling. Many of the common links are right on the front page and links are provided on the left for the major categories of settings areas. This makes finding what you need quick and easy instead of having to hunt around in SharePoint 2007. See the new design in Figure 2-2.

The new Central Administration has also embraced the Office Ribbon interface, providing a host of functionality right at the top of the page. See the ribbon in Figure 2-3.

FIGURE 2-2

FIGURE 2-3

This allows SharePoint to drive more functionality from the same page, without requiring the user or administrator to click back and forth to find individual or configuration options.

SAY GOODBYE TO SHARED SERVICE PROVIDERS

The new service application architecture is a major improvement over the previous Shared Service Provider (SSP) architecture in SharePoint 2007. If you worked with SSPs in 2007 you'll remember the scaling nightmare they caused. SharePoint 2007's ability to associate only one SSP to a web application, and then require that web application to get all of its services from that SSP, causes lots of problems for enterprise deployments.

This new architecture applies to all SharePoint 2010 editions including Foundation. Several areas of the application structure should be discussed because they apply to the configuration you will be doing later in the book. The next few points reference Figure 2-4.

➤ **Web Application** — This is the highest level of organization in SharePoint. It is commonly mistaken for a website, but a web application can contain many sites and workspaces. This is the IIS application that is created when you install SharePoint. A default web application is created for you, usually located at http://<ServerName>.

➤ **Service Application Group** — This is what gets associated with a web application. When you create a default web application, it is set up to use the default service application group. It's important to remember that the default application group has all applications contained in it. If the default group does not meet your needs, you can always create a custom group just for a particular web application. If you'd like to create a group you can reuse over and over with different web applications, you will need to use the *New-SPServiceApplicationProxyGroup* cmdlet.

➤ **Service Application Connections** — These connections are configured for you automatically but are nonetheless a critical piece of the service application framework. They provide the connectivity between the web application and the instance to a particular service application that is running in the associated service application group. To see them, you can go into IIS (Internet Information Services) and drill down into the SharePoint Web Services web application. You will see the service applications connections and their web services as shown in Figure 2-5.

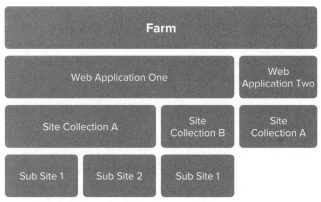

FIGURE 2-4

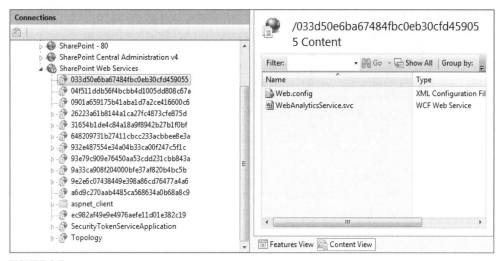

FIGURE 2-5

➤ **Service Application** — The service application is the main focal point of this stack. When you create a new service application, SharePoint automatically creates the accompanying services, connections, and databases. This is the user-facing portion of this stack visible within SharePoint along with the services that make up the service application in Central Administration.

➤ **Service Application Services** — These are the real powerhouses in the service application architecture. When a request is made to PerformancePoint, for example, it goes through all the connections listed previously and hits the service application. The service application facilitates the request, but all the work is done by the PerformancePoint service itself running on one or more servers in the farm.

➤ **Service Application Databases** — Not all the service applications have a storage requirement. When a service application creates a database you will need to supply the name and the rest is done for you. You can modify database options from Management Studio, but if you want to rename the databases, you need to do this with PowerShell cmdlets.

IMPROVED AUTHENTICATION CONTROL

This section covers the improved authentication functionality in SharePoint. The new Claims Based Authentication is discussed first, then we move on to a more general overview of SharePoint Authentication.

Claims Based Authentication

SharePoint 2010 uses a new authentication method called Claims Based Authentication. Its goal is to work with open standards and protocols so it will work with any corporate identity system, not just Windows and Active Directory. Identity is represented in token form and once that token is verified by some directory system containing user name and password information it will be authenticated. The best part about this new system is that it doesn't depend on just user name and password.

Claims Based Authentication (CBA) is a big topic and is explored only at a summary level here. CBA delivers a common way for applications to get identity information from users, no matter whether they are inside or outside the organization. That information is stored in a security token. This token holds one or more claims about the user. This is metadata about the user that may include user name, password, organizational information, location information, and device information; all to be used to ensure identification can be accomplished on any system, even those that require more than user name or password authentication.

Implementing this requires a few technologies including something new called Windows Identity Foundation:

➤ **Windows Identity Foundation (WIF)** — This was formerly called "Geneva framework," and it provides a set of application programming interfaces or APIs that help developers build applications to use custom security tokens and enterprise single identity models.

➤ **Active Directory Federated Services 2.0 (ADFS)** — This was formally called "Geneva Server," and provides WIF functionality and single sign on solutions. It combines Active Directory as the identity store and Lightweight Directory Access Protocol (LDAP), SQL, or a customized store to hold attribute information.

➤ **Windows CardSpace 2.0** — This is an identity selection technology that provides a solution for replacing user names and passwords by storing them in a visual information card.

You can see more details in the example of a Claims Based Authentication request in Figure 2-6.

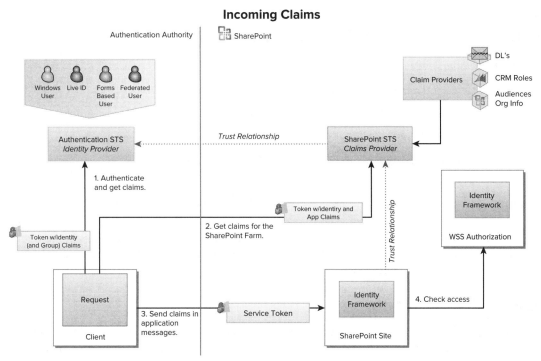

FIGURE 2-6

SharePoint Authentication

If you're not planning on using advanced authentication features and require a more standard "out-of-the-box" security infrastructure, Classic Mode Authentication (CMA) is for you. You have the option based on which tier of server and application you're working with, but overall most organizations try to steer toward one or another.

Classic mode refers to integrated Windows security and supports the following authentication methods:

➤ Anonymous

➤ Basic

➤ Digest

➤ Certificate

➤ NTLM

➤ Kerberos

ADDITIONAL SHAREPOINT FEATURES

SharePoint offers even more under the hood. These features include:

➤ Full administration support with PowerShell

➤ Improved SharePoint high-availability support

➤ Additional usability improvements throughout the environment

You get a chance to review these new features in the Try It section.

TRY IT

In this Try It you will explore the new SharePoint architecture by looking for things in the Central Administration control panel. You will also explore the new graphical interface features and see how they help you do things faster.

Lesson Requirements

In this lesson you test your knowledge of the new technical architecture with a scavenger hunt of sorts. You are going to identify services and applications within Central Administration and explore the new ribbon interface. This Try It is about exploring. You will use this architecture to create and deploy service applications later in the book.

Hints

➤ Remember that the applications and services can be accessed directly from the homepage of Central Administration.

➤ Use the ribbon interface to change the view of the list you're working with and to control your personal perspective on SharePoint options.

Step-by-Step

1. Start by opening Central Administration (Start ➪ All Programs ➪ SharePoint 2010 Products ➪ Central Administration).

2. Find the section of Central Administration that is used for managing service applications.

3. Once you are there, change your view using the ribbon interface.

4. Click Excel Services Application and you can see the types of options available under this new architecture.

5. Find the section of Central Administration where you manage the services on the server.

6. Once you are there, change your view using the ribbon interface.

Congratulations, you've just completed your exploration of the new SharePoint architecture.

 Please select Lesson 2 on the DVD to view the video that accompanies this lesson.

3

SharePoint Central Administration Overview

Once SharePoint is installed and configured, now may be a good time to look at the Central Administration Interface available in SharePoint 2010. This lesson provides a general overview of Central Administration. This overview includes discussions on how to navigate and use the Central Administration Interface, managing and maintaining a SharePoint site, and important Business Intelligence SharePoint services.

WHAT IS CENTRAL ADMINISTRATION?

SharePoint Central Administration is the interface that should be used by administrators to perform several common tasks. You can access it by clicking Start ➪ All Programs Microsoft SharePoint Products ➪ SharePoint 2010 Central Administration. On the Central Administration homepage you see that all tasks are divided into eight categories, as shown in Figure 3-1.

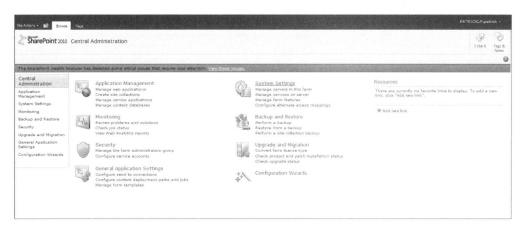

FIGURE 3-1

Directly beneath each category title are additional links to more commonly needed tasks. The categorization of the tasks makes it easier for administrators to perform common day-to-day setup and configurations. For example, you can start creating site collections or configuring service accounts directly from the homepage. In addition, you can start a backup, manage security, or monitor and review problems by simply clicking the corresponding link on the homepage.

BI SERVICE APPLICATIONS

As mentioned earlier, the Central Administration homepage has been divided into eight categories. Typically, when configuring your SharePoint site for Business Intelligence (BI) you will spend most of your time in the Application Management, Monitoring, and Security areas. If your SharePoint installation is farmed, you may also utilize a few options in the System Setting section. Nevertheless, you should take some time and review each category and become familiar with what's available in each.

In the Application Management section you configure services, web applications, and other items such as databases and site collections. Four subcategories are located under the Application Management section. Understanding the function of each subcategory and what you can do in each is pivotal in properly configuring your SharePoint site for BI. Following is a short tour in the Application Management area.

Click the Manage Services Applications link under the Application Management category. When you click the link, you are directed to a page that lists all the service applications that were available during the initial installation and configuration as shown in Figure 3-2.

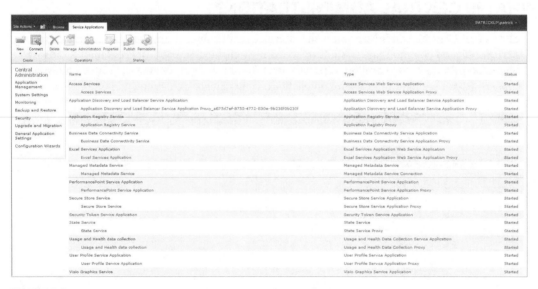

FIGURE 3-2

Among all the services that are available to you as part of SharePoint 2010, a few are vital to your BI and SharePoint configuration. Those services include PerformancePoint, Excel Services, Secure Store Services, Visio Graphic Services, and Business Connectivity Services.

PerformancePoint Services (PPS) is a management service that can be used by everyone in your organization to analyze and monitor business activities at all levels. PPS provides flexible tools for creating scorecards, reports, grids, dashboards, charts, and Key Performance Indicators (KPIs). Each of the aforementioned components provides you with functionality to interact with various server components. What makes PPS even better is that it was created with the end user in mind. You, as the developer, can bundle all of your built components into a dashboard and publish to a SharePoint page.

Excel Services is another service that was designed to help you and your organization increase use of Business Intelligence by data analysis. Using Excel Services you can publish Excel workbooks that have been created by you and your end users on a SharePoint server. Any workbook that is published can be managed and secured in a manner that meets your organization's needs.

Visio Graphic Services is yet another visualization service that is part of SharePoint 2010. Visio Services allows users to share and view Visio drawings. End users can publish their Visio Web Drawings to a SharePoint site. The only limitation is that you must be using Microsoft Visio Professional 2010 or Microsoft Visio Premium 2010.

The final two services, Secure Store Service and Business Data Connectivity (BDC) Server, both provide a mechanism for storing some secure resource. The BDC stores external content types and related objects. For example, it will store connectivity information or a named set of fields such as product. The Secure Store Service stores a set of credentials. It can use that account to associate it with an identity or group from an external system. Coupling the two, BDC and the Secure Store Service deliver a mechanism for authenticating users to external sources.

BASICS OF SITE MANAGEMENT

The Central Administration Interface provides a great central collection of tools that eases the process of managing your SharePoint site. If you are just starting your SharePoint BI initiative, the first step would probably be to create a site collection. To accomplish this, open Central Administration if it is not already open. Click the Application Management category. You are presented with the page shown in Figure 3-3.

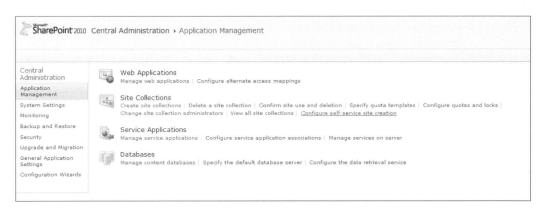

FIGURE 3-3

Under Site Collections click the Create Site Collections link. On the Create Site Collection page, you can create the site based on several available templates. If you click the Enterprise tab located in the Select Template section, you will be able to choose the Business Intelligence Center template.

This prebuilt site template takes advantage of many of the key BI elements of SharePoint 2010 as shown in Figure 3-4.

You can customize the site to include scorecards, dashboards, data connections, indicators, and many other BI elements. In addition, you can see examples of each of the elements by clicking the links that will direct you to more information about each. Libraries are also available that allow you to manage PPS and create data connections.

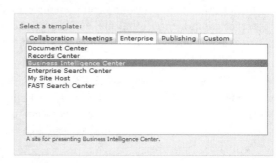

FIGURE 3-4

To create a BI site in SharePoint you must open Central Administration, if it is not already open. Next, click Create Site Collection under the Application Administration category. Then give your site a title and specify a unique URL for the site. Next, select the Enterprise tab in the Select a Template section and choose the Business Intelligence Center template. Finally, in the section labeled Primary Site Collection Administrator, type a site administrator user name in the textbox labeled User name. Click OK and your site will be created.

TRY IT

In this Try It you learn to create a Business Intelligence Site Collection.

Lesson Requirements

Prior to building your Business Intelligence Site Collection you should have a web application created and configured.

Hints

➤ Create Sites Collections is located under the Application Management Section on the Central Administration page.

➤ Ensure that you select the correct site template when creating the collection.

Step-by-Step

1. Open the SharePoint Central Administration Interface.

2. Select Home ➪ All Programs ➪ Microsoft SharePoint 2010 Products ➪ SharePoint 2010 Central Administration.

3. Click the Create Site Collections link located in the Application Management category as shown in Figure 3-5.

4. You will be redirected to the Create Site Collection page. If needed, change the web application to the one that has been created for your examples.

5. On the right, in the textbox labeled Title, type **24HourSharePointBI** as shown in Figure 3-6.

FIGURE 3-5

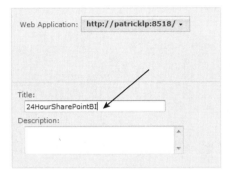

FIGURE 3-6

6. Type **24HourSharePointBI** in the textbox labeled URL.

7. Click the Enterprise tab in the Select a Template section and choose Business Intelligence Center as shown in Figure 3-7.

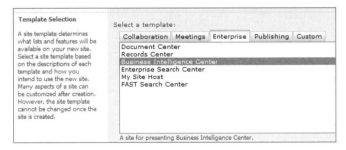

FIGURE 3-7

8. In the Primary Site Collection Administrator section type the site administrator in the textbox labeled User name.

9. Click OK.

10. You are redirected to your site collection as shown in Figure 3-8.

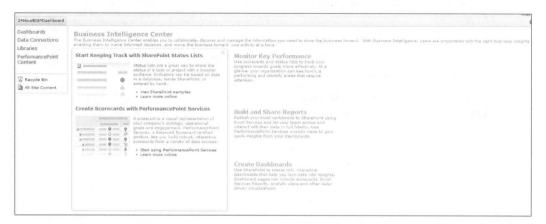

FIGURE 3-8

 Please select Lesson 3 on the DVD to view the video that accompanies this lesson.

Data Security Overview in SharePoint 2010

SharePoint 2010 has introduced new features to handle security. On the SharePoint Central Administration page is a section labeled Security that allows administrators to manage user access, user policies, and configure service accounts. You can view all the available options by clicking the Security link on the Central Administration page, as shown in Figure 4-1.

FIGURE 4-1

MANAGED ACCOUNTS

SharePoint 2010 introduced the concept of Managed Accounts. This provides administrators greater control over domain accounts that are assigned to services and components that are part of SharePoint. To configure the managed accounts, select the Configure Managed Accounts link under the Security category, as shown in Figure 4-2.

FIGURE 4-2

To add a new user, click the Register Managed Account link in the top-left corner of the Managed Accounts page and the dialog shown in Figure 4-3 will appear.

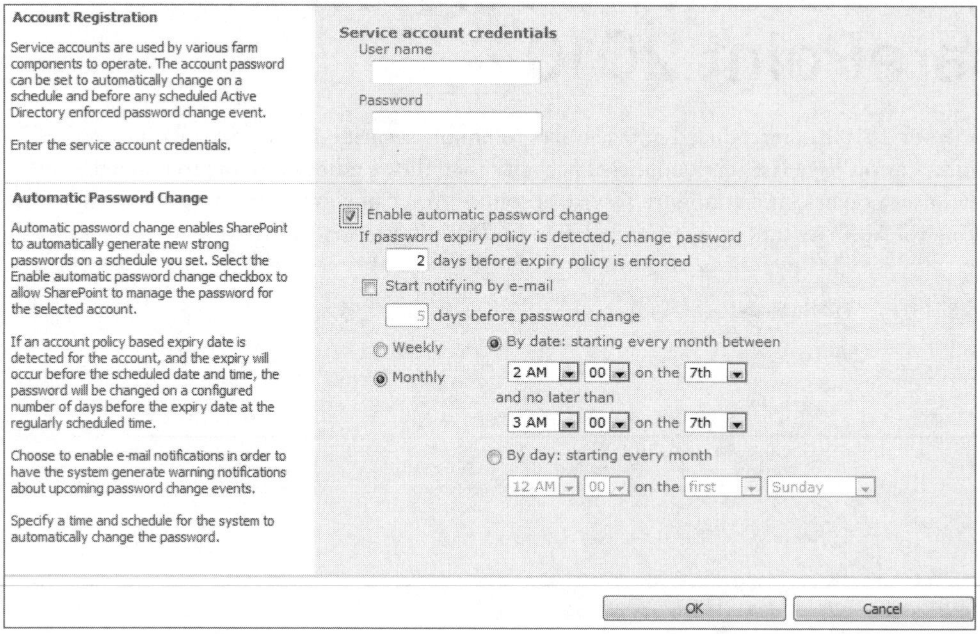

FIGURE 4-3

Enter the username and password for the user you would like to add. Click OK to add the user. You can also allow SharePoint to automatically manage and handle password changes for any domain account added as a Service Account. To do this, simply check the box labeled Enable Automatic Password Change. When this option is enabled SharePoint will generate a new strong password based on the schedule that you specify. In addition you can have an e-mail notification sent before the password is changed.

Please note that when you allow SharePoint to handle your password changes you will not know the password. Therefore, careful consideration should be taken when deciding whether or not to allow SharePoint to manage your passwords. If the password is changed in Active Directory you will be required to change the password from the Managed Accounts page. To change a password, click the Edit icon under the Edit column of the Managed Account list. Check the box labeled Change Password Now. You can either allow SharePoint to generate a password, set an account password to a new value, or use the existing password.

Finally, you can also remove the account from SharePoint by clicking the X in the Remove column of the Managed Account list. Prior to removing the account you must disassociate it from any SharePoint service. As mentioned earlier, if you allow SharePoint to manage the passwords for an account, you will not know them. Therefore, prior to removing the account you should change the password.

UNATTENDED SERVICE ACCOUNT

Before using PerformancePoint Services to access any external data you must configure the unattended service account. This is a single shared user account that is used to access data sources. Before you select an account you must ensure that is has access to all the data that will be used in your Dashboard.

To configure the account, click the Manage Service Applications link under the Application Management category. Select the PerformancePoint Service Application Service then click the PerformancePoint Service Application Settings link on the next page. On that page, as shown in Figure 4-4, enter a valid user name and password for the unattended service account.

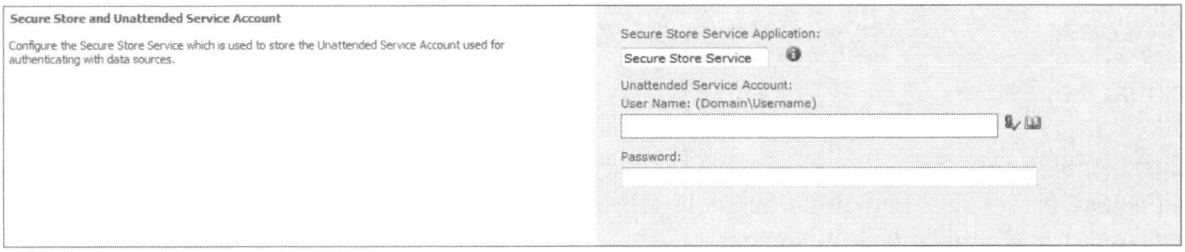

FIGURE 4-4

Accept the defaults for the other settings and click OK. Your account has been configured and you can now start creating and deploying your PerformancePoint Dashboards.

OFFICE AUTHENTICATION OPTIONS

In SharePoint 2010 all of the Microsoft Office products are more integrated than in any of the previous SharePoint versions. As a result, this can increase collaboration and productivity across teams and departments. Individuals are now able to communicate seamlessly through the use of several of the new features. Because this book is focused on BI, this section primarily discusses Excel integration. However, you should note that because all the Office products have the same look and feel, once you are familiar with Excel it will be easy to switch back and forth between the various Office products.

Importing and exporting Excel workbooks into SharePoint enables end users to share work and data quickly and more efficiently. You can allow your users to save workbooks from Excel or upload workbooks directly into SharePoint. However, if the data in the spreadsheet is from an external source, SQL Server, or Analysis Services, you must ensure that you correctly configure the authentication options.

When data is imported into Excel from an external data source you must ensure that the correct authentication option is selected. To import data into Excel, first open Excel then select the Data tab on the ribbon. Finally, select From Other Sources and choose From SQL Server. The Data Connection Wizard will start, as shown in Figure 4-5.

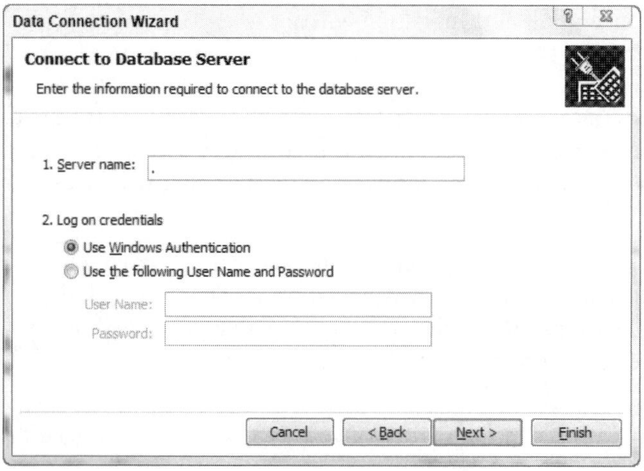

FIGURE 4-5

Enter an SQL Server that you have access to and select Windows Authentication or enter a valid user name and password. Then on the Select Database and Table screen, as shown in Figure 4-6, choose a database and a table that has some data.

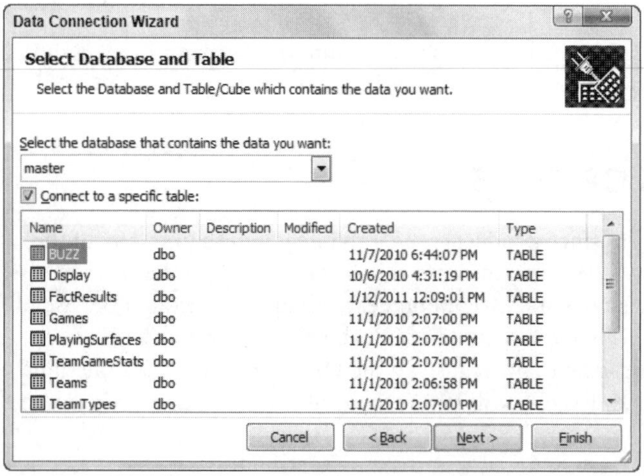

FIGURE 4-6

Finally, on the Save Data Connection File and Finish screen you will configure how the data will be accessed. Click the button labeled Authentication Settings. You have three options. The first is Windows Authentication, which uses the logged-on user's identity to authenticate to the data source. This is typically the default method for connecting to an SQL Server or Analysis Services data source. It is also considered to be the most secure method for accessing external data.

The second choice is SSS, which is Single Sign On. This method relies on a database that stores the credentials for accessing the external data. In this case, Excel Services will obtain the credentials required to authenticate to the SQL Server. The final choice, None, means that credential retrieval should not take place. This does not mean that authentication will not occur. Because you have configured an unattended service account, the data will be accessed using that account. Therefore, you should select None. Once you have imported the data, you have two ways to publish the workbook to SharePoint. First, you can upload the workbook directly from SharePoint. Second, you can publish the workbook from Excel. To upload the workbook from SharePoint, open Internet Explorer and browse to the web application, 24HourSharePointBI, that you created in the Try It section of Lesson 3. Once there, click the All Site Content link in the left navigation pane, as shown in Figure 4-7.

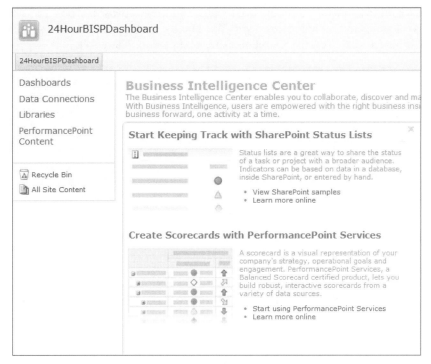

FIGURE 4-7

Here you can create your own document library or you can select an existing library. For now, just select Documents from the list of available Document Libraries. Next, click the Add Document link and the Documents – Upload Document screen will appear, as shown in Figure 4-8.

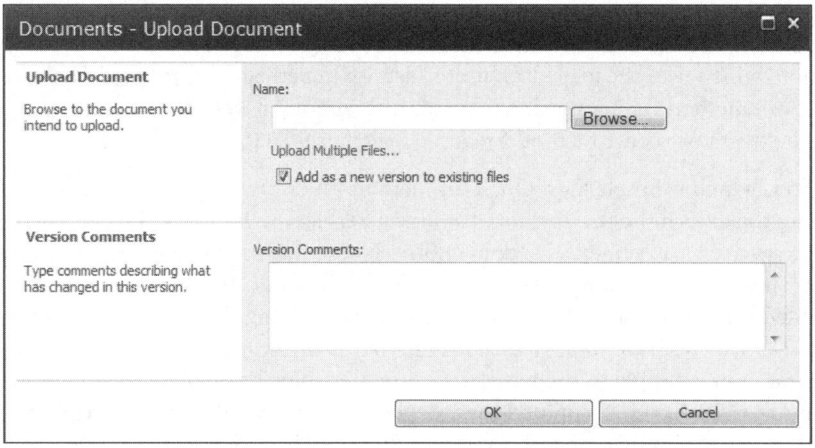

FIGURE 4-8

Before uploading the workbook, you must save it to a location on your machine. Save it as **Lesson4Workbook.** Back on the upload screen, browse to where you saved the workbook and select it. Then you can add versioning and version notes if you like. Finally, click OK to upload the workbook. The workbook is now available on the SharePoint site, as shown in Figure 4-9.

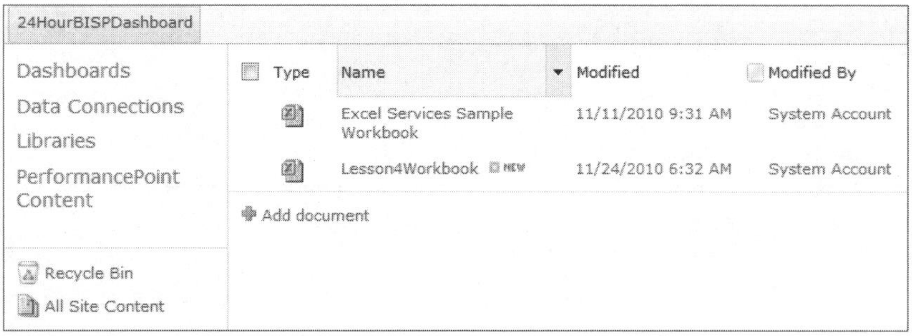

FIGURE 4-9

BEST PRACTICES

When storing Excel workbooks and accessing external data inside of SharePoint 2010, you should consider a couple of best practices before deciding on your methodology. First, in regard to storing workbooks, you should store them in the SharePoint 2010 content database. Excel workbooks can be accessed from UNC paths and HTTPS websites. However, by storing them in the content database, SharePoint will maintain an access control list for the files. Through the use of Excel Services, SharePoint will use claims-based authentication to improve security so that you can authenticate to various environments from Office applications, SharePoint services, and other web farms. In short, claims-based authentication is a method of authentication that is flexible and requires less specific information about the requesting user. This method of authentication trusts external systems by doing a proof of identity check instead of requesting a user name and password.

In addition to storage location of files, you should also consider your authentication method when accessing external data. As mentioned in the previous section, three types of authentication are supported by Excel Services. As a best practice, it is recommended that you use Integrated Windows Authentication because Excel Services depends on claims-based authentication. With this approach, data can be accessed by users without the need to provide their credentials more than once.

TRY IT

In this Try It you learn to configure the unattended service account for PerformancePoint Services. Then you upload an Excel workbook that contains data from the AdventureWorksR2 database into SharePoint.

Lesson Requirements

Before you set up the unattended service account for PerformancePoint Services, ensure that you have created an account that has the appropriate data access permissions. You will also need the AdventureWorks2008R2 database, which you can download from `www.codeplex.com`. You will also need to know the name of your SQL Server.

To complete this lesson, you configure an unattended service account. Then you export data from SQL Server into an Excel workbook. Finally, you publish the workbook from Excel to SharePoint.

Hints

> ➤ To configure the unattended service account, you have to successfully configured the Secure Store Service.

> ➤ In addition, you must generate a new key to ensure that the unattended service account can be configured.

> ➤ To publish the workbook from Excel to SharePoint, click the File tab in the Excel ribbon menu. Then choose the Save & Send option, which will expose several save options.

Step-by-Step

1. Open SharePoint 2010 Central Administration.

2. Click the Manage Service Application link under the Application Management category.

3. Locate and select the PerformancePoint Service Application, as shown in Figure 4-10.

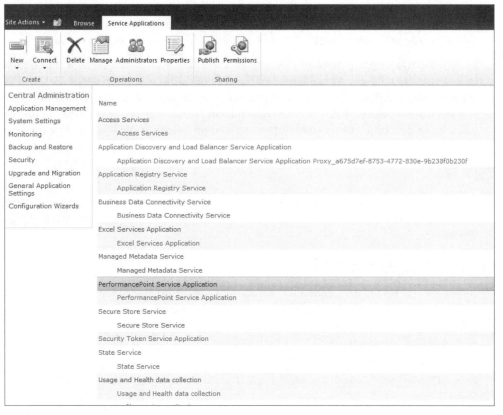

FIGURE 4-10

4. Click the Manage button located on the menu bar.

5. Click PerformancePoint Service Application Settings as shown in Figure 4-11.

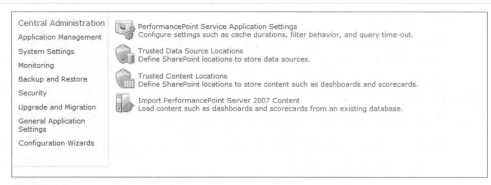

FIGURE 4-11

6. On the Application Settings page enter a valid user name and password.

7. Accept all defaults for the additional items and click OK.

8. Open Microsoft Excel 2010.

9. Click the Data tab and select the From Other Sources option.

10. Select From SQL Server in the drop-down list that appears.

11. Enter a server name and either choose Windows Authentication or enter a user name and password.

12. Click Next.

13. On the Select Database and Table screen, as shown in Figure 4-12, choose AdventureWorks2008R2 and select the Employee table.

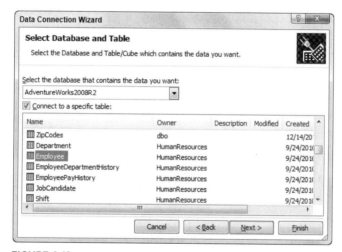

FIGURE 4-12

14. Click Next.

15. On the next screen click the Authentication Settings button.

16. Select the radio button labeled None.

17. Click OK.

18. Click Finish.

19. On the Import Data screen select Table and ensure that you specify **A1** as the starting point for the table.

20. Click OK.

21. Click File in the menu bar.

22. Choose the Save & Send option.

23. Select Save to SharePoint, as shown in Figure 4-13.

FIGURE 4-13

24. Double-click Browse for Location.

25. In the URL bar type `http://<yoursite>/Documents`. Replace <yoursite> with web application URL that was created in Lesson 3.

26. In the FileName textbox name the workbook `Lesson4TryIt.xlsx`.

27. Click Save and the workbook is published to SharePoint.

 Please select Lesson 4 on the DVD to view the video that accompanies this lesson.

SECTION II
Configuring SharePoint for Business Intelligence

▶ **LESSON 5:** Creating and Configuring Excel Services Applications

▶ **LESSON 6:** Creating and Configuring PerformancePoint Services Applications

▶ **LESSON 7:** Creating and Configuring Visio Services Applications

▶ **LESSON 8:** Creating and Configuring PowerPivot for SharePoint Services Applications

▶ **LESSON 9:** Creating Your First SharePoint Site for Business Intelligence

▶ **LESSON 10:** Configuring Reporting Services for SharePoint Integration

▶ **LESSON 11:** Implementing Business Connectivity Services in SharePoint

Creating and Configuring Excel Services Applications

Excel Services is a feature set for SharePoint 2010. With Excel Services you can take sharing Excel workbooks to the next level. Excel Services allows easy collaboration among an entire organization without the need to worry about pulling down the latest version of the file or even having Excel 2010 installed on a workstation. The service has three main parts:

➤ **Excel Calculation Services** — Used to load and calculate workbooks

➤ **Excel Web Access** — Renders the HTML page the user sees in the browser

➤ **Excel Web Services** — A web service designed to separate calculations from the front end

Using these three components, workbooks can be viewed online through a web browser, data permissions can be set, and reports can be created.

CREATING AN EXCEL SERVICES APPLICATION

The first step to working with Excel Services in SharePoint 2010 is to create an Excel Services application. Application management is done through the SharePoint Central Administration site. To open Central Administration navigate to the following location Start ➾ All Programs ➾ Microsoft SharePoint 2010 Products ➾ SharePoint 2010 Central Administration. Under the heading Application Management is a Manage Service Applications link as shown in Figure 5-1. This is a list of all the service applications currently configured. Here you can create and configure your entire Excel Services application, including trusted locations, caching options, and the unattended service account.

The first step is to create a new Excel Services application if one is not already present. To do this click New on the ribbon in the top left. The drop-down menu has a list of all the service applications that can be created; select Excel Services Application. The Create New Excel Services Application screen will appear. Choose a name for the application, enter a name for the new application pool, configure the security account, and whether you want the application to be added by default to the farm's proxy list. Finally, click OK and the Excel Services Application will be created.

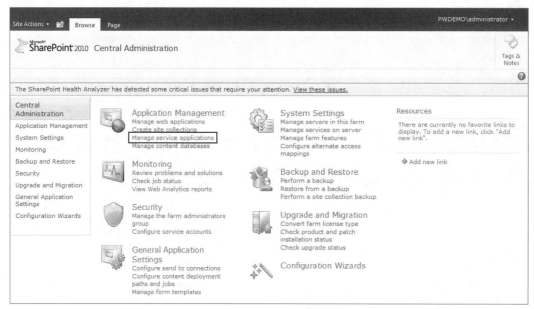

FIGURE 5-1

ENABLING EXCEL SERVICES

Once you have an Excel Services application set up, the next step is to allow your site to be able to use the features. To do this you must add the site that will be using the application to the trusted locations list.

Inside Central Administration under Manage Service Applications, click the name of the Excel Services application you want your site to be associated with. Next, select Trusted File Locations from the list of configuration options. This lists all the locations where Excel workbooks can be stored and accessed by Excel Services. Click the Add Trusted File Location button and enter the location where the workbooks will be stored. This can be the site URL or the URL of the library where they are housed. If the site URL is selected be sure to check the box next to Children Trusted so that all URLs inside your site will be trusted automatically as shown in Figure 5-2. Click OK and the location will be added to the list. Any workbooks not listed in the trusted locations will not be allowed to be accessed by Excel Services.

The final step is to be sure that the Excel Services service application is associated with your site or web application. Back in the Application Management section of Central Administration choose Configure Service Application Associations. Locate your site on the list and click its name. The Configure Service Application Associations screen will appear with a list of all the service applications. If Default is selected, all the default applications will be checked. If the Excel Services application is not selected, change the drop-down to Custom and place a check in the box next to Excel Services.

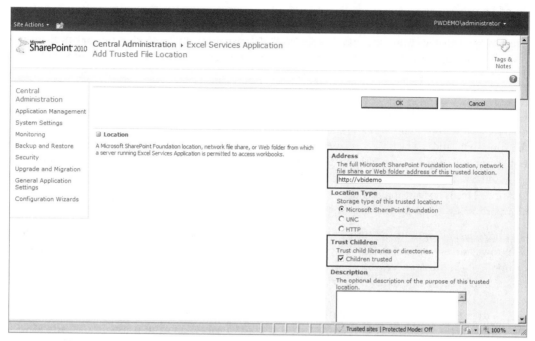

FIGURE 5-2

CONFIGURING EXCEL SERVICES SECURITY AND AUTHENTICATION

The Excel Services trusted file locations, data providers, and data connection libraries are the main ways that security for Excel files will be handled on your SharePoint site. In the trusted file locations you will need to put any document libraries, filesystems, and websites from where Excel workbooks can be opened. If you try to open a file not listed in the location an error will be displayed letting you know that it is not a trusted Excel location. This will occur only if you attempt to open the file in the browser. If the file is not in one of these locations it can still be downloaded to your local machine or opened directly in Microsoft Excel, but Excel Services cannot access it. By default the location of `http://` with Children Trusted is configured when an Excel Services application is created. For instructions on adding any specific libraries and locations to the trusted locations list, see the "Enabling Excel Services" section of this lesson.

The trusted data provider list is a set of connections that will be used by Excel Calculation Services. Just like the trusted file locations, Excel Services can use the data provider only if it is on this list. If outside data is needed for the Excel workbook for use by Excel Calculation Services, such as a connection to a SQL Server, the connection can be stored in a library on the SharePoint site in the form of an `.odc` (Office Data Connection) file. These files can be generated from within an Excel workbook and exported to a library. Any connections that are used by Excel Services will need to be inside a trusted data connection library.

To add a new trusted connection library for Excel Services, open Central Administration and navigate to your Excel Services application under the Manage Service Applications section. Click Trusted Data Connection Libraries and select Add Trusted Data Connection Library in the top-left corner. Next, enter the URL of the document library that contains your .odc files and click OK. The library will need to exist before adding the URL to this list. For more information on deploying the .odc file see Lesson 12.

Excel workbooks can be stored in a number of locations including the content database, a UNC path, or an HTTP website. This will affect the security settings that are chosen under the Global Settings for your application. The file access methods include Impersonation and Process Account. Selecting Impersonation requires user authentication when connecting to a workbook. Process Account, however, allows anonymous access by using the Excel Services process account to access files stored in a UNC location. This is not a recommended solution because it allows access to all files in which the process account can see affecting all trusted file locations, thus causing a security issue.

You have several options for authentication when creating data connections for Excel. These include Windows authentication, Secure Service Store authentication, and None. See Figure 5-3 for an example of the authentication options in Excel. Windows authentication uses the user's Windows account to authenticate data connections. Secure Store Service can be used to assign a single user or a group of users access by using the secure store database similar to how credentials are assigned for the unattended service account. Finally, you can choose the authentication type None. When you choose None the provided connection string is used. If a user name and password are already supplied in the connection string, a connection is made under that user. If the connection string uses Windows authentication, the credentials of the unattended user account are used.

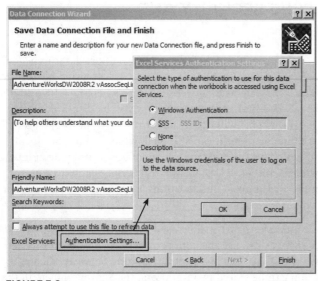

FIGURE 5-3

The unattended service account is used when connecting to non-Windows environments, as well as when the authentication method is None in the Excel Services authentication setting for a data connection. This account is linked to Excel Services by entering the application ID of the unattended service account created in the Secure Store Service. To create an unattended service account access Central Administration ➪ Manage Service Applications ➪ Secure Store Service.

If it is your first time doing any setup in the Secure Store Service application a message will be displayed that reads "Before creating a new Secure Store Target Application, you must first generate a new key for this Secure Store Service Application from the ribbon" as shown in Figure 5-4. To do this click Generate New Key on the ribbon and enter a passphrase that will be used as part of the database encryption. Be sure to remember this or store it in a secure location in case you need to reference it again later. Once the processing is complete click New in the top-left corner of the page. Enter a name for the service Application ID, which must be unique and cannot be changed. Enter a display name, which will only be used for identification, and an e-mail address for an application contact. From the Target Application Type drop-down select Group, then change the Target Application Page URL to None.

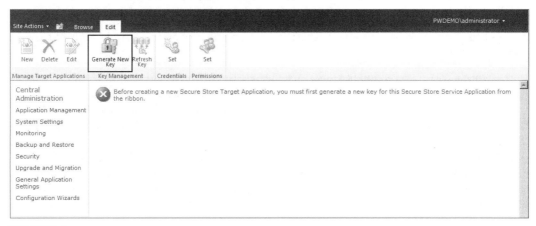

FIGURE 5-4

On the next page verify that the Field Type of Windows User Name and Windows Password are selected. Add the application administrators, which can edit the users assigned to the application at a later date, and at least one user that you would like to be added now. These values can be modified at a later date by those assigned to the administrators group. Click OK and the application will be created. Next place a check in the box next to the Application ID that was just created and click Set Credentials from the ribbon. At this point enter the credentials of the user to be assigned as the unattended services account.

The final step is to assign the unattended service account to the Excel Services application. Back on the Global Settings page of the Excel Services application (available from Central Administration ➪ Application Management ➪ Manage Service Applications ➪ *Name of Excel Services Application*) enter the Application ID of the newly created application from the Secure Store Service in the External Data section and click OK to apply the settings.

REPORTING AND CACHING OPTIONS

Excel workbook caching is also controlled through the Global Settings for the Excel Services application. This is handled by setting the memory utilization and workbook cache options.

Under the Memory Utilization section there is an option for maximum private bytes. This is the number of megabytes of available memory that Excel Calculation Services will be allowed to use on the server where the application is running. By default this is set to a value of –1, which represents 50 percent of physical memory. If there is 2048 MB of physical memory, then by default Excel Calculation Services would be allowed to use 1024 MB of that.

The next option, Memory Cache Threshold, is the percentage of the maximum private bytes that inactive objects are able to take up. Therefore Excel Calculation Services can store information that is currently not being used up to a certain percentage. Assuming the 1024 MB of memory available and a 50 percent threshold, 512 MB of memory can be used for inactive objects. If the threshold is exceeded, unused objects will be dropped from the cache to make room for new objects. This value can be set to zero to disable calculation services from caching inactive objects.

Finally, the Maximum Unused Object Age value will set how long objects are kept in the cache. If set to –1 they will be kept indefinitely. Alternatively, a number of minutes can be entered from 1 to 34560, or 24 days.

In the Workbook Cache section of Global Settings are three more caching options. A filesystem location can be specified to cache files in the Workbook Cache Location box. This is the location where any workbooks that are currently in use by Excel Calculation Services will be stored. If this is left empty the cache will be in the default system temporary directory. The Maximum Size of Workbook Cache sets the amount of disk space that the cache location is able to use. This is a value in MB and can be any positive whole number. Finally, a check box for caching unused files will allow workbooks that are no longer used by Calculation Services to be stored in a cache location. If the location fills these, workbooks will be dropped first. An example of the cache settings is shown in Figure 5-5.

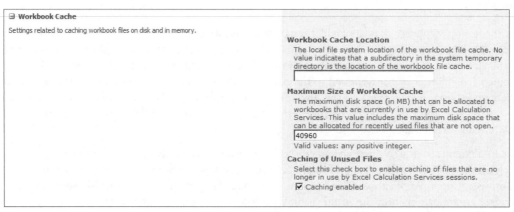

FIGURE 5-5

Now that you have learned about creating an Excel Services application and how to configure the security options, try creating your own in the next section.

TRY IT

In this Try It you learn how to create an Excel Services application, associate an unattended service account, and add a document library as a trusted location.

Lesson Requirements

For this lesson you will need a SharePoint site already created that contains a document library where Excel files will be stored. You will also need access to the Central Administration site to create the Excel Services application. You will create the Excel Services application and add an unattended service account for access purposes as well as the location of your document library to the trusted locations.

Hints

➤ You will need credentials for setting up the unattended service account.

➤ The Excel Services application will be created in the Central Administration site.

➤ You will add a specific document library to the trusted file locations.

➤ The document library should already be created and contain an Excel file.

Step-by-Step

1. Open the SharePoint 2010 Central Administration site.

2. Click Manage Service Applications under the Application Management section.

3. From the ribbon click New and select Excel Services Application.

4. In the Name box type **Excel Services**. For Application Pool switch to Use Existing Application Pool and select SharePoint Web Services Default from the drop-down. Your screen should now look like Figure 5-6.

5. Click OK.

6. Click Secure Store Service where you will create the unattended service account.

7. If necessary follow the instructions on the screen to create a key for the application.

8. Click New from the ribbon.

9. Enter **ExcelServices** in the Application ID box, **Excel Services** in the Display Name box, an administrator's e-mail address in the Contact e-mail box, select Group on the Target Application Type drop-down, and set the Target Application Page URL to None as shown in the Figure 5-7.

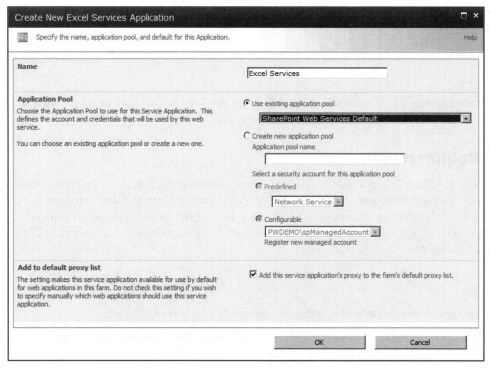

FIGURE 5-6

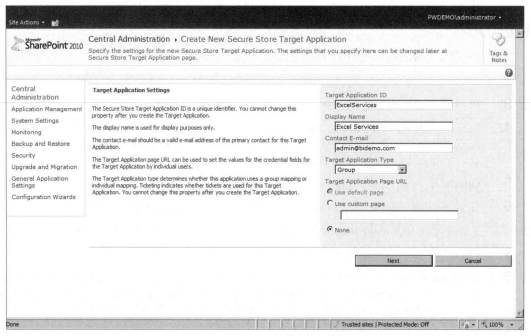

FIGURE 5-7

10. Click Next.

11. Verify the fields listed are Windows User Name and Windows Password. Click Next.

12. Add a list of application administrators in the Target Application Administrators box.

13. In the Members box add all users and user groups that should be mapped to the unattended credentials and click OK.

14. Check the box next to the newly created entry and click the Set icon above Credentials on the ribbon.

15. Enter the user name and password of the account you want to map to and click OK.

16. Return to the Manage Service Applications page (available by clicking Application Management on the left pane).

17. Select Excel Services from the list.

18. Select Global Settings and scroll down to the bottom and locate the External Data section.

19. In the Application ID box type `ExcelServices` exactly how it was entered in the Secure Store Service screen.

20. When your screen looks like Figure 5-8 click OK.

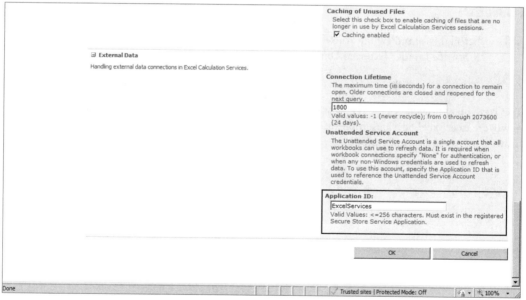

FIGURE 5-8

21. Click Trusted File Locations on the Application Management screen.

22. Click Add Trusted File Location in the top left of the screen.

23. Enter the URL to your document library and check the box next to Children Trusted as shown in Figure 5-9.

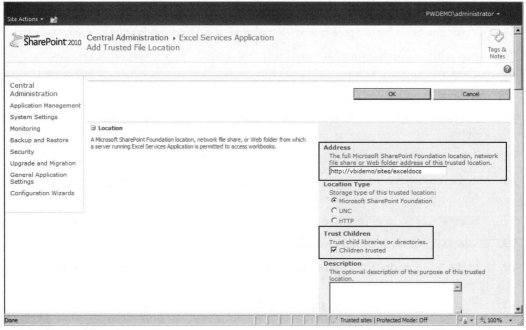

FIGURE 5-9

24. Scroll down and switch Allow External Data to Trusted Data Connection Libraries And Embedded under External Data.

25. Click OK.

You have just allowed your Excel workbooks in the document library to use the resources of your newly created Excel Services application! If your library is set up to open documents in the web browser you can now click an Excel workbook and it will open in the browser.

 Please select Lesson 5 on the DVD to view the video that accompanies this lesson.

Creating and Configuring PerformancePoint Services Applications

Using PerformancePoint in your SharePoint site requires installing the PerformancePoint Service application, as well as its dependencies, which in this case is the Secure Store Service. The Secure Store Service is a service used to store credentials for connecting to data sources using PerformancePoint.

In this lesson you learn how to install and configure the PerformancePoint and Secure Store service applications in order to enable PerformancePoint functionality on your SharePoint site.

ENABLING PERFORMANCEPOINT SERVICES

You have a series of steps to take in configuring PerformancePoint Services for use in a SharePoint 2010 environment.

Note that running the Farm Configuration Wizard will do many of the initial configuration steps.

The first step in installing PerformancePoint Services is to ensure that the Enterprise Features are installed. To do this, go to Upgrade and Migration in the Central Administration site, and click Enable Enterprise Features. This is necessary only once for any Enterprise Features. Once you have done this, enable these features on any existing sites by clicking Enable Features on Existing Sites. This will enable the Enterprise Features across all existing sites — you can do this manually if you want to enable the features only on some sites.

The next steps will be done for you if you run the configuration wizard, but are covered here for completeness. Return to the Central Administration site, and under System Settings, select Manage Services on server. Ensure that both PerformancePoint Services and Secure Store Service are running.

Next up, you need to check that the service application is associated with your web application.

Under Application Management is a link to Configure Service Application Associations, where the web applications are linked to specific services as shown in Figure 6-1.

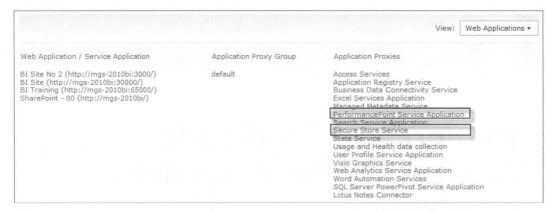

FIGURE 6-1

If the PerformancePoint service application is not associated with your web application, you will add it here by clicking the link under Application Proxy Group and selecting it from the list.

As the final installation step, you will need to create a Service Application for the PerformancePoint Services. Under the Application Management heading, select Manage Service Applications. Click New and select PerformancePoint Service. Set the Service Application Name to PerformancePoint Service.

You will also need to set the application pool — create a new application pool for each service application even if they share service accounts.

CONFIGURING PERFORMANCEPOINT SERVICES SECURITY AND AUTHENTICATION

In a web server environment, you experience what is known as a "double hop" when connecting to a database, as shown in Figure 6-2.

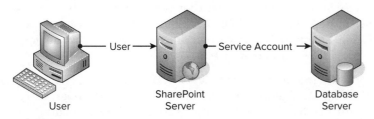

FIGURE 6-2

In the double hop problem, when connecting to a web server that connects to a database, the initial connection to the web server is made under your own credentials, and then the connection to the database is made using the credentials that the web service runs under — in the case of PerformancePoint, this is the service account for PerformancePoint.

This is not always the desired outcome, because giving a service account access to a database is not a good security practice.

You have two possible solutions: Kerberos and the Secure Store Service, each with its own advantages and disadvantages

Kerberos, Per-User, Unattended Service Account

Kerberos, a solution developed at MIT, is one of the solutions often used for this. When Kerberos is set up (a task that is outside the scope of this book), a Kerberos token is given to the web server by the Kerberos server, allowing it to delegate (pass on) the user account used to authenticate as shown in Figure 6-3. Without this token, the web server cannot use the user account.

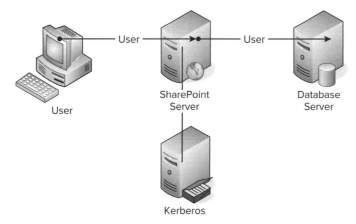

FIGURE 6-3

The advantage to Kerberos is that the authentication is "Per-User," that is, the authentication that is used is the account the user uses. The disadvantage is that the setup is complex, requires Active Directory changes, and needs to be set up for each server involved.

The Secure Store Service, shown in Figure 6-4, is SharePoint's answer to the authentication challenge. A secure store is used to store user credentials that applications will use to connect to data sources. PerformancePoint Services, however, makes an idiosyncratic use of the Secure Store Service, and will always use the credentials assigned to a specific Secure Store Service application, rather than allowing one to specify which service to use.

As you did for PerformancePoint, you need to check that the Secure Store Service application is associated with your web application.

Under Application Management is a link to Configure Service Application Associations, where the web applications are linked to specific services.

You will need to create a Service Application for the Secure Store Service. Under the Application Management heading, select Manage Service Applications. Click New, then select Secure Store Service. Set the Service Application Name to Secure Store Services.

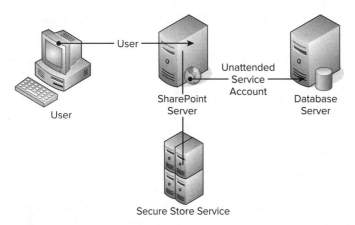

FIGURE 6-4

Set the application pool — create a new application pool for each service application even if they share service accounts.

Finally, choose a database to use, and click OK.

Now that the Secure Store Service is set up, you need to create a Secure Store Service Application. As opposed to "the" secure store service application, this application is the credential store for other applications.

The steps to be taken are:

1. Create a key for encryption.

2. Create a new Secure Store Application.

3. Assign credentials to the new application.

From Central Administration, choose the Manage Service Applications option under Application Management and click the Secure Store Service.

Figure 6-5 shows the applications that have been set up to use the Secure Store Service — remember that PerformancePoint will always use the first application.

If no applications are listed, you will need to start by generating a new key. This is the key that will be used to encrypt the credentials stored in the Secure Store Service, so ensure that you save the passphrase in a secure location.

Now that you have created a key to encrypt the user names, you will create the secure store application that PerformancePoint will use to authenticate when connecting to data sources.

Click New, and then enter the settings for the application. The Target Application ID should be descriptive, and normally using the same name for the ID and the Display name is suggested.

The contact e-mail needs to be a mail address of someone responsible for administering SharePoint.

The Target Application Type is an important step — always choose Group. The other options are intended for purposes in applications unlike the usage PerformancePoint makes of this service.

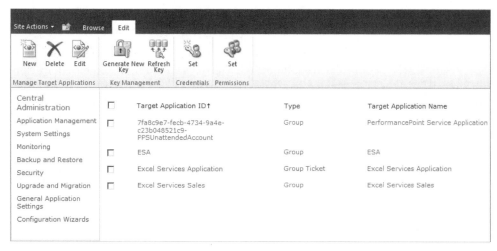

FIGURE 6-5

The next page, Add Field, is also intended for custom applications making use of the Secure Store Service, and thus you should leave the two fields (Windows User Name and Windows Password) as they are, then click Next.

In this step, Specify The Membership Settings, you will be setting up the administrators for this application — set yourself and any user who will be changing the user account in the Target Application Administrators field.

The other item set up here is the group or groups of users that will use the application, in the Members field. Make sure to include any users that will be using PerformancePoint in any manner. If this will potentially be your entire user base (for example, if you intend to have dashboards on your intranet) you can use the All Authenticated Users windows group.

The final step in setting up your Secure Store Service application is assigning the credentials it will use when connecting to a data store. To do so, click the checkbox next to your application, and then click the Set Credentials button in the ribbon. These will be the credentials PerformancePoint uses to connect to data sources.

REPORTING AND CACHING OPTIONS

In the Central Administration homepage, go to the Manage Service Applications link under Application Management. Click PerformancePoint Service Application. Of the three settings links, you can safely ignore Trusted Data Source Locations and Trusted Content Locations, because they default to All SharePoint locations.

You can also ignore the Import PerformancePoint Server 2007 Content option.

Click PerformancePoint Service Application Settings.

The settings that you are interested in here are the Unattended Service account and the Cache setting.

First, the unattended service account: Click Edit User and you will be asked to enter a user name and password — this will set the user used by PerformancePoint Services to access data sources.

PerformancePoint does caching at a data source level, and the only caching option available at this level is the KPI Icon Cache option. The default here is 10 seconds, and, unless you have long running dashboards (that is, they take longer than 10 seconds to load), you will most likely not need to change this.

TRY IT

In this Try It you install and configure the Secure Store Service and PerformancePoint Services features in SharePoint.

Lesson Requirements

In this lesson, you will enable Enterprise Features in order to use PerformancePoint, and install the PerformancePoint and Secure Store services.

You will then configure the Secure Store Service to support PerformancePoint, and configure PerformancePoint to use an unattended service account.

You will not create a new site or site collection.

Hints

> ➤ Run the Farm Configuration Wizard, and then review the settings.

Step-by-Step

1. Open the Central Administration site by clicking Windows ➪ All Programs ➪ Microsoft SharePoint 2010 Products ➪ SharePoint 2010 Central Administration.

2. Click Upgrade and Migration in the left-hand menu.

3. Click Convert Farm License Type.

4. If the Current License does not say SharePoint Server with Enterprise Client Access License, enter your product key and click OK.

5. Click Upgrade and Migration in the left-hand menu.

6. Click Enable Enterprise Features.

7. If Use these Features is not grayed out, click the Enterprise (Requires Enterprise client license) radio button and click OK.

8. Click Configuration Wizards in the left menu.

9. Click Launch the Farm Configuration Wizard.

10. Click the Start the Wizard button.

11. If no existing managed account is available, click Create New Managed Account and enter the managed account and password.

12. Ensure that the check boxes for Secure Store Service and PerformancePoint Service Application are checked — a service that is already installed will be checked and grayed out. A Processing window will be shown — this may take some time.

13. A window to create a new top-level website will be shown — click Skip.

14. The final window will document what is installed on the farm — click Finish to complete the wizard.

15. Click Application Management in the menu on the left.

16. Click Manage Services on the Server.

17. Click Start next to the Secure Store Service if it is stopped.

18. Click Start next to the PerformancePoint Service if it is stopped.

19. Click Application Management in the menu on the left.

20. Click Manage Services Applications as shown in Figure 6-6.

FIGURE 6-6

21. Click Secure Store Service.

22. If the list of applications is empty, click Generate New Key.

23. Enter a passphrase, and store it in a safe location.

24. Click New to create a new Secure Store Service Application.

25. Set the Target Application ID and Display Name, add a Contact E-mail, and set Target Application Type to Group as shown in Figure 6-7. Click Next.

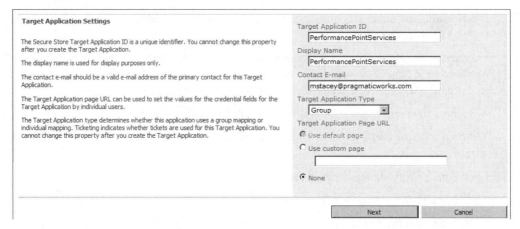

FIGURE 6-7

26. On the Add Field page, click Next.

27. Set the Target Application Administrators field to the user you are logged in with, and set the Members field to All Authenticated Users [All Users] as shown in Figure 6-8.

FIGURE 6-8

28. Check the check box next to the newly created application, and click Set ⇨ Credentials in the ribbon as shown in Figure 6-9.

29. Select the user to use for accessing data sources when using this Secure Store Service application.

30. Click Application Management on the left-hand menu.

31. Click Manage Service Applications.

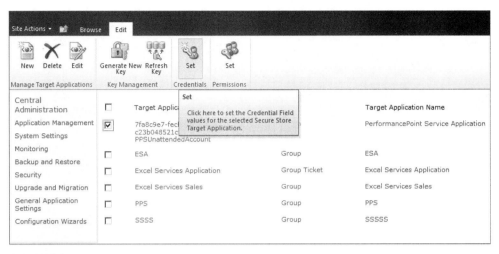

FIGURE 6-9

32. Click PerformancePoint Service Application.

33. Click PerformancePoint Service Application Settings.

34. Click Edit User. Set the user name and password to the password used for accessing data sources as shown in Figure 6-10.

FIGURE 6-10

 Please select Lesson 6 on the DVD to view the video that accompanies this lesson.

Creating and Configuring Visio Services Applications

Visio Services is a new service application in SharePoint 2010 designed for sharing Visio Web Drawings. Similar to other service applications in SharePoint 2010, Visio Services allows distribution and viewing of Visio Web Drawings in the browser, eliminating the need to have Microsoft Visio installed on the client machine. This means that one developer can create Visio documents and share them across the company. Visio Services also allows for interactivity to be included in drawings. By using the Visio Access Web Part, an end user will have the ability to navigate from one Visio drawing to the next through built-in links. Data refreshes are also handled by the Visio Services application, allowing for visual updates to be pushed down each time the Visio drawing is opened.

It is worth noting that only Visio Web Drawings are rendered in the browser by Visio Services. These are files that have the extension .vdw and can be uploaded to a document library or sent to the SharePoint site directly from Visio Professional Premium. Visio documents with the extension .vsd, which are standard drawings, are not supported to be shown in the browser by Visio Services. Web Drawings cannot be created using the Standard version of Microsoft Visio, only Premium and Professional.

CREATING A VISIO SERVICES APPLICATION

Before you are able to use all the features of Visio Services in your SharePoint site, you must create a Visio Services application. In SharePoint 2010 application management is handled through the SharePoint Central Administration site. This is the location where you will need to go to create your new Visio Services application. To open the Central Administration site, click the Start menu and navigate to the Microsoft SharePoint 2010 Products folder under the Programs section. Next, click SharePoint 2010 Central Administration and enter your credentials or an administrator's credentials when prompted. From the homepage, open the Application Management section and click the link for Manage Service Applications under the Service Applications heading.

This page contains a list of all the service applications currently configured. Click New on the ribbon at the top of the page and select Visio Graphics Service. The New Visio Graphics Service Application wizard opens as shown in Figure 7-1.

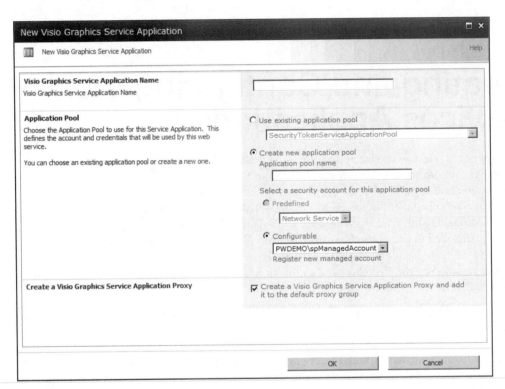

FIGURE 7-1

Fill out the form, provide a name, and create a new application pool for this service application.

ENABLING VISIO SERVICES

Once the Visio Service application has been created, it needs to be added to your site's Application Proxies. To do this, open the Application Management page in the Central Administration site. Click Configure Service Application Associations in the Service Application section. Find your web application in the list and check to be sure the Visio Services application is listed in the Application Proxies list as shown in Figure 7-2. If it is not listed, click the link in the Application Proxy Group column and place a check in the box next to the Visio Services application.

FIGURE 7-2

CONFIGURING VISIO SERVICES SECURITY AND AUTHENTICATION

Two situations need to be addressed when dealing with Visio Services security. The first is a drawing that has no external data, and the second is a drawing that does contain external data. All Visio drawings need to be stored inside a SharePoint library in order for Visio Services to render the drawing in the browser. That said, if there is no external data, meaning no data connections are present in the file, all security is handled by the SharePoint library.

In the event that the drawing has external data, be it from a SharePoint list, an Excel workbook, or from a database, other security methods are used. If the data is stored in a SharePoint list, the drawing and list must be in the same farm and the user's credentials will be used and therefore must have access to the list. The same situation holds true for Excel workbooks. They must be in the same farm and the user needs access to both. In each of these situations all security is handled by SharePoint.

In the event that a drawing uses a connection to a database, a number of different connection methods may be used, including Windows authentication, Secure Store Service, and the unattended service account. With the Windows authentication method the current user's credentials will be used for the connection. For both the other methods an .odc (Office Data Connectivity file created in Excel) file will need to be generated and stored on the SharePoint server. This will determine if the secure store or unattended service account will be used. With the secure store option a user will be mapped to another account for the connection. These can be assigned based on a single user or a group level. In similar fashion, the unattended service account will map your credentials to another account and use that for authentication. The difference is that everyone is mapped to the same account when using the unattended service account.

To configure the unattended service account, open SharePoint Central Administration and navigate to the Manage Service Applications page under Application Management. If a Secure Store Service application does not exist, click New and create one. Before creating an account, you must generate a new key as shown in the error message in Figure 7-3.

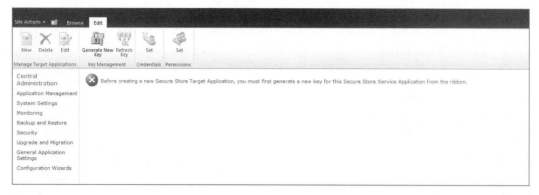

FIGURE 7-3

Be sure to make note of the passphrase because it will not be stored anywhere automatically for you to reference later. Next, click New on the ribbon and enter an Application ID, Display Name, and Contact Email, and switch the drop-down from Individual to Group. Click Next and be sure that the resulting page shows Windows User Name and Windows Password as the fields. Click Next and enter the application administrators and the application members. Administrators have the option to add and remove members at a later date. Click OK. The next step is to assign the account to be used. Place a check in the box next to the Application ID desired, choose Set Credentials from the ribbon, enter the user name and password for the Windows account to be used, and click OK. Finally, back in the Global Settings for the Visio Services application enter the Application ID in the box at the bottom of the screen.

REPORTING AND CACHING OPTIONS

Several caching options are available to your Visio Services application. These can have a large effect on performance and should be monitored in the initial site setup so that a happy medium can be found among them. All caching options are found under the Global Settings section of the application, which you can access through Central Administration ➪ Application Management ➪ Manage Service Applications. See the location of the Manage Service Applications link in Figure 7-4.

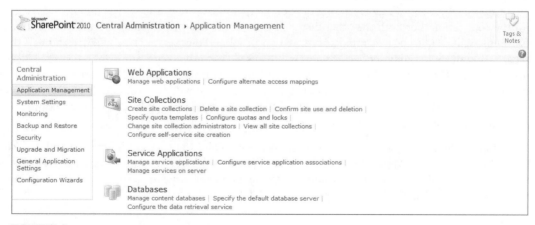

FIGURE 7-4

The setting for Maximum Web Drawing Size will limit how large of a drawing can be rendered in the browser by Visio Services. Though allowing for larger drawings will allow more files to be opened, this could have a detrimental effect on server performance. Drawings that are opened will stay in the cache up to the amount of time entered in the setting for Maximum Cache Age. This value is in minutes and has a maximum of 34,560 minutes or 24 days.

OTHER CONSIDERATIONS

Many factors will affect the performance of your Visio Services application. These are further affected by the setting chosen in the Global Settings section of the service application but also include things such as the amount of memory on the server where the service is running. Always be sure to plan for the maximum server impact. This means that you want to plan for the time when the most users will be rendering the largest Visio drawings. This becomes more important when your SharePoint farm has more than one application server. If everyone is preparing for a 10 AM status meeting on Monday morning, a lot of users may be hitting Visio applications, PerformancePoint applications, and Excel applications all at the same time. It would be wise to spread these service applications out so they are not all running on the same server to boost overall system performance. Therefore, each server is processing one item at a time instead of three. You have many other factors to keep in mind as well, which include but are not limited to:

➤ Number of drawings

➤ Size of each drawing

➤ Whether your drawings are pulling from external data sources

➤ If external data sources are used, performance will be tied to those sources as well.

Now that you know how to configure a Visio Services application, go to the Try It section and test out your new knowledge.

TRY IT

In this Try It you learn how to create a new Visio Services application and associate it with your SharePoint site.

Lesson Requirements

For this lesson you need access to the Central Administration site to create a new Visio Services application. You also need to have an account to map to for the unattended service account.

Hints

➤ You need to create an account in the Secure Store Service application for the unattended service account.

➤ You need credentials for mapping the unattended service account.

➤ The Visio Services application will be created in Central Administration.

Step-by-Step

1. Open SharePoint 2010 Central Administration from the Start menu.

2. Authenticate your session when prompted with the credentials of an Administrator.

3. Click the Application Management link on the left menu.

4. Click Manage Service Applications in the Service Applications section.

5. Click New on the ribbon at the top of the screen and select Visio Graphics Service as shown in Figure 7-5.

6. When the New Visio Graphics Service Application Wizard opens, enter **Visio Services** as the name for your application.

7. Keep the button next to Create New Application Pool selected and enter a name for the pool.

8. Select a security account for the application pool from either the predefined list or a custom account from the Configurable list.

9. Click OK to create the application.

10. You will be brought back to the Manage Service Applications screen. Click Secure Service Store on the list of applications.

FIGURE 7-5

11. If this is the first time you have set up an account in the Secure Service Store, you will need to generate a new key. Follow the onscreen instructions to create a new key. Be sure to store the passphrase in a secure location because it will not be stored automatically and it may need to be referenced from time to time.

12. Click New from the ribbon to create a new account.

13. Enter **VisioUnattendedAccount** or another unique value in the Target Application ID. Make note of this value because you will need it soon.

14. Enter **Visio Services** in the Display Name box. This will show in the list of the Secure Store applications.

15. Enter the Visio Services' primary contact e-mail address in the Contact E-mail box.

16. Change the drop-down for Target Application Type to Group.

17. When your screen looks like Figure 7-6, click Next.

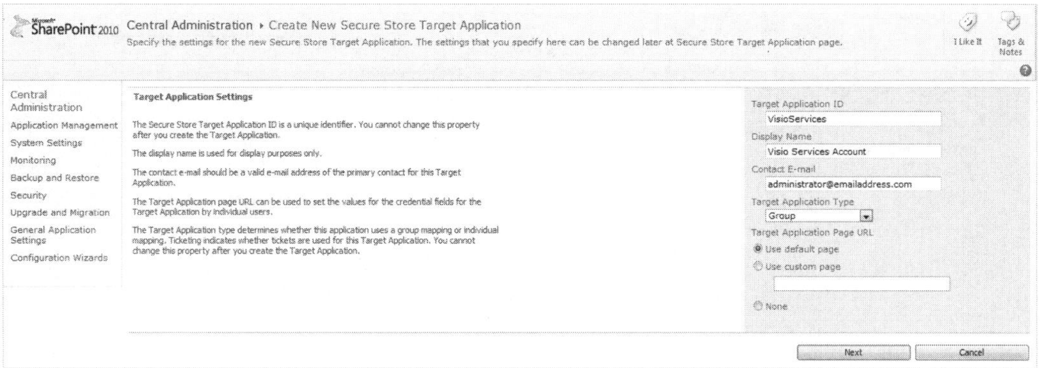

FIGURE 7-6

18. When the next screen loads, be sure it has the fields listed as Windows User Name and Windows Password. Click Next.

19. Add a list of application administrators in the Target Application Administrators box.

20. In the Members box add all users and user groups that should be mapped to the unattended credentials and click OK.

21. Check the box next to the newly created entry and click the Set icon above Credentials on the ribbon, as shown in Figure 7-7.

FIGURE 7-7

22. Enter the user name and password of the account you want to map to and click OK.

23. Return to the Manage Service Applications page (available by clicking Application Management on the left pane).

24. Select the Visio Services application from the list and click Global Settings.

25. Scroll down to the Unattended Service Account option and enter **VisioUnattendedAccount** in the Application ID box.

26. Your settings screen should now look like Figure 7-8. When it does, click OK.

27. Go back to the Application Management section one last time and select Configure Service Application Associations.

Monitoring	**Minimum Cache Age**	5
Backup and Restore	The minimum number of minutes (between 0 and 34560) that a Web Drawing is cached in memory. Smaller values allow more frequent data refresh operations for users, but increase CPU and memory usage on the server.	
Security		
Upgrade and Migration		
General Application Settings	**Maximum Cache Age**	60
Configuration Wizards	The number of minutes (between 0 and 34560) after which cached Web Drawings are purged. Larger values decrease file I/O and CPU load but increase memory usage on the server.	
	Maximum Recalc Duration	60
	The number of seconds (between 10 and 120) before data refresh operations time out.	
	External Data	**Unattended Service Account**
	Handling external data connections in Visio Graphics Service.	The target application ID in the registered Secure Store Service that is used to reference Unattended Service Account credentials. The Unattended Service Account is a single account that all documents can use to refresh data. It is required when connecting to data sources external to SharePoint, such as SQL.
		Application ID:
		VisioUnattendedAccount
		Valid Values: <=256 characters. Must exist in the registered Secure Store Service Application.

FIGURE 7-8

28. If the Visio Services application is not listed in the far-right column, click the link in the Application Proxy Group column.

29. Check the box next to the Visio Services application and click OK.

You are now ready to upload a few .vdw drawings for Visio Services to render and for your users to see.

 Please select Lesson 7 on the DVD to view the video that accompanies this lesson.

Creating and Configuring PowerPivot for SharePoint Services Applications

PowerPivot is a tool new in Office 2010 that provides a type of in memory OLAP tool, which is available in the familiar interface of Excel. It gives end users the ability to analyze data in a similar fashion that an Analysis Services cube would provide. For the purposes of this lesson though we will focus on the configuration of PowerPivot with SharePoint, but for a more in depth discussion on PowerPivot and when it is appropriate to use, read Lesson 13.

PowerPivot is one of the most difficult and time consuming of the Business Intelligence tools to configure for SharePoint. It requires a separate install of an Analysis Services instance and special considerations depending on whether SharePoint is installed on a standalone machine or on an existing farm. In this lesson's Try It section you walk through the steps for properly configuring a standalone instance, which is the best way to get you up-and-running the fastest.

SQL SERVER AND SHAREPOINT INSTALLATIONS

Before you can begin installing SQL Server or SharePoint you will need to ensure your machine is properly prepared. You will also need to have the proper editions of products to install. Use this checklist before beginning the installation:

➤ The operating system is Windows Server 2008 R2 or Windows Server 2008 Service Pack 2 or higher and must be 64-bit.

➤ SharePoint 2010 Enterprise.

➤ SQL Server R2 Enterprise Edition.

➤ Domain account available that can be used for configuration and setup.

Standalone vs. Existing Farm

Performing a standalone installation on a single server is the simplest way to start learning PowerPivot in SharePoint. This type of installation is performed when you know ahead of time that you would like to have the PowerPivot functionality as part of your SharePoint instance.

This installation has two major steps:

1. Install a SharePoint 2010 instance without running the configuration wizard.

2. Install SQL Server 2008 R2 and select SQL Server PowerPivot for SharePoint for a New Server on the Setup Role page.

After the SQL Server install is complete you will find your SharePoint site is configured and a PowerPivot site has become your homepage. You can use the Try It section of the lesson as a detailed step-by-step guide for following this installation type, so here the emphasis is more on the setup for an existing farm.

The alternative to the standalone install is to perform the PowerPivot installation on an existing SharePoint farm to which you would like to add the feature. You would do this if you have already installed SharePoint and have decided now to add the PowerPivot functionality.

This installation method follows many of the same steps as the standalone method, but following the completion of the SQL Server install your SharePoint site will not be ready.

Installing SQL Server PowerPivot for SharePoint

To get install SQL Server PowerPivot for SharePoint, follow these steps:

1. Log on to the computer that has the SharePoint 2010 instance already installed and start the SQL Server 2008 R2 installer.

2. When the setup menu opens click Installation ➪ New Installation or add features to an existing Installation.

3. Click OK after the Setup Support Rules complete.

4. Install the Setup Support Files and click Next when the support files complete installation.

5. If you already have an instance of SQL Server installed on this server an Installation Type page will appear. If this is true for you, select New installation or features. PowerPivot for SharePoint must have its own instance. If you have not previously installed SQL Server then this page will not appear.

6. On the next dialog you will be required to enter your product key. After entering your key click Next.

7. You will then be required to accept the licensing terms. Click the checkbox to accept and click Next.

8. Click Install to install all the Setup Support Files to be installed.

9. In the Setup Support Rules dialog click Next.

10. Select SQL Server PowerPivot for SharePoint and set the Add PowerPivot for SharePoint To drop-down box to Existing Farm, as shown in Figure 8-1.

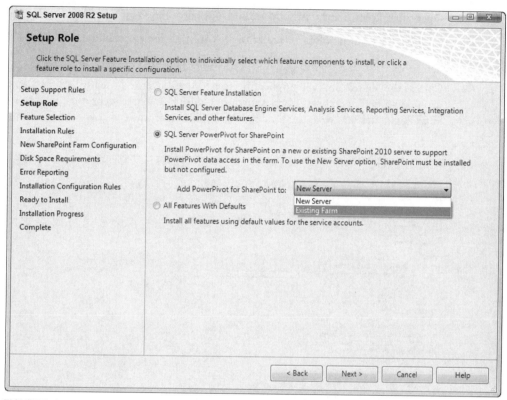

FIGURE 8-1

11. In the Feature Selection dialog click Next.

12. Click Next again in the Installation Rule dialog after the Install Rules Check completes.

13. The instance name that will be created for the SQL Server Analysis Server will be PowerPivot. Accept the defaults and click Next.

14. On the Disk Space Requirements dialog click Next.

15. On the Server Configuration page provide a domain account for Analysis Services. This account must be a domain account (a Windows administrator account is not good enough here) and can be changed later from SharePoint Central Administration. Click Next when this is complete.

16. Click Add Current User so the account you are logged in as will be added as an Analysis Services administrator, then click Next.

17. Click Next on the Error Reporting dialog to continue.

18. In the Installation Configuration Rules dialog click Next.

19. Click Install after reviewing the summary information.

Deploying the PowerPivot Solution to SharePoint

To deploy a PowerPivot workbook, follow these steps:

1. Open SharePoint Central Administration and select the System Settings heading.

2. Click Manage Farm Solutions under the Farm Management heading.

3. Click powerpivotwebapp.wsp and select Deploy Solution.

4. Choose the SharePoint web application to add the PowerPivot feature in the Deploy To drop-down box and click OK, as shown in Figure 8-2. These steps must be repeated for all SharePoint sites you wish to allow the PowerPivot features.

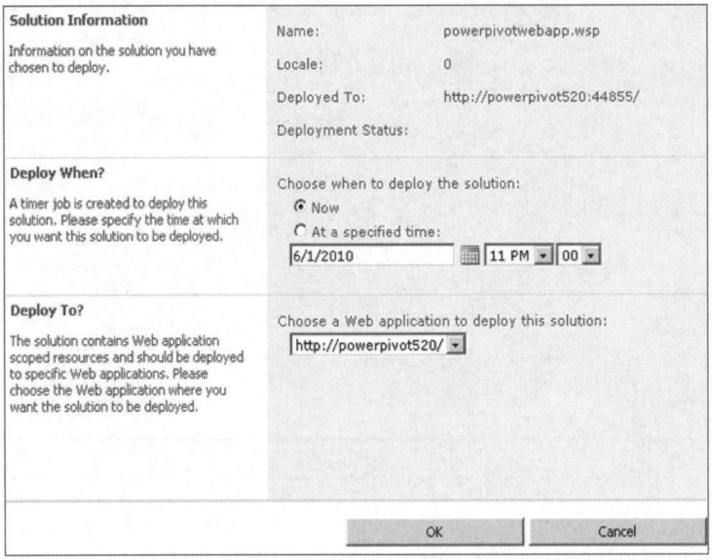

FIGURE 8-2

Creating the PowerPivot Service Application

To create a PowerPivot service application, follow these steps:

1. Open SharePoint Central Administration and select Manage Service Applications under the Application Management heading.

2. Click New and select SQL Server PowerPivot Service Application, as shown in Figure 8-3.

3. Give the Application pool a name and check Add the proxy for this PowerPivot service application to the default proxy group. Click OK.

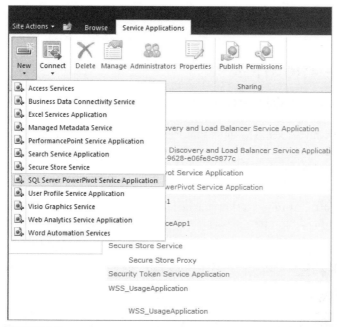

FIGURE 8-3

Activating the PowerPivot Feature on Site Collections

To activate PowerPivot on a SharePoint site, follow these steps:

1. Open your web browser and enter the URL `http://<YourServerName>`.

2. Click Site Actions and then Site Settings.

3. Click Site Collection Features under the Site Collection Administration heading.

4. Click Activate next to the PowerPivot Feature Integration Site Collections, as shown in Figure 8-4.

FIGURE 8-4

You have now successfully configured PowerPivot for an existing farm. As you can see many more steps are involved in doing an existing farm installation. When the standalone install completes you can start working, whereas the existing farm installation has several configuration steps even after completion of the installer. Make sure to walk through the Try It section for the step-by-step instructions on configuring a standalone install.

The next section describes how you can set up a Secure Store Service, which will be used for scheduling a data refresh of your PowerPivot data.

POWERPIVOT AUTHENTICATION

As you have just found out, both installation types require that you skip the configuration wizard that comes with SharePoint. A side effect of this is that some settings that would be configured automatically must now be manually set. The most important of these settings is the Secure Store Service, which is most often used for the scheduling of a data refresh to automatically update PowerPivot data inside an Excel workbook. This is done by setting up a Secure Store Target Application in SharePoint Central Administration.

After opening SharePoint Central Administration, navigate to Manage Service Applications under the Application Management heading. From the service applications list as shown in Figure 8-5 select the Secure Store Service.

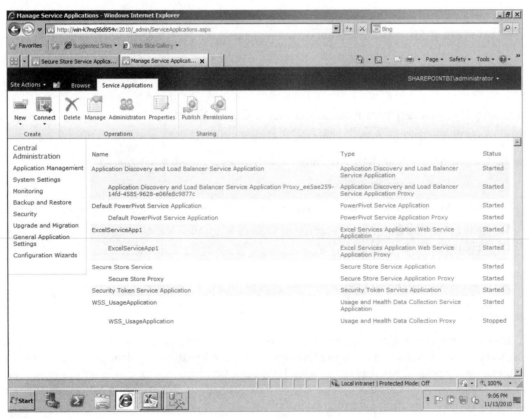

FIGURE 8-5

You must first select Generate New Key as shown in Figure 8-6, which is generated from a passphrase you provide. It is very important for you to record this passphrase because it will not be stored for later reference.

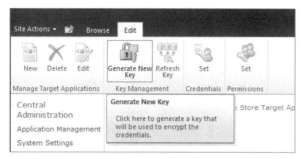

FIGURE 8-6

Next, click New in Manage Target Applications. The Target Application ID is the name that users will type in when setting up a data refresh that uses credentials that are stored, so make sure it is a name that is easy to remember. Provide a Target Application ID, Display Name, and Contact E-mail, and change the Target Application Type to Group as shown in Figure 8-7. Click Next.

Target Application Settings

The Secure Store Target Application ID is a unique identifier. You cannot change this property after you create the Target Application.

The display name is used for display purposes only.

The contact e-mail should be a valid e-mail address of the primary contact for this Target Application.

The Target Application page URL can be used to set the values for the credential fields for the Target Application by individual users.

The Target Application type determines whether this application uses a group mapping or individual mapping. Ticketing indicates whether tickets are used for this Target Application. You cannot change this property after you create the Target Application.

Target Application ID

PowerPivotDataRefresh

Display Name

PowerPivotDataRefresh

Contact E-mail

Administrator@SharepointBI.com

Target Application Type

Group

Target Application Page URL

○ Use default page

○ Use custom page

◉ None

| Next | Cancel |

FIGURE 8-7

Leave the defaults for the field names of Windows User Name and Windows Password and click Next. In the Target Application Administrators box provide the users who should have administrative access to the application settings. In the Members section provide either user and/or group accounts that will be entering this target application for data refreshes and click OK, as shown in Figure 8-8.

The Target Application has now been created and can be used for scheduling PowerPivot workbook data refreshes.

Return to Manage Service Applications under the Application Management heading. Select the PowerPivot Service Application and then click Configure Service Application Settings under the Actions heading. Find the Data Refresh section and change the PowerPivot Unattended Data Refresh Account to the Target Application ID created in the earlier steps, shown in Figure 8-9.

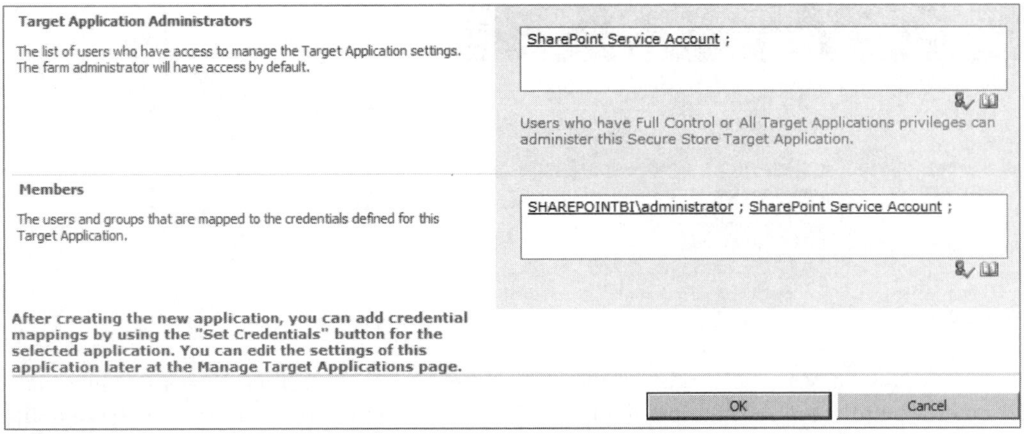

Target Application Administrators

The list of users who have access to manage the Target Application settings. The farm administrator will have access by default.

SharePoint Service Account ;

Users who have Full Control or All Target Applications privileges can administer this Secure Store Target Application.

Members

The users and groups that are mapped to the credentials defined for this Target Application.

SHAREPOINTBI\administrator ; SharePoint Service Account ;

After creating the new application, you can add credential mappings by using the "Set Credentials" button for the selected application. You can edit the settings of this application later at the Manage Target Applications page.

OK   Cancel

FIGURE 8-8

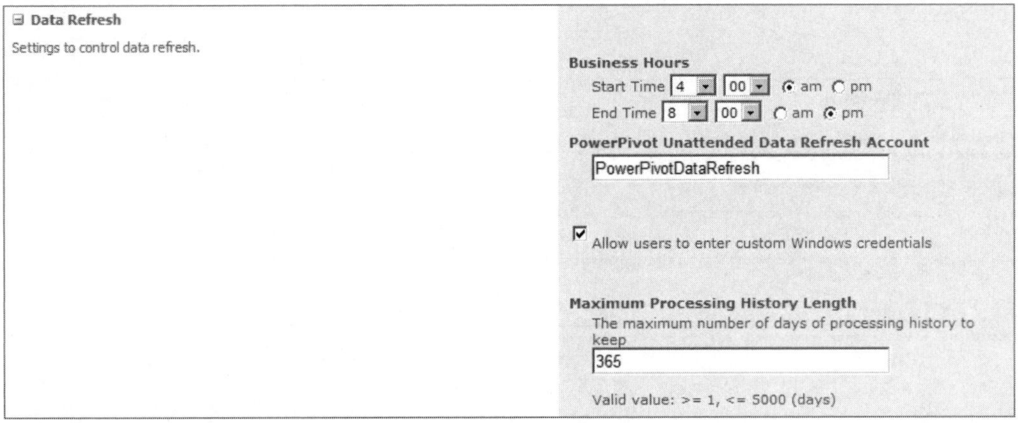

☐ **Data Refresh**

Settings to control data refresh.

Business Hours
Start Time 4 ▾ 00 ▾ ⦿ am ○ pm
End Time 8 ▾ 00 ▾ ○ am ⦿ pm

PowerPivot Unattended Data Refresh Account

PowerPivotDataRefresh

☑ Allow users to enter custom Windows credentials

Maximum Processing History Length
The maximum number of days of processing history to keep

365

Valid value: >= 1, <= 5000 (days)

FIGURE 8-9

TESTING YOUR CONFIGURATION

Now that the Secure Store Target Application is configured you can test it by attempting to schedule a data refresh on an Excel workbook with PowerPivot data using the Secure Store Service. Navigate to the PowerPivot Gallery on your PowerPivot site and find an Excel workbook that you have already deployed. You may be required to install Silverlight to continue. Click the Manage Data Refresh button as shown in Figure 8-10.

When the Manage Data Refresh page opens, turn on data refresh by checking the Enable box. Set Schedule Details to Once, set Earliest Start Time to Specific Earliest Start Time, and set it to 15 minutes from your current time for testing purposes. Normally you would leave this option at the default After Business Hours.

Next, provide an e-mail in the E-mail Notification section that will be notified in the event of a data refresh failure. Finally, in the Credentials section select Connect Using the Credentials Saved in Secure Store Service (SSS) to Log On to the Data Source. Enter the ID Used to Look up the Credentials in the SSS ID Box. In the ID box provide the Target Application ID that you created in the previous section and click OK. Your configuration should look similar to Figure 8-11.

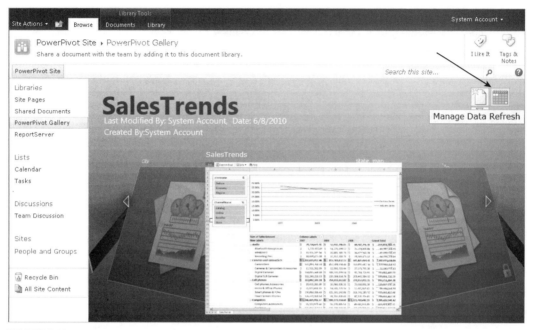

FIGURE 8-10

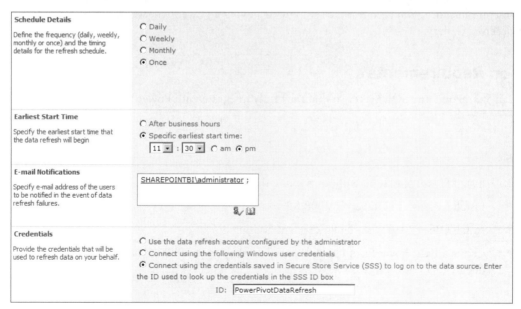

FIGURE 8-11

You can verify that the data refresh was successful by clicking Manage Data Refresh again to see the list of refreshes that have occurred, as shown in Figure 8-12.

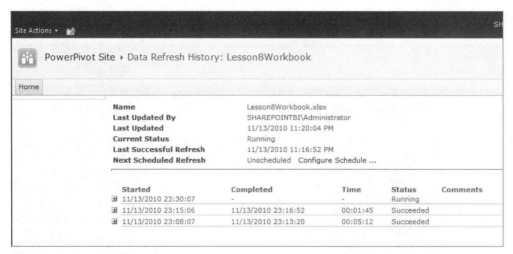

FIGURE 8-12

TRY IT

In this Try It, you learn how to successfully install and configure a PowerPivot-ready standalone SharePoint instance. You then test the setup by deploying a PowerPivot workbook to a SharePoint PowerPivot Gallery.

Lesson Requirements

Install SharePoint and SQL Server so that they fully integrate with PowerPivot documents that are deployed to the server.

Hints

- ➤ Install SharePoint 2010 without running the configuration wizard.
- ➤ Install Microsoft SQL Server 2008 R2.
- ➤ Install Office 2010 with the PowerPivot add-in.
- ➤ Create a basic PowerPivot example based on the AdventureWorksDW2008R2 database and deploy to a PowerPivot Gallery.

Step-by-Step

1. Log on as the administrator to the desired server for the installation of SharePoint.

2. Run the `PrerequisiteInstaller.exe` from the SharePoint install DVD to ensure all the necessary prerequisites are installed prior to running the full setup. When this is complete restart the machine and log back in as the administrator.

3. Run the `setup.exe` from the SharePoint install DVD and select Install SharePoint Server.

4. After accepting the licensing agreement click Continue.

5. Figure 8-13 shows the next dialog, which asks if you would like to do a Standalone or Server Farm installation. Here you must choose Server Farm because PowerPivot is supported only in Server Farm mode.

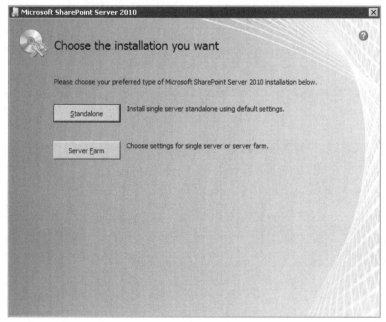

FIGURE 8-13

6. In the Server Type dialog choose Complete — Install All Components, then click Install Now to begin the installation as shown in Figure 8-14.

7. When this installation completes you will be given the option to configure SharePoint by checking Run the SharePoint Products Configuration Wizard Now, as shown in Figure 8-15. Do not check this option because you will use the PowerPivot for SharePoint SQL Server installer, which configures SharePoint as part of the New Farm install option.

8. Exit the SharePoint installation and launch the SQL Server 2008 R2 installer.

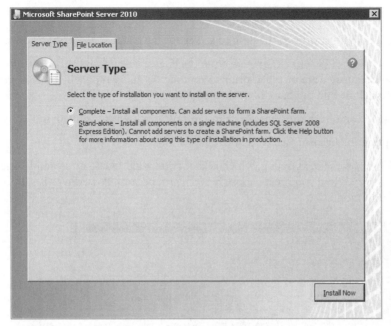

FIGURE 8-14

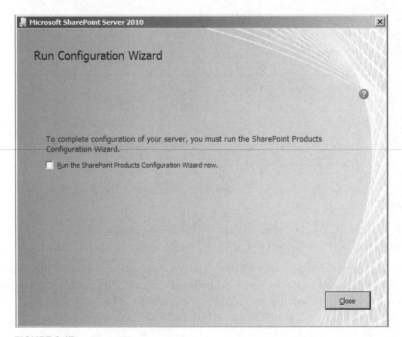

FIGURE 8-15

9. Select the Installation page and click New installation or add features to an existing installation.

10. Click OK once the Setup Support Rules complete.

11. On the next dialog you will be required to enter your product key. After entering your key click Next.

12. You will then be required to accept the licensing terms. Click the checkbox to accept and click Next.

13. Click Install to install all the Setup Support Files to be installed.

14. In the Setup Support Rules dialog click Next.

15. Select SQL Server PowerPivot for SharePoint, as shown in Figure 8-16, and click Next.

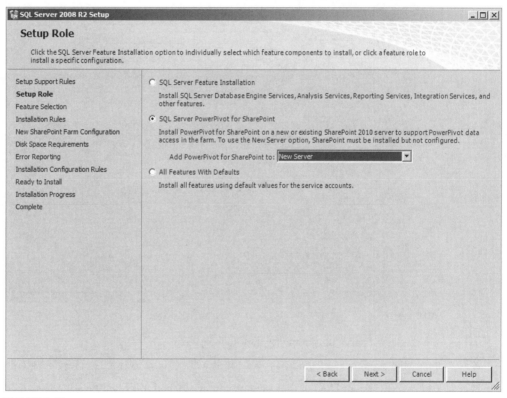

FIGURE 8-16

16. In the Feature Selection dialog click Next.

17. Click Next again in the Installation Rule dialog after the Install Rules Check completes.

18. The instance name that will be created for the SQL Server Engine and SQL Server Analysis Server will be PowerPivot. Accept the defaults and click Next.

19. Specify credentials for the Server Farm Account, as shown in Figure 8-17. This account must be a domain account (Windows administrator account is not good enough here) and can be changed later from SharePoint Central Administration.

20. You will also be required to provide a passphrase, which will be used when adding additional servers to the farm.

21. Provide a port number, which will be used for hosting SharePoint Central Administration, and click Next.

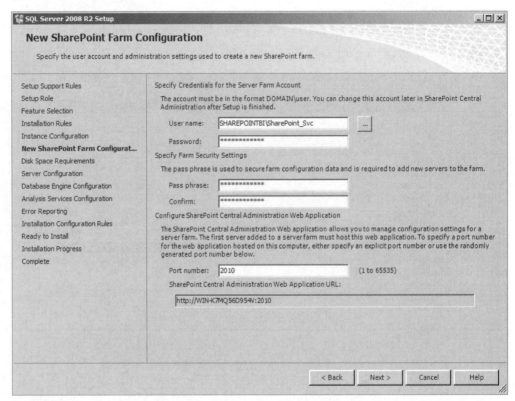

FIGURE 8-17

22. On the Disk Space Requirements dialog click Next.

23. Select the account name and password that will be used to run each service and click Next.

24. Click Add Current User so the account you are logged in as will be added as an administrator of the Database Engine and click Next.

25. Click Add Current User so the account you are logged in as will be added as an administrator of the Analysis Server and click Next.

26. Click Next on the Error Reporting dialog to continue.

27. In the Installation Configuration Rules dialog click Next.

28. Click Install after reviewing the summary information.

29. After the installation process completes, test your SharePoint site. Open Internet Explorer and enter the URL `http://<YourServerName>`. This may take up to several minutes to load the first time, but will look like Figure 8-18 once it completes.

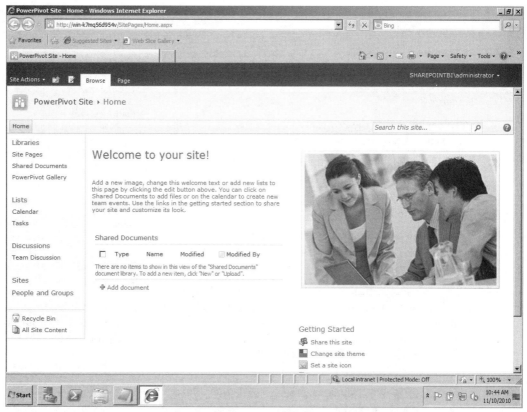

FIGURE 8-18

30. Ensure that the PowerPivot add-in for Excel 2010 has been downloaded and installed. You can find the download at `http://tinyurl.com/PowerPivotDownload`.

31. Open Excel 2010 where you will create a basic PowerPivot document that can be deployed to your new SharePoint instance.

32. Select the PowerPivot tab and click the PowerPivot Window button in the ribbon.

33. After the PowerPivot for Excel window opens select From SQL Server in the From Database drop-down box.

34. Type in the server name where the Adventure Works sample database has been installed and select AdventureWorksDW2008R2 from the Database Name drop-down box. Click Next.

35. On the Choose How to Import the Data page leave the default Select from a list of tables and views to choose the data to import and click Next.

36. From the table list select FactInternetSales and click the Select Related Tables button. This should give you a total of six tables selected. Click Finish when this is correct.

37. After the wizard completes, import the data from these tables into PowerPivot and click Close.

38. Click the PivotTable button in the ribbon and click OK when it asks to create the PivotTable in a new worksheet.

39. From the FactInternetSales table check the Order Quantity field.

40. From the DimSalesTerritory table check the fields SalesTerritoryGroup, SalesTerritoryCountry, and SalesTerritoryRegion. Your worksheet should look like Figure 8-19.

41. To deploy this to the PowerPivot site select the File tab and choose Save & Send.

42. Click Save to SharePoint and click the Save As button. In the top of the Save As window, type in the SharePoint site that was created earlier: `http://<YourServerName>`.

43. Open the PowerPivot Gallery and rename the file `Lesson8Workbook`, as shown in Figure 8-20, and click Save.

44. This will automatically open Lesson8Workbook in the web browser. You can optionally navigate to the PowerPivot Gallery through the SharePoint site and select the gallery from the navigation bar. This will allow you to view your documents in the carousel view as shown in Figure 8-21. (You may be prompted to install Silverlight to view the PowerPivot Gallery.)

Row Labels	Sum of OrderQuantity
⊟ **Europe**	**18089**
⊟ **France**	**5558**
France	5558
⊟ **Germany**	**5625**
Germany	5625
⊟ **United Kingdom**	**6906**
United Kingdom	6906
⊟ **North America**	**28964**
⊟ **Canada**	**7620**
Canada	7620
⊟ **United States**	**21344**
Central	20
Northeast	27
Northwest	8993
Southeast	39
Southwest	12265
⊟ **Pacific**	**13345**
⊟ **Australia**	**13345**
Australia	13345
Grand Total	**60398**

FIGURE 8-19

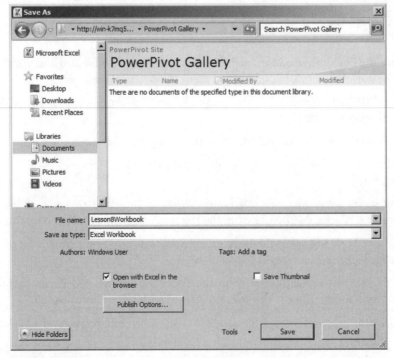

FIGURE 8-20

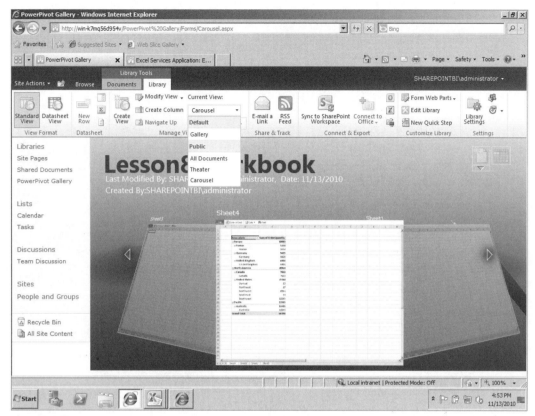

FIGURE 8-21

Congratulations! You have configured a standalone instance of SharePoint with PowerPivot integration and deployed your first PowerPivot workbook to a PowerPivot Gallery.

 Please select Lesson 8 on the DVD to view the video that accompanies this lesson.

Creating Your First SharePoint Site for Business Intelligence

A SharePoint site is the principal method for collaboration in any SharePoint setup, whether that is in a standalone server or a farmed server. The SharePoint site is where all users go to find their libraries that contain Excel files, view custom dashboards, or even check on something simple like the status of an item that is part of a task list. All of these different components are essential to the day-to-day operations of many companies, and as such, need to be configured correctly in your site. With the addition of several new site templates in SharePoint 2010 the configuration has become easier than ever. You have a lot of different options to choose from, so this lesson is here to help you make the correct choices.

UNDERSTANDING WEB APPLICATIONS, SITE COLLECTIONS, AND SITES

Before creating a site in SharePoint it is essential you understand the hierarchy of the SharePoint site. What is the difference between a site and a web application? Does a site collection belong to a web application or the other way around? The following list shows an outline of the site hierarchy.

- ➤ Web Application
  - ➤ Site Collection 1
    - ➤ Site 1
    - ➤ Site 2
  - ➤ Site Collection 2
    - ➤ Site 1
- ➤ Sub Site 1

At the top of this hierarchy is the web application. In its simplest form this is a website in IIS. You will notice in Figure 9-1 that both Central Administration and the custom application (called SharePoint – 80) are shown as separate entries in the IIS Manager. Naturally, because the web application is at the top, it must be created before you can create a new site.

FIGURE 9-1

Directly below the web application is the site collection. A site collection is exactly what the name implies; it is a group of sites. When you create a site collection, what is known as a top-level site is created as well. All the sites within a collection have shared administrator settings and common features. In your organization you may have a single site collection with a single site, a single site collection with multiple sites, or multiple site collections each with multiple sites. Each configuration has advantages and disadvantages ranging from security implications, performance, maintenance (that is, backups), and even navigation. These situations are out of scope for this book, but be sure to research this ahead of time because it could potentially be very difficult and time consuming to change your mind at a later date. There is not necessarily a one-to-one ratio of web applications to site collections. This can be a one-to-many relationship; as mentioned before, this will depend on your organization's size and needs.

Sites are the smallest unit in this hierarchy and make up the site collection. These can be created as anything from a blank page to an entire site preconfigured and waiting for content by using one of the built-in templates. As mentioned, the site is the go-to location for all the business needs. You can think of a SharePoint site just as you would any other website on the Internet. A site will have different pages, each serving a specific function; for instance, storing a list of tasks, navigation features such as the ability to go back to the previous page, and interactivity through the use of links that will take you directly to a subpage or an external page. A site will have its own unique link and can be customized to meet a specific need such as for blogs, wikis, or team collaboration as in the case of the Business Intelligence site. Because a site is generally for a specific purpose only certain people will have access to it. For instance, a site customized for the Human Resources department would not allow someone from the sales department access. From this point in the hierarchy there are subsites, which are just sites created under the directory of an existing site.

You can see in Figure 9-2 the possible different sites that could be associated under a site collection. In this case the company has a site collection called ABC Widgets and a site for each department.

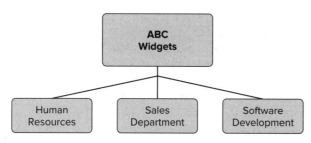

FIGURE 9-2

CREATING A SITE IN SHAREPOINT 2010

In this lesson you create a basic site using a template included in SharePoint 2010 called the Business Intelligence Center. To get started, open Central Administration by clicking the Start menu, navigating to Microsoft SharePoint 2010 Products, and selecting SharePoint 2010 Central Administration. Click the link that says Application Management and then select Manage Web Applications under the Web Application heading. This will list all the current web applications currently in your SharePoint setup. Make note of any ports that are being used already in the Port column on the right side of the screen because there can be only one web application associated with a given port. At the very least SharePoint Central Administration will be on this list. Click New from the ribbon at the top. The Create New Web Application screen will appear as shown in Figure 9-3.

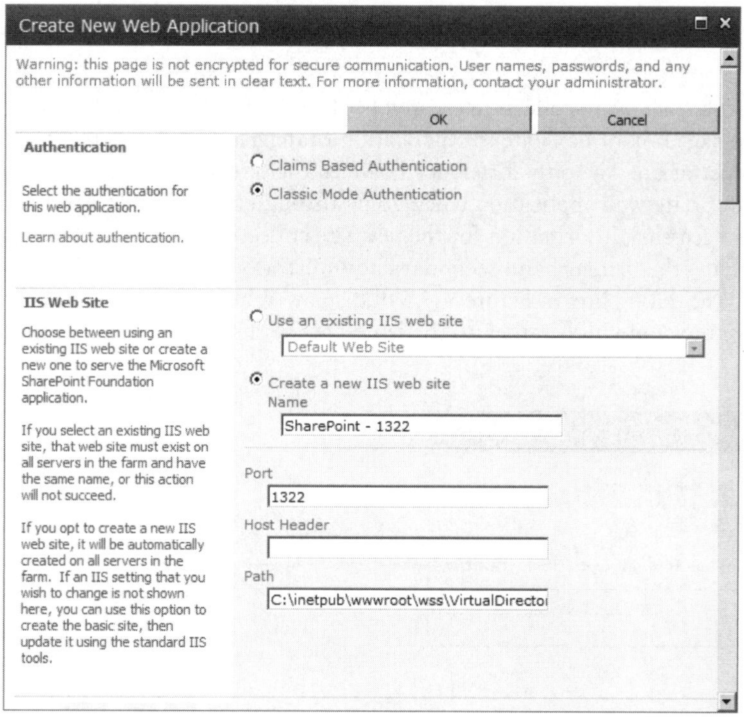

FIGURE 9-3

Keep the option for Create a New IIS Web Site selected and enter a name for your application in the box. Enter the port on which you want the site to operate as well. Any information entered here will be applied to all servers in the farm. Any of the IIS fields here as well as all additional IIS settings not listed here can be changed at any time through the IIS Manager on the server. Keep the option for Create New Application Pool selected, change the name if desired, and select a security account for the application pool. Under Database Name and Authentication enter the necessary information for connecting to the database. Generally the default is fine in this location. If you have a secondary server that is mirroring your primary database enter that server name in the Failover Database Server box. Finally, click OK at the bottom and your web application will be created. The message shown in Figure 9-4 will be displayed.

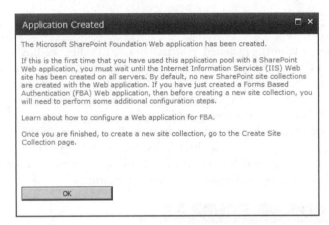

FIGURE 9-4

As indicated in the message, there is no site collection created by default. To create a collection either click the link in the message box or navigate to Application Management ⇨ Create Site Collections in Central Administration. The only difference between the screens that will appear is an option to select the appropriate web application when going through the link in Central Administration. Enter all the necessary information for the new site collection including a name, selecting a template, and entering the primary and secondary administrators. Click OK. The site collection will be created and the dialog box in Figure 9-5 will display. When you navigate to the URL displayed in the message box you will be taken to the template site that was selected in the previous step.

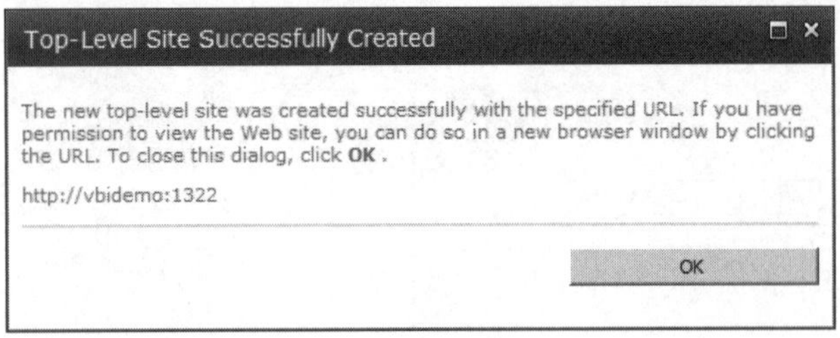

FIGURE 9-5

The top-level site that was just created is your basis for everything else in your SharePoint site. If you would like to add more sites to this web application you can do so by going to the site URL that was provided in the previous message box and logging in with an account that has administrator access. From the Site Actions drop-down, select New Site as shown in Figure 9-6. Fill out the resulting form by entering a name, URL, and picking a template. The final option is to decide if you would like the navigation bar at the top of the page to mimic what is listed on the current top-level site. Selecting No allows the subsequent site to have navigation independent of the top-level site. Now, when visiting the homepage created from the site collection, the name you entered will be listed on the navigation bar. Clicking the name, which will be a hyperlink, will bring you to the new site you just created.

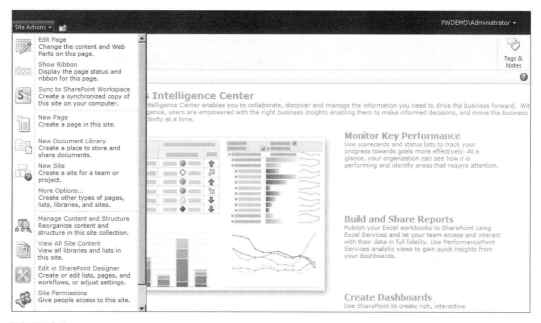

FIGURE 9-6

SITE OPTIONS AND TEMPLATES

Regardless of the type of site you have selected you should be aware of some other options for your site. Many different items can be added to your site. These come in a variety of forms such as libraries for storing different types of documents and information, as well as blank pages and Web Parts where you can add custom code and embed items like reports. To add these items click Site Actions in the top-left corner of any site page and select More Options. All of these items are there to customize your SharePoint site to allow for the type of functionality you desire. For instance, you would select the Data Connections library for storing .odc files for use by Excel Services. You may opt for a report library in which to store Reporting Services reports. Regardless of the use of the site, there is a library that is right for you.

SharePoint 2010 has several new templates included to help get you started. The templates in SharePoint will create a shell with a good foundation to get you started on whatever your desired functionality is. The templates are broken down into sections as shown in Figure 9-7. As you highlight each template the description below the box will change. The Blank Site template will create an empty page with links to Libraries, Lists, and Discussions. It is up to you to decide exactly what type of libraries you need as well as what pages you want displayed. The Team Site is a great option for setting up a project collaboration page. It will create document libraries, task lists, discussion pages, and a calendar so everyone can be on the same page from the start of your project. Several of the options under the Enterprise tab are great choices as well. An obvious choice if you have picked up this book is the Business Intelligence Center. This is also the option mentioned earlier in this lesson.

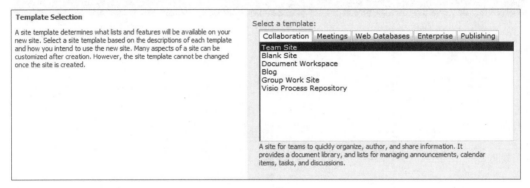

FIGURE 9-7

BUSINESS INTELLIGENCE SITES

Getting the right site components can be difficult when starting a new SharePoint site. You want to ensure that you have the right libraries, the correct pages, and all the proper features enabled. Building a Business Intelligence site for your organization is no different. Keep the following factors in mind when building your site:

➤ What kind of reporting tools you use (Excel, Reporting Services, and so on)

➤ How you want data represented (Files, dashboards, lists)

➤ What kind of end user applications are used (Excel, Access, Visio)

➤ Document size (Download files or render in browser)

Each of these topics presents its own unique setup requirements. There is a pretty solid base of libraries and pages to add to your site to make sure it can handle all your needs, and with a little tweaking here and there will make your site work for you.

Libraries are very useful and important when it comes to storing your Business Intelligence data. The Document library is the basis for storing all types of documents. This includes Word, Excel 97 and 2007-2010, and PowerPoint presentations. One of the great features of the Document library is the ability to check documents in and out. This will help ensure that no one makes changes to a document just to have another version uploaded by someone else that was based on a previous version. The Report library is perfect for storing SQL Server Reporting Services reports. It will allow you to do versioning for your organization to keep track of changes as well. Another important library, especially if you will be employing the assistance of the Reporting Services Web Part, is the Data Connections library. This library is the perfect way to organize all your data connections for SSRS reports and .odc files for use in a variety of other features.

A further draw of SharePoint is the ability to use Web Parts. These will allow you to take portions of Excel files or SSRS reports, a graph of sales by store for instance, and display it directly in the web page. Each time the data is loaded it can be set to refresh so it is constantly up-to-date each time the page is opened. Web parts give the user a snapshot of only the most useful information so they don't have to download three Excel workbooks and view two reports to get just a single piece of information from each. With Web Parts available to display Excel workbooks, SSRS reports, charts, graphs, PerformancePoint scorecards, and many more information sources, the value of a well-designed dashboard using Web Parts can be invaluable to any organization.

Of course the ability to add many of these options comes from ensuring that your site has the appropriate features enabled. Many of these topics are covered in other lessons in this section of the book. Each of the other lessons in this section give you the instructions necessary to get things such as Excel Services and PerformancePoint Services configured so you can add them to your dashboard. If your organization is using SQL Server Reporting Services there is a special Web Part just for displaying SSRS reports in your browser.

As was mentioned earlier, the Business Intelligence Center template is a great starting point for your SharePoint site. If it doesn't meet all your requirements, or has too many features, it is a good tool to be able to see what some of the default settings are on different libraries and lists.

Now that you have learned how to create a new SharePoint web application and site, put that knowledge to the test in the Try It section.

TRY IT

In this Try It you learn how to create a new web application, site collection, site, and library. Once created, this site will be the foundation for displaying Business Intelligence data from a variety of sources.

Lesson Requirements

After the top-level site is created, add another site called Sales Department, where the sales team can house and share their internal SSRS reports, and where you can later create a dashboard for the sales manager.

Hints

➤ You need to create a new web application.

➤ Choose the Business Intelligence Center as your site template.

➤ Choose a team site as the template for the Sales Reports site.

➤ Add an additional library called Reporting Services Reports.

➤ The library type should be a report library.

Step-by-Step

1. Open SharePoint Central Administration by clicking the Start menu and choosing Microsoft SharePoint 2010 Products ⇨ SharePoint 2010 Central Administration.

2. Enter an Administrator's credentials when prompted.

3. Click Manage Web Applications under the Application Management section.

4. Click New from the ribbon at the top.

5. When the Create New Web Application Wizard opens be sure Classic Mode Authentication is selected.

6. Select the Create a New IIS Web Site option and enter `SharePointBI` in the Name box.

7. Scroll down to Application Pool and select Create New Application Pool.

8. In the Application Pool Name box enter **SharePointBI**.

9. Select a security account for the application pool.

10. Click OK.

11. Click OK when the Application Created screen appears.

12. You will be brought back to the Web Applications Management screen. It should now look similar to Figure 9-8.

13. Click the Application Management link on the left side of the screen.

14. Under Site Collections select Create Site Collections.

15. Click the drop-down next to Web Application and select Change Web Application.

16. A screen will appear showing all the web applications. Select SharePointBI from the list.

17. In the Title box enter **Business Intelligence Site**.

18. In the Template Selection section click the tab labeled Enterprise.

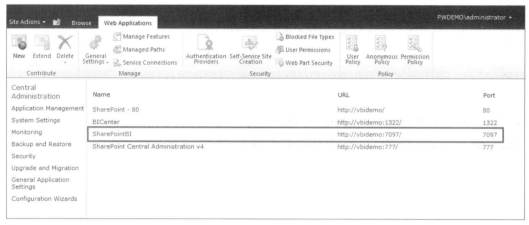

FIGURE 9-8

19. Highlight Business Intelligence Center.

20. Your screen should now look like Figure 9-9.

21. Enter a primary and secondary (secondary is optional) site collection administrator in the appropriate fields.

22. Click OK.

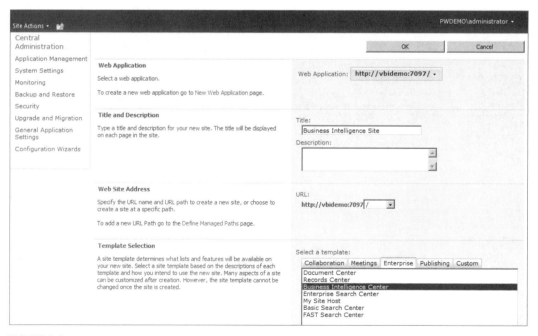

FIGURE 9-9

23. Your site has now been created. A screen will appear that has a message, a link to the site, and an OK button. Click the link to the site to open it.

24. If prompted, enter your credentials.

25. Click the Site Actions drop-down in the top-left corner of the page.

26. Select New Site from the list.

27. For the Title enter **Sales Department**.

28. In the URL Name box enter **SalesDepartment** (with no space).

29. In the Template Selection section, choose Team Site.

30. Choose Yes in the Navigation Inheritance option so the navigation from the top-level site will show up here as well.

31. Click Create.

32. You will be brought to your new team site; click Site Actions in the top-left corner again.

33. Select More Options from the list.

34. Under the Libraries section, click Report Library.

35. Enter **Sales Team Reports** in the Name field and click Create when your screen looks like Figure 9-10.

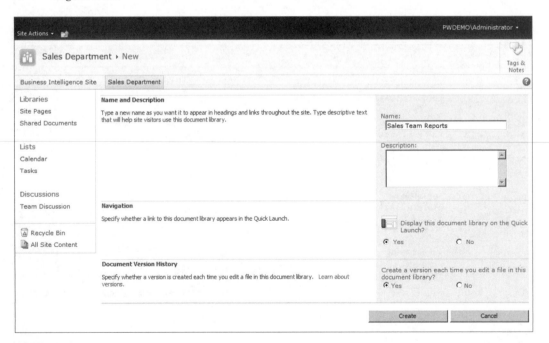

FIGURE 9-10

The final step is to enable your site to be able to take advantage of service applications such as Excel Services, which will allow Excel files to be used in Web Parts and opened in the browser. See the other lessons in Section II for more information on how to configure each individual service application you would like to take advantage of.

Congratulations! You have just created a new SharePoint web application, a site collection, and a custom site for the sales department with a library where they can store all the sales reports they develop in SSRS.

 Please select Lesson 9 on the DVD to view the video that accompanies this lesson.

10

Configuring Reporting Services for SharePoint Integration

Reporting Services integration with SharePoint has been available for several iterations of both tools now. With each version, configuring the integration has become much less problematic. Major steps have been taken to simplify the process so the integration is seamless. In this lesson you walk through the steps needed to configure either a new instance of Reporting Services for SharePoint integration or change an existing native mode instance of Reporting Services to SharePoint integrated mode.

CONFIGURING REPORTING SERVICES FOR SHAREPOINT INTEGRATED MODE

You may have noticed while stepping through the SQL Server installer that, if you included Reporting Services as part of the installation, the installer asked whether you would like to install in SharePoint integrated mode. Selecting Install the SharePoint Integrated Mode Default Configuration, shown in Figure 10-1, will save you the trouble of manually converting the report server databases, which are created with every installation of Reporting Services, to be in SharePoint integrated mode. When installing Reporting Services for the very first time this is all you must do to have it ready for SharePoint integration.

If you have previously installed Reporting Services in native mode, without SharePoint integration, you must manually make the switch to integrate the two products. To start the process of manually converting from native mode to integrated mode, open the Reporting Services Configuration Manager and connect to the instance of Reporting Services you want to change. The Reporting Services Configuration Manager is found by navigating to Start ➪ All Programs ➪ Microsoft SQL Server 2008 R2 ➪ Configuration Tools ➪ Reporting Services Configuration Manager. Ensure the service is started and then select the Database page, shown in Figure 10-2.

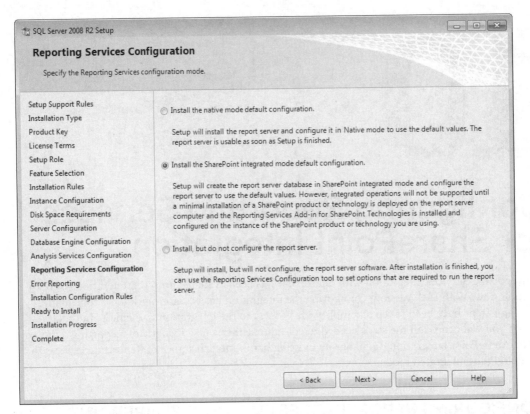

FIGURE 10-1

Click the Change Database button, which opens the Report Server Database Configuration Wizard. Select Create a New Report Server Database, and click Next. Choose the database engine instance on which you want to create the new integrated report server database, and click Next. Figure 10-3 shows that you must switch the Report Server Mode property from Native Mode to SharePoint Integrated Mode, and click Next. Complete the rest of the wizard using the defaults.

You have now configured Reporting Services to work in SharePoint integrated mode, and if you attempt to view reports using the Report Manager (http://ServerName/Reports) you will receive the following error:

```
This operation is not supported on a report server that is configured to run in
SharePoint integrated mode. (rsOperationNotSupportedSharePointMode)
```

You have a few more steps to do on the SharePoint side to complete the integration, which are discussed in the next section.

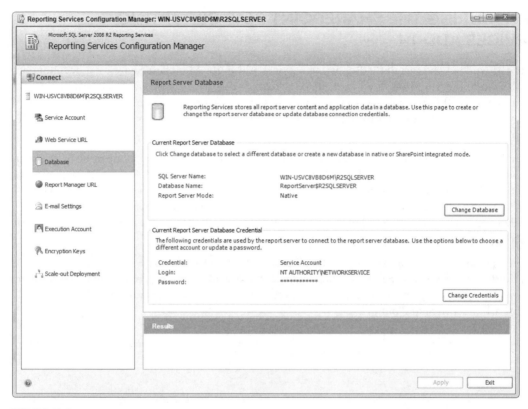

FIGURE 10-2

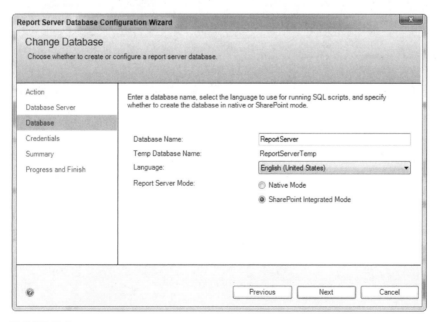

FIGURE 10-3

CONFIGURING THE SHAREPOINT 2010 REPORTING SERVICES ADD-IN

First, download and install the Reporting Services add-in for Microsoft SharePoint Technologies 2010. Go to the Microsoft download site (www.microsoft.com/downloads) and search for SharePoint 2010 Reporting Services Add-in to ensure you get the most up-to-date version. After downloading the add-in, run the installer, in which you will be able to specify whether you will be deploying to a SharePoint farm or a standalone instance of SharePoint.

With the add-in installation complete, you can now configure the feature by opening SharePoint Central Administration and clicking General Application Settings. Look for the Reporting Services section: if this section is missing, the add-in did not properly install. Select Reporting Services Integration and specify the report server site in the Report Server Web Service URL (http://servername/reportserver), shown in Figure 10-4. You will also need to set up security credentials before you click OK.

You then have the option to configure the "Set server" defaults to change some of the default options set for Reporting Services. These include, but are not limited to, a property to limit report snapshots and a property to configure which version of Report Builder launches when you click Report Builder in SharePoint.

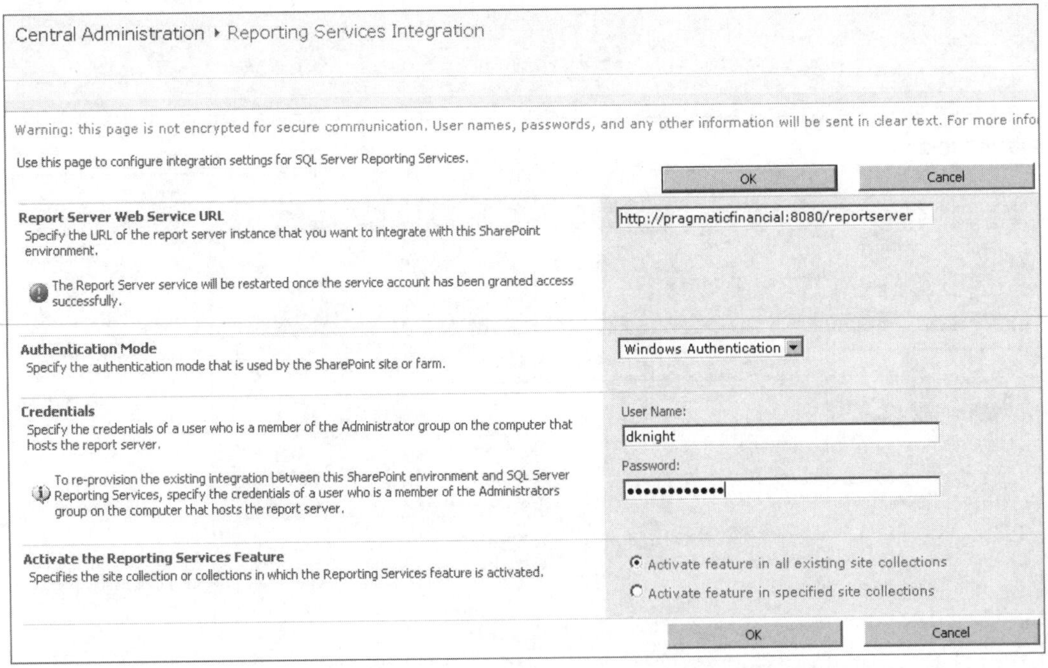

FIGURE 10-4

Now that you have completed the configuration needed to integrate Reporting Services and SharePoint, you are ready to test it by attempting to deploy reports.

TESTING THE REPORTING SERVICES CONFIGURATION

Deploying to SharePoint is a lot like deploying to the regular report server. After you have opened Business Intelligence Development Studio (BIDS), right-click the Report Server project and select Properties. In the Deployment section, shown in Figure 10-5, first point the TargetServerURL property to the SharePoint URL. Then point the four properties labeled Target above this one to the appropriate library to which you want to deploy. Once you have finished configuring, right-click the project, and, this time, select Deploy.

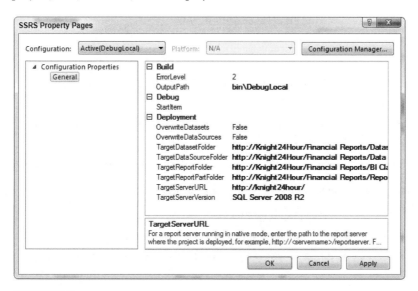

FIGURE 10-5

Once your reports complete deployment you can navigate to the SharePoint library to which you just chose to deploy and select the report to view it in SharePoint.

TRY IT

In this lesson, you learned when installing Reporting Services for the first time that it is very simple to make it SharePoint ready. It only requires that you select Install the SharePoint Integrated Mode Default Configuration during installation.

So, this Try It focuses on the more difficult task of changing an existing Report Server configuration from native mode to SharePoint integrated. Then you will configure SharePoint to use this newly reconfigured Report Server database.

Lesson Requirements

This lesson assumes that Reporting Services has already been installed previously but you would like to change it from native mode to SharePoint integrated. You will then install the Reporting Services add-in for Microsoft SharePoint Technologies 2010 and configure SharePoint to complete the integration.

Hints

➤ Use the Reporting Services Configuration Manager to change the Report Server database type.

➤ Install the Reporting Services add-in for Microsoft SharePoint Technologies 2010.

➤ Use SharePoint Central Administration to configure the add-in.

Step-by-Step

1. Go to Start ➪ All Programs ➪ Microsoft SQL Server 2008 R2 ➪ Configuration Tools ➪ Reporting Services Configuration Manager.

2. Click Connect after selecting the Report Server instance you would like to change from native mode to SharePoint integrated.

3. If the Report Server is not already started you must click Start on the Report Server Status page.

4. Select the Database page, shown in Figure 10-6, and click Change Database.

5. Select Create a New Report Server Database and click Next.

6. Provide the Server Name where this new SharePoint integrated Report Server database will be created. Click Test Connection to ensure you have access to the server before you click Next.

7. Give the Report Server database a name, as shown in Figure 10-7, select SharePoint Integrated Mode, and click Next.

8. Set the permissions that will be used for Reporting Services accessing the SQL Server Report Server database and click Next.

9. Click Next on the Summary page.

10. The last screen will actually create the new Report Server database for you. Once this completes click Finish and close out of the configuration manager. You are now ready to install and configure the SharePoint integration.

11. Go to www.microsoft.com/downloads and search for the latest version of the Reporting Services add-in for Microsoft SharePoint Technologies 2010. Download and install the add-in.

12. Configure the add-in on SharePoint Central Administration by selecting General Application Settings.

13. Under the Reporting Services heading select Reporting Services Integration.

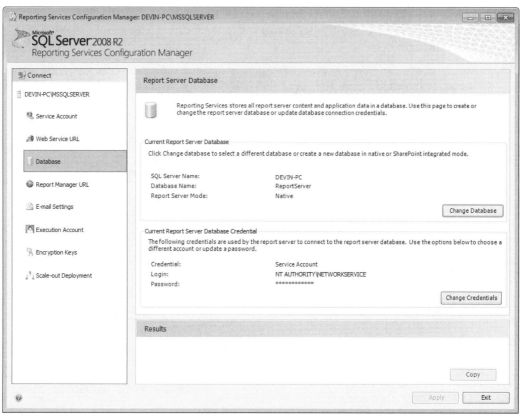

FIGURE 10-6

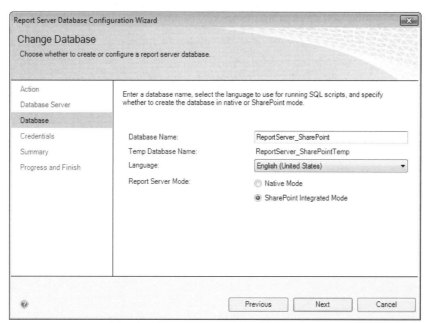

FIGURE 10-7

14. Provide your Reporting Services Web Service URL, which usually looks like `http://servername/reportserver`, and change the Authentication Mode to Windows Authentication.

15. Specify an account of a user that is an Administrator on the machine that hosts the Report Server, as shown in Figure 10-8. And click OK. This will configure the feature and by default will also activate it on all existing sites.

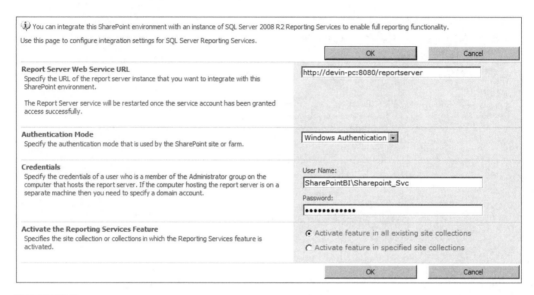

FIGURE 10-8

Congratulations! You have configured an existing instance of Reporting Services for SharePoint integration.

 Please select Lesson 10 on the DVD to view the video that accompanies this lesson.

11

Implementing Business Connectivity Services in SharePoint

In this lesson, you learn how to create a BCS list connected to a table in SQL Server, which enables the editing of data in SQL tables directly from SharePoint.

WHAT IS BCS?

BCS, short for Business Connectivity Services, is a technology built within SharePoint for the purpose of connecting to external data sources, such as SQL or other ODBC data sources, as well as web services, with the advantage that other components of SharePoint will treat these data sources as if they were SharePoint lists. This connection allows for full CRUD (Create/Read/Update/Delete) operations. BCS solutions can be designed using either SharePoint Designer or Visual Studio, with differing levels of complexity and capability. Using Visual Studio exposes a greater level of functionality, with the full flexibility of being able to write in C# (or your .NET language of choice). Of course, this full flexibility comes with the requirement that you write code — this has benefits especially when connecting to web services. This lesson covers only SharePoint Designer, because it is adequate for updating dimension tables in a data warehouse.

BUSINESS CONNECTIVITY SERVICES VS. BDC

SharePoint 2007 introduced the Business Data Catalog (BDC) as a technology to connect external data sources within SharePoint. This technology used XML documents to map an external data source, store a defined subset of that data as an index inside SharePoint, and then expose that data within SharePoint. This becomes really powerful when using data from a LOB (Line of Business) system, or even Exchange. One use would be storing an index for where to retrieve data, along with some fields to identify the data — for example, a name and surname from Exchange — and then retrieving other information, such as business unit or title.

Two limitations of this approach are immediately apparent: this data is read-only, and the mapping needs to done by hand in XML.

In SharePoint 2010, these limitations were both addressed by extending the BDC system to include read/write capabilities, and by introducing new features to SharePoint Designer to allow working with BCS.

DESIGN PRINCIPLES IN BCS

At its heart, BCS is based on external content types. An external content type is an extension of the content type within SharePoint. A content type is a reusable schema for lists, and an external content type extends this concept to include the data access capabilities. When using SQL, an external content type is mapped to a table, including the connection details to connect to the server. The schema details store the structure of the table — the columns and their data types, as well as any keys that are needed to uniquely identify a record.

Acting on external content types are *operations* — these are the actions that can be performed. At a minimum these need to include a read list (to show the entire list) and read item (to read a single item), but can also be expanded to include insert, update, and delete. Whereas the Create, Update, Edit, and View List Item operations all act on a single item in the list, View List returns a list of results, and to make this manageable, filters need to be added. These filters can be limit filters, to return items in a paged manner, or they can be filter parameters, allowing the user to select a value to filter the returned items.

Creating only View List Items and View Item operations is useful when using BCS purely for indexing external content in SharePoint.

Once operations have been created, a list based on the content type must be added. This list, like any SharePoint list, will have ListItems, AddItems, and ViewItems pages created that can then be edited — either as SharePoint pages in SharePoint Designer, or they can be replaced with either InfoPath forms or custom ASPX pages using Visual Studio.

The final piece of the design principles is the association of content types — this represents exactly the relational principles from a database, and allows for such functionality as drop-down selection boxes.

The relationship of all these items is shown in Figure 11-1.

INSTALLING AND CONFIGURING BCS

The Business Data Connectivity service needs to be running and set up in order to use the functionality. BCS is an enterprise feature, and as such SharePoint Enterprise features need to be enabled.

Open up the SharePoint Central Administration site, and click Manage Service Applications under Application Management. On this page, first check for a service with type Business Data Connectivity Service Application, as shown in Figure 11-2.

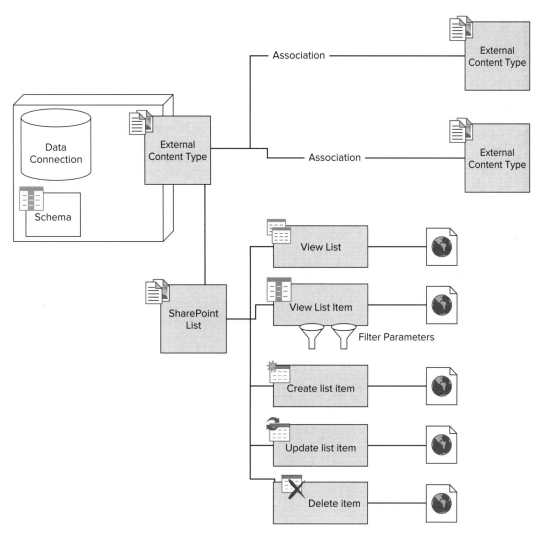

FIGURE 11-1

Central Administration	Name	Type	Status
Application Management	Access Services	Access Services Web Service Application	Started
System Settings	Access Services	Access Services Web Service Application Proxy	Started
Monitoring	Application Discovery and Load Balancer Service Application	Application Discovery and Load Balancer Service Application	Started
Backup and Restore			
Security	Application Discovery and Load Balancer Service Application Proxy_fd5d3840-b54d-4be3-9fd3-638e7412b3e7	Application Discovery and Load Balancer Service Application Proxy	Started
Upgrade and Migration	Application Registry Service	Application Registry Service	Started
General Application Settings	Application Registry Service	Application Registry Proxy	Started
Configuration Wizards	Business Data Connectivity Service	Business Data Connectivity Service Application	Started
	Business Data Connectivity Service	Business Data Connectivity Service Application Proxy	Started

FIGURE 11-2

If you don't see this entry, you need to add it. Click New ➪ Business Data Connectivity service, as shown in Figure 11-3.

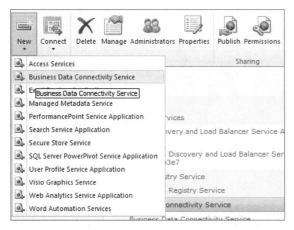

FIGURE 11-3

On the settings screen, give your service application a name, and name the database and the application pool similarly, as shown in Figure 11-4.

Name	Service Application Name
Enter the name of the Business Data Connectivity Service Application. The name entered here will be used in the list of Service Applications displayed in the Manage Service Applications page.	BCS
Database	Database Server
Use of the default database server and database name is recommended for most cases. Refer to the administrator's guide for advanced scenarios where specifying database information is required.	MGS-2010BI\SQL2k8r2
	Database Name
Use of Windows authentication is strongly recommended. To use SQL authentication, specify the credentials which will be used to connect to the database.	BCS_Service_DB
	Database authentication
	⦿ Windows authentication (recommended)
	◯ SQL authentication
	Account
	Password
Failover Server	Failover Database Server
You can choose to associate a database with a specific failover server that is used in conjuction with SQL Server database mirroring.	
Application Pool	◯ Use existing application pool
Choose the Application Pool to use for this Service Application. This defines the account and credentials that will be used by this web service.	SecurityTokenServiceApplicationPool
	⦿ Create new application pool
You can choose an existing application pool or create a new one.	Application pool name
	BCS
	Select a security account for this application pool
	◯ Predefined
	Network Service
	⦿ Configurable
	MGS\administrator
	Register new managed account

FIGURE 11-4

Click OK twice to finish the installation.

CREATING A NEW BCS LIST IN SHAREPOINT 2010

SharePoint Designer is a separate tool, available for a free download from Microsoft. To get to the download page, choose Site Actions ➪ Edit in SharePoint Designer, and you will be taken to the download page. Ensure that you install the version that is the same as your Office install. If you have 32 bit Office installed (the default), install 32 bit SharePoint Designer. PowerPivot works better with 64 bit versions, so if you have to decide whether to use 32 bit or 64 bit, use 64 bit and make sure that both Office and SharePoint Designer are the same version. Any development in BCS starts with SharePoint Designer, and as per the design principles mentioned in the preceding section, will start by creating an External Content Type, as shown in Figure 11-5.

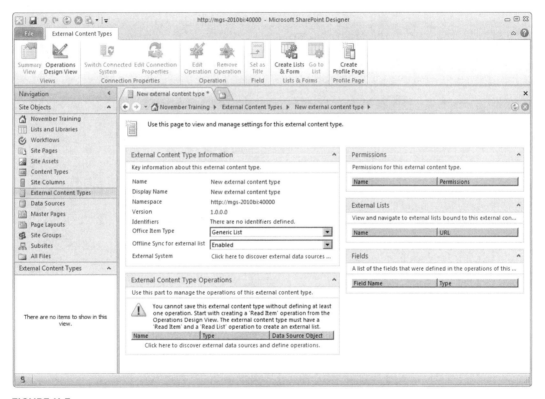

FIGURE 11-5

Name the content type, and click the Click Here to Discover External Data Sources link — you enter connection details to the SQL server where the data is stored, and choose a table to add operations to. This is also where you add associations, as shown in Figure 11-6.

Choosing Create All Operations is often the quickest approach — a wizard is included to guide you through the process, and helps set up the filters as well as map the keys. The three steps of the wizard are shown in Figures 11-7 through 11-9.

In the first step of the wizard, you set the name and display name, as shown in Figure 11-7.

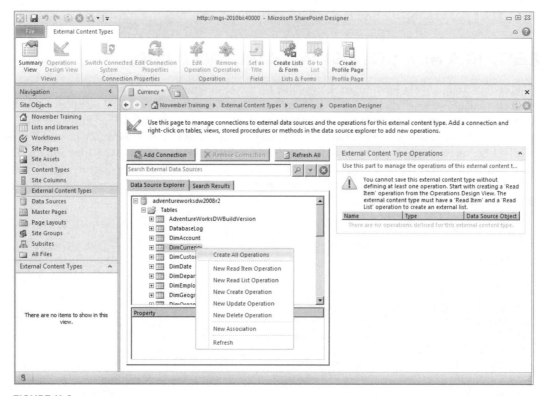

FIGURE 11-6

In the second step of the wizard, the individual column properties are defined, as shown in Figure 11-8.

➤ **Identifier** — This identifies keys in the table.

➤ **Field** — Maps to the check box selecting whether this field is included.

➤ **Display Name** — The name as it will be displayed in SharePoint.

➤ **Foreign Identifier** — Clicking this button opens a window to link another external content type.

➤ **Required** — This field is required to be filled in when adding new items.

➤ **Read-Only** — Fields that can't be edited by a user, for instance, an IDENTITY field.

➤ **Office Property** — This is used only when mapping BCS to office documents.

➤ **Show in Picker** — When another external content type links to this one, this check box defines which fields appear in the picker box to select the foreign key used.

➤ **Timestamp Field** — This field is a SQL timestamp.

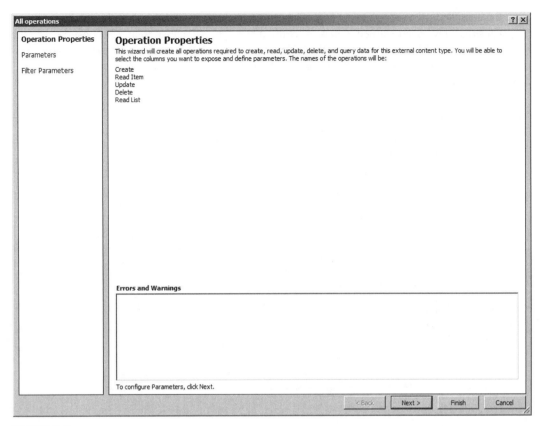

FIGURE 11-7

The Filter Parameters are set in the third step of the wizard, as shown in Figure 11-9. The parameter types that you are interested in are Limit and Comparison. A limit parameter is simply a limit on the number of results returned — this is necessary when doing lookups from another content type, because the picker used to choose a specific item may need to be constrained if there are many results.

A comparison filter is used to enable a user to search for specific items in the picker. When creating a comparison filter, you choose an operator — equal to, less than, and so on — and the field to filter on.

After the wizard has been run, you can save the External Content Type, as it has been created in its most basic form.

The next step is to create a SharePoint list based on the external content type. Click Create Lists & Form in the ribbon, set the name of the library, and click OK to create the list. To view the list, click Lists and Libraries, and double-click your list. Here you can change properties such as whether the list appears in the navigation, or edit the associated pages.

Finally, the security in SharePoint itself needs to be set up for this external content type. Open up SharePoint Central Administration, go to Application Management ➪ Service Applications, and click Business Data Connectivity Service. This brings up a screen showing all the external content types that have been defined. Click the content type you have just created, choose Set Object Permissions, and add the users who will have permissions to interact with this content type. Once permissions have been granted, you can return to the list in SharePoint Designer and click Preview in Browser to view your work.

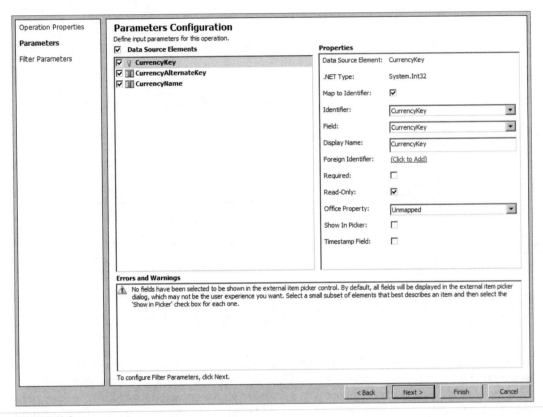

FIGURE 11-8

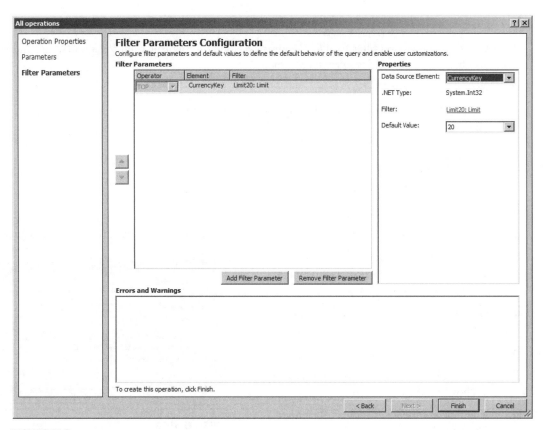

FIGURE 11-9

TRY IT

In this Try It, you create two external content types, associate them, and set up a list to edit entries.

Lesson Requirements

You create external content types for the DimReseller and DimGeography tables, and create an association between the two. Create an external list based on DimReseller that enables reading, inserting, and updating items.

Hints

➤ Create a comparison filter for DimGeography based on EnglishCountryRegionName, and another one based on StateProvinceName.

➤ Use 20 for all limit filters.

➤ For Reseller, create operations, then an association, and then only create the foreign key identifiers.

Step-by-Step

1. Open SharePoint Designer.

2. Click External Content Types under Site Objects.

3. Create a new external content type by clicking the icon at the top left corner of the designer.

4. Name the external content type `Geography` by clicking on the New External Content Type text next to the Name.

FIGURE 11-10

5. Click the Click Here to Discover External Data Sources and Define Operations link.

6. Click Add Connection.

7. Select SQL Server for the data source type, as shown in Figure 11-10.

8. Right-click DimGeography and Create All Operations.

9. Click Next on the Operation Properties page.

10. Select Show in Picker for City, StateProvinceName, and EnglishCountryRegionName.

11. Click Next to move to the last page of the wizard.

12. Click Add Filter Parameter.

13. Click the Click To Add button that is next to Filter.

14. Change the filter name to **Limit**.

15. Change the filter type to Limit and click OK.

16. Change the default value to 20.

17. Click Add Filter Parameter.

18. Click the Click To Add button that is next to Filter.

19. Change the filter name to Country.

20. Change the filter type to Comparison.

21. Change the filter field to EnglishCountryRegionName.

22. Click the Is Default check box.

23. Check Use to Create Match List in External Item Picker and click OK.

24. Change the Data Source Element to EnglishCountryRegionName.

25. Change the default value to United States.

26. Click Add Filter Parameter.

27. Click the Click To Add button that is next to Filter.

28. Change the filter name to State.

29. Change the filter type to Comparison.

30. Change the filter field to StateProvinceName.

31. Click Use to Create Match List in External Item Picker and click OK.

32. Change the Data Source Element to StateProvinceName.

33. Change the default value to Alabama.

34. Make sure to change the Operator to OR, so that a search can be done on either state or country, as shown in Figure 11-11.

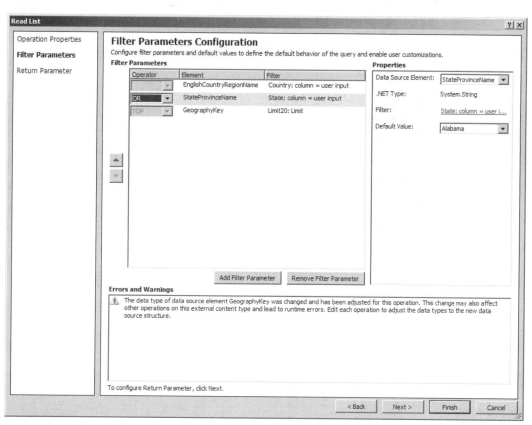

FIGURE 11-11

35. Click Finish.

36. The Geography external content type is now created; now create the Reseller external content type.

37. Click External Content Types.

38. Create a new external content type.

39. Name the external content type Reseller.

40. Click the Click Here to Discover External Data Sources and Define Operations link.

41. Click Add Connection.

42. Select SQL Server for the data source type.

43. Right-click DimReseller and Create All Operations.

44. Click Next on the Operation Properties page. Don't try to add a foreign key identifier yet, because you haven't added an association.

45. Click ResellerName and check Show in Picker, as shown in Figure 11-12.

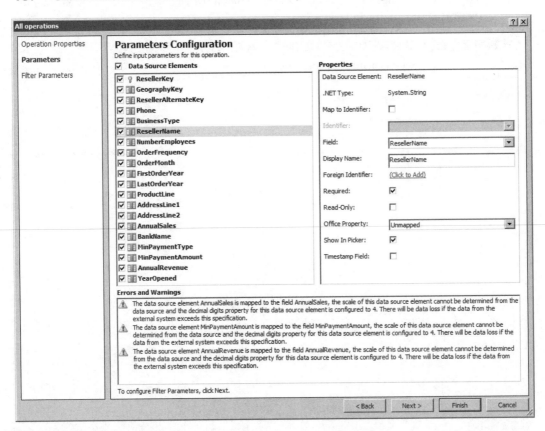

FIGURE 11-12

The scale warnings can be safely ignored — they are related to the use of the money data type in SQL and won't cause any problems.

46. Click Next.

47. Click Add Filter Parameter.

50. Click the Click To Add button that is next to Filter.

51. Change the filter name to Limit

52. Change the Filter Type to Limit and click OK.

52. Change the default value to 20 and click Finish.

53. Right-click DimReseller and choose New Association, as in Figure 11-13.

54. Click the Browse button and choose Geography.

The fields to map will be automatically picked up, as shown in Figure 11-14.

56. Click Next.

57. Select GeographyKey from the Reseller fields, and click Map to Identifier, as shown in Figure 11-15.

58. Click Next.

59. Click Next on the Filter Parameters page — you aren't going to filter the association.

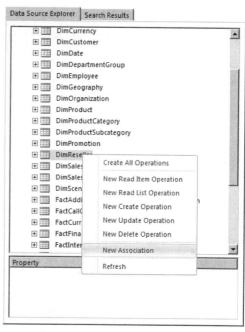

FIGURE 11-13

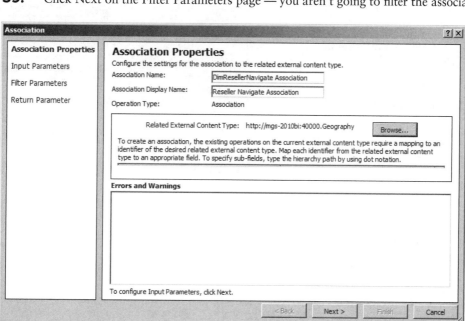

FIGURE 11-14

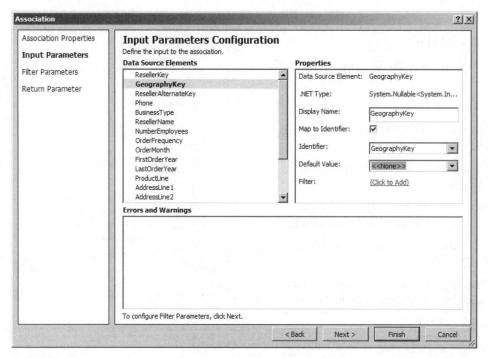

FIGURE 11-15

60. Leave the return parameters as the defaults, and click Finish and then Save.

61. Click Create Lists & Form in the ribbon.

62. Fill in the list name, as shown in Figure 11-16, and click OK.

63. Click Lists & Libraries in the navigation pane on the left, and click the Reseller list to bring up the page shown in Figure 11-17.

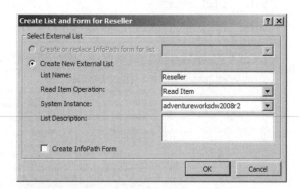

FIGURE 11-16

64. Open SharePoint Central Administration.

65. Click Manage Service Applications under Application Management.

66. Click Business Connectivity Data Service to display the list of External Content Types, as shown in Figure 11-18.

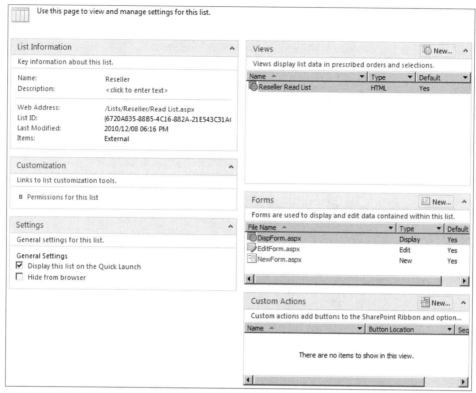

FIGURE 11-17

FIGURE 11-18

67. Click the box next to Geography, and then click Set Object Permissions.

68. Search for the user groups you wish to add permissions for (or your current user name during development), and click Add. Check all the permissions boxes, as shown in Figure 11-19, and click OK.

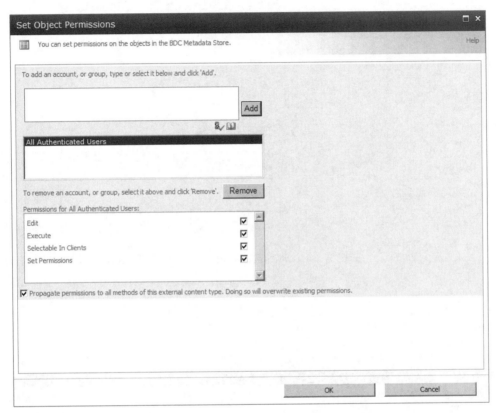

FIGURE 11-19

69. Set the same object permissions for Reseller.

70. Go back to your list in SharePoint Designer, and click Preview List to see the list, as shown in Figure 11-20.

71. Hover over any of the ResellerKey entries to show the arrow, click it, and then click Edit Item.

72. Here you can edit any of the values in this reseller record, or click the Select Item button under Geography to open up a picker screen. These two screens are shown in Figure 11-21.

73. Enter Tennessee in the search box, click the search icon, and choose Pigeon Forge. Click OK.

74. Click Save to save the changes to the database.

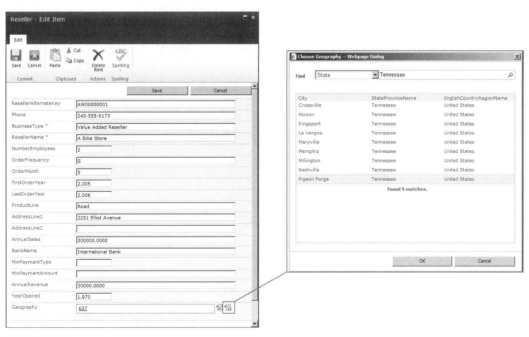

FIGURE 11-20

FIGURE 11-21

 Please select Lesson 11 on the DVD to view the video that accompanies this lesson.

SECTION III
Applying SharePoint 2010 Business Intelligence in Office

▶ **LESSON 12:** Developing and Deploying Excel Services Analytics Applications

▶ **LESSON 13:** Developing and Deploying PowerPivot Analytics Applications

▶ **LESSON 14:** Developing and Deploying Visio Services Analytics Applications

12

Developing and Deploying Excel Services Analytics Applications

Excel Services is a very powerful tool available in SharePoint 2010. With Excel Services you can create workbooks and deploy them to SharePoint to be used across your entire organization. They can be viewed in the browser, downloaded for later viewing, checked out so no one person's changes are overwritten, refreshed, and even embedded into dashboards. In this lesson you learn the basis for creating Excel reports and deploying them to SharePoint for use by Excel Services. You also integrate a portion of an Excel workbook into a dashboard. After this lesson you should have a deeper understanding of how to use Excel Services in your SharePoint environment.

For information on setting up and enabling Excel Services for your SharePoint site, see Lesson 5.

DEVELOPING AN EXCEL SERVICES REPORT

Whether the purpose of your Excel report is to simply share data, show data comparison between actual and projected values, embed into a dashboard, or something in between, the beginning stages of report development are the same. Two things will always be a part of your report: a data source and data.

Data Sources

Data sources are the foundation for building an Excel report. This is the method through which you will keep the spreadsheet data up to date from a wide range of sources. Two types of connections exist: embedded and linked. Embedded connections are stored as a part of the Excel workbook and will be carried along with the file. Linked connections, however, rely on a data connection from another source, in this case an .odc (Office Data Connection) file. One major advantage to using linked connections over embedded is the ability to update. If a server or user ID changes, you simply update the .odc file and all workbooks using that connection are updated, whereas embedded connections would each have to be changed manually and potentially affect a large quantity of documents. Three settings are available to tell the Excel Services application how to handle external data connections as seen in Figure 12-1.

➤ **None** — This is the default setting and means that no external data connections are allowed.

➤ **Trusted data connection libraries only** — The only external connections that are allowed must be stored in a data connection library.

➤ **Trusted data connection libraries and embedded** — Connections stored in data connection libraries are allowed as well as those embedded in workbooks.

Knowing which of these options has been chosen is vital to being able to develop an Excel report because it lets you know which type of connection, if any, can be used in your workbook. To check these settings, open the SharePoint 2010 Central Administration ⇨ Application Management ⇨ Manage Service Applications ⇨ Excel Services Application ⇨ Trusted File Locations ⇨ *Location where your files are stored* ⇨ External Data section.

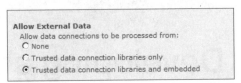

FIGURE 12-1

If your SharePoint environment is not going to allow external connections, you can still create reports and simply display cached data. This is going to limit the use and lifespan of the reports, however, because the data in the source may be refreshed weekly, daily, or hourly and become out of date. For this reason it is not recommended to use reports that can't be refreshed in web parts to build a dashboard because someone would have to manually update that particular spreadsheet each time the data was changed.

Creating a Data Source

Creating a data source is a very simple task in Excel 2010. Simply select the tab labeled Data from the ribbon at the top. In this book we focus on the sources from SQL Server and Analysis Services. These options are shown in Figure 12-2. If your organization has an Analysis Services cube already created, Excel is a great way to display the data for everyday use and connecting to it has never been easier. Choose the drop-down labeled From Other Sources and select either From SQL Server or From Analysis Services. Here a simple wizard will walk you through creating your connection. Enter the server name and authentication and click Next. The following screen gives you a drop-down list of all the databases and a list of the tables or cubes that it contains depending on whether you chose SQL Server or Analysis Services. Once you choose the

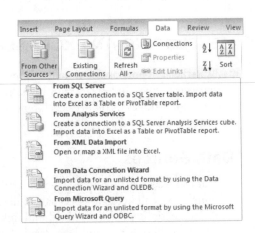

FIGURE 12-2

table or cube you want to report from, click Next. Give your data source a name in the box labeled Friendly Name. Connection options can be changed in the Authentication Settings of the Excel Services section if need be to match your environment. Finally, click Finish.

A box pops up for you to indicate how to display the data and where to display it. More information on ways to display the data are discussed later in this lesson.

If you have created a connection previously on your machine, you can use that as well. Again, from the Data tab in Excel 2010, select the button that says Existing Connections. A list of all the connections that currently reside on your machine can be found here. These are generally stored inside of the Documents folder. This screen also lists any connections already inside the workbook as well as on the network. An example is shown in Figure 12-3. Selecting any of these connections brings up the same screen asking how to display the data and what cell to start displaying it in.

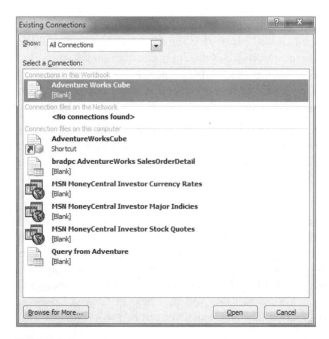

FIGURE 12-3

Another way to add connections to your document is through the Connections link on the Data tab. This link is also visible in Figure 12-2 directly below the Data tab. This shows any connections already in the workbook and also allows you to add additional sources by clicking Add in the upper-right corner of the screen. The same box will appear that shows when going through the Existing Connections option mentioned earlier, except you will not be prompted to display the data. This will simply add the connection for later use.

Several other ways exist to connect to data, including custom queries. This particular option is available in the From Other Sources drop-down of the Data tab. It allows you to create a connection to a variety of sources and even build a custom query that can include joining between tables. A simple wizard walks you through this process if that method fits your needs.

Each of these methods has demonstrated how to embed connection information into workbooks. What if you want to create a linked connection? The process is very similar. Start by creating an embedded connection using any method previously mentioned. Then, from the Data tab, click Connections to display all the connections currently in the workbook. Highlight the connection you would like to be linked and click Properties from the options on the right. On the Definition tab choose the button labeled Export Connection File. At this point a standard file save screen will appear. Browse to a location on the file system to store the connection file, or skip a step and enter the URL to the SharePoint connection library where you want to deploy this connection (`http://sharepointurl/site/BISite/DataConnectionLibrary`).

Notice that after saving the `.odc` file the location in Connection File has changed to this new location. If you choose to save it to the file system, upload it to a Data Connection Library but do not close the Connection Properties window in Excel. After uploading the file click Browse next to the location of the connection file in the Connection Properties window. Enter the URL for the SharePoint library and select the connection file that was just uploaded. In either case you can check the option for Always Use Connection File. This will ensure that the data is always accessed through the connection file rather than trying to use the embedded connection information shown in the connection string. This is especially useful if you want to be able to manage all your connections externally. There is no risk of having the data pulled from a development server coded in the connection string as opposed to the production server listed in the connection file.

If you are using connection files, be sure to list the connection library in the Excel Services application settings under the Trusted Data Connection Libraries link. This link is accessed through Central Administration just below the Trusted File Locations link mentioned earlier in this lesson.

Displaying Data

Once your sources have been added, data can be displayed using a variety of methods. The easiest way to get started is through the From Other Sources Wizard at the end when prompted to choose the way data is presented along with the location on the spreadsheet. If, however, there is an existing connection, you can add data presentation by going to the Insert tab from the ribbon at the top of Excel and choosing from options such as the PivotTable. When selecting this option, change the option from Select a Table or Range to Use an External Data Source. Click the Choose Connection button and select any connection from the section labeled Connections in this workbook.

The data you display can be in one of many formats. These formats could include a standard spreadsheet table, pivot table, chart, or graph. Each of these presentation methods has its own advantages. The intent behind the report should be taken into consideration when preparing it. Different ways of displaying the data may not be available depending on the source.

Table

The raw data displayed in a table can give you detailed specifics for a particular store, employee, or product. Oftentimes, this amount of data is overwhelming and ends up taking away from the true purpose of making business decisions. This option is available with an SQL Server source but not with an Analysis Services source. To display data in table format, select Table when using either the From Other Sources or Existing Connections options for adding connections. A sample table is shown in Figure 12-4.

PivotTable

With a PivotTable, such as the one pictured in Figure 12-5, you can group data by date, customer, region, or any number of other methods. Now, instead of the values being displayed representing a single entry in a sales detail table, it will give a sum of sales broken down by product (columns) and grouped by week (rows). Here you can add any field to the filter, columns, rows, or values section to modify the table as you see fit. Hierarchies display very well and can be quite useful with a PivotTable. This format is much more user friendly when it comes to making business decisions because you see performance over a period of time rather than by individual sale. Pivot tables can be added when creating connections or from the Insert tab and selecting the PivotTable option.

	A	B	C	D	E
1	SalesOrderID	SalesOrderDetailID	CarrierTrackingNumber	OrderQty	ProductID
2	43659	1	4911-403C-98	1	776
3	43659	2	4911-403C-98	3	777
4	43659	3	4911-403C-98	1	778
5	43659	4	4911-403C-98	1	771
6	43659	5	4911-403C-98	1	772
7	43659	6	4911-403C-98	2	773

FIGURE 12-4

	A	B	C	D	E	F	G	H
1	Internet Gross Profit Margin	Countries						
2	Year	Australia	Canada	France	Germany	United Kingdom	United States	Grand Total
3	⊞ CY 2005	40.38%	39.99%	40.13%	40.19%	40.21%	39.89%	40.15%
4	⊞ CY 2006	40.84%	39.85%	40.43%	40.36%	40.71%	40.43%	40.53%
5	⊞ CY 2007	41.08%	43.48%	41.27%	40.91%	41.02%	42.43%	41.60%
6	⊞ CY 2008	40.22%	43.13%	41.43%	41.64%	41.30%	42.05%	41.45%
7	Grand Total	40.68%	41.96%	41.08%	41.02%	41.00%	41.54%	41.15%

FIGURE 12-5

Graphically

Finally, charts and graphs give a quick visual comparison. Graphs are particularly helpful to show one store's performance against another or total revenue by quarter over the past five years. A pie chart, for instance, may be useful to see revenue breakdown between the different product categories that your company sells. Charts can be added when creating connections or by selecting a chart or graph from the Insert tab and choosing a range of existing data from a sheet within your workbook. A sample chart is shown in Figure 12-6 that breaks down the company's profit margin visually.

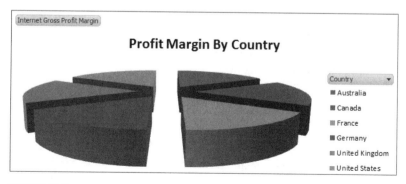

FIGURE 12-6

Make note of anything that you would like to display in a web part because you will need the name that is shown in Excel for that object. You can find this by selecting the object, a pie chart for instance, and looking in the top-left corner of the screen where the cell is usually listed.

DEPLOYING AND MANAGING EXCEL SERVICES REPORTS

After development, deploying Excel Services reports is as easy as saving to any regular file system location. All you will need is the URL and permissions to access the SharePoint library where the Excel workbooks will be stored.

Deployment Options

When it comes time to deploy your reports, there are two simple options, uploading manually from outside Excel and directly from Excel. Each method has its own advantages. Uploading from outside Excel is generally preferred if you have multiple reports to deploy.

Upload

If you choose to deploy your reports by uploading them, open your SharePoint site in your web browser. Next, navigate to the library where the workbooks will be stored. Click the link at the bottom of the list labeled Add Document and browse to the workbook on your machine. Watch out for other workbooks with the same name because the option for Overwrite Existing Files is enabled by default. This will add the Excel workbook to the library. It can now be accessed by anyone with permissions to view files in that library as well as used in web parts in other places in the SharePoint site.

From Excel

With your workbook still open in Excel, click File and select Save & Send. Click the link for Save to SharePoint and select a location already listed or click Browse for a location. In the address bar at the top of the screen enter the URL for the SharePoint library where this workbook will be saved and press Enter. In the File Name box type a name for the workbook and click Save. You can also do this same thing by using File and selecting Save As, entering the library URL in the address bar giving the workbook a name, and clicking Save.

Managing documents is a simple task with SharePoint 2010. Overwriting files is only a checkbox away when uploading changes. Another option for updates is to check out the document for editing rather than downloading a copy. When editing is completed, just choose Save in Excel and the changes will be saved directly to the SharePoint document in the library. Just be sure to remember to check the document back in. Versioning is a built-in option for each document library. In the library settings choose Versioning Settings under the General Settings heading. Here you can tell SharePoint to keep no previous versions, only major versions, or a combination of major and minor versions. These options are shown in Figure 12-7.

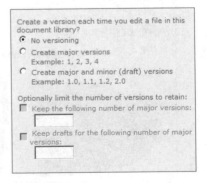

FIGURE 12-7

Once your Excel workbooks have been deployed to SharePoint, you may choose to share them through use of just the document library or add pieces of them into web parts. From any page where you can add web parts, such as the homepage of your Business Intelligence Center, click the drop-down located in the top-left of the screen labeled Site Actions and select Edit Page. This will allow you to add web parts and rearrange items. Click the link in the location where you would like the Excel data to be displayed that says Add a Web Part. Under Categories select Business Data, choose Excel Web Access in the Web Parts pane, and click Add. The Excel web part will be added and you will need to click the link labeled Click Here to Open the Tool Pane in order to modify the rest of the settings. In the tool pane select a workbook by navigating to one stored in a library on the site. Then in the Named Item box enter the name of the object you want to display. This is where making note of the chart name, such as Chart 1, comes in handy. The same name that you noted when you were creating the workbooks should be entered here. If no named item is given, the entire workbook will be displayed in the web part. Change any other settings and click OK. Your Excel workbook has now been added to the page.

Just like the Trusted Data Connection Libraries, workbooks must be stored in a trusted file location. Be sure your unattended service account is also configured. This will ensure there are no problems with selecting None as the authentication method instead of Windows Authentication in your data connections. These locations and accounts are managed through Central Administration in the Excel Services web application settings. More information is available on setting these options in Lesson 5.

Keep in mind that all Excel workbooks must be in libraries specified in trusted file locations and all .odc connection files must be stored in data connection libraries specified in trusted data connection libraries. Both of these settings are found in Central Administration.

Now that you know how to create and deploy Excel workbooks and data connection files, put your knowledge to use in the Try It section.

TRY IT

In this Try It you create a new Excel workbook to pull data from an Analysis Services cube and display the data in a PivotTable and Chart. You then upload it to your Business Intelligence Center.

Lesson Requirements

When creating the report, use data that will be relevant for making quick business decisions. Be sure not to overload the report with fields that will not bring any added value to the report. This should be a simple, concise report that could be integrated into a dashboard.

Hints

➤ Connect to the AdventureWorks2008R2 cube.

➤ Create a PivotTable and a Bar Chart.

➤ PivotTable rows will display the year and columns customer geography.

➤ Use a linked data source.

➤ Add the chart to a web part.

Step-by-Step

1. Open Microsoft Excel 2010 from the Start menu.

2. Select the Data tab from the ribbon at the top of the window.

3. Click the From Other Sources drop-down.

4. Select From Analysis Services.

5. Enter the server name where your cube is located.

6. Click Next.

7. Choose Adventure Works DW 2008R2 from the drop-down list of database names.

8. Check the box next to Connect to a Specific Cube or Table and highlight the Adventure Works cube in the bottom pane, as shown in Figure 12-8.

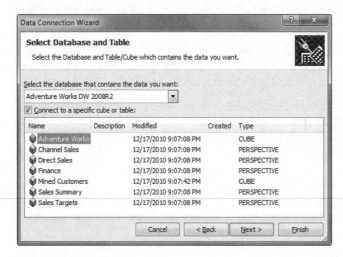

FIGURE 12-8

9. Click Next.

10. Change the Friendly Name to `AdventureWorks2008R2Cube`.

11. Click the Authentication Settings button and select Windows Authentication from the list of options and click OK.

12. Click Finish.

13. From the Import Data box choose PivotChart and PivotTable Report and choose Existing Worksheet to place the data in cell A1, as shown in Figure 12-9.

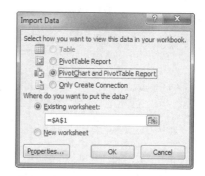

14. A placeholder for the chart and table will be created and the PivotTable field list will be shown on the right side of the screen.

15. From the drop-down list under Show Fields Related To select Internet Sales, as shown in Figure 12-10.

FIGURE 12-9

16. From the list of fields locate Internet Sales Amount and drag it to the Values area below the fields list. Notice the table and chart both change automatically to reflect this field

17. Locate Customer Geography and add it to the box labeled Legend Fields. This will add the geography to the top of the table.

18. Locate Date in the fields and expand the Calendar folder.

19. Find Date.Calendar Year and drag it to the area labeled Axis Fields. This will add the date vertically on the left side of the table.

20. Click Cell B1 that contains the text Column Labels and change the text to read **Countries**.

FIGURE 12-10

21. Click Cell A2 that contains the text Row Labels and change the text to read **Year**.

22. The report should now look like Figure 12-11.

23. Select the Data tab on the ribbon.

24. Click Connections to show all the connections inside this workbook.

25. With the Adventure Works Analysis Services connection highlighted click Properties.

26. Click the Definition tab.

27. Click Export Connection File.

28. Enter the URL for your data connections library.

29. In the File Name box type **AdventureWorksCube** and click Save.

The Web File Properties window will be displayed.

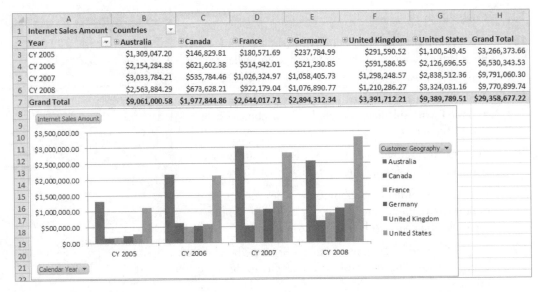

FIGURE 12-11

30. Change Content Type to Office Data Connection File and click OK.

31. Check the box next to Always Use Connection File.

32. When your screen looks like the image in Figure 12-12, click OK.

33. Click Close.

34. Click File, then Save As and enter the URL for your document library in the address bar at the top.

35. Name your workbook **SalesComparison** and click Save.

36. Open your web browser and navigate to your BI Center homepage.

37. Click Site Actions and select Show Ribbon. Click Edit Page on the left side of the ribbon.

38. Click the link labeled Add a Web Part, select Excel Web Access from the Business Data category, and click Add.

39. Click the link to open the tool pane.

40. Click the ellipsis next to the workbook field and navigate to find the SalesComparison workbook you just uploaded. Click OK.

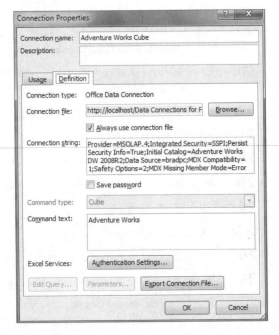

FIGURE 12-12

41. In the Named Item text box enter **Chart 1**. This is the name Excel gave the chart created earlier.

42. Scroll down and click OK.

43. Click Stop Editing from the ribbon.

You have just created and deployed an Excel workbook to your SharePoint site! You can now access the entire workbook and view it in your browser by navigating to the library where it is stored and clicking the name of the workbook. Adding the web part is not a required part of deployment. Your report is now ready to share with the rest of your colleagues. Just give them the URL to the library and they can access the worksheet and download any data changes.

 Please select Lesson 12 on the DVD to view the video that accompanies this lesson.

13

Developing and Deploying PowerPivot Analytics Applications

The end goal of most Business Intelligence projects is to provide data in an easy-to-understand and easy-to-access way for end users to make decisions. No other Business Intelligence tool can fulfill these requirements more than PowerPivot. PowerPivot provides extreme computation power inside a tool that most end users are familiar with and would prefer as their data visualization tool anyway: Excel.

CHOOSING THE RIGHT TOOL FOR THE JOB

PowerPivot can function in two capacities. The first method is PowerPivot for Excel, which is a standalone application. Users can develop high-powered in-memory analytics on their personal machines, which are all self-contained using highly efficient compression algorithms. If users want to share what they have created with others, that leads to the second method, PowerPivot for SharePoint.

PowerPivot for SharePoint allows users to share data models and analysis in a centralized location so the power of the tool is no longer restricted to an end user's desktop. In Lesson 8 you learned how to configure and install PowerPivot for integration with SharePoint 2010 using SQL Server 2008 R2. That lesson set the stage for this one, where you start learning how to develop PowerPivot content and then deploy it to SharePoint.

SQL Server Analysis Services shares many similar features with PowerPivot, but is thought to be a more Enterprise-ready tool, meaning it has additional functionality and scalability features. So the question you must ask yourself before preparing for a project is whether you should use PowerPivot or Analysis Services. For smaller, departmentalized projects PowerPivot is a great solution to provide quick analysis, whereas Analysis Services may take more time to build but it can be easily scaled out to thousands of users.

Figure 13-1 describes instances where you may choose one tool over the other. It describes Personal BI as a great example for PowerPivot to shine. A single user, often a business user, develops a PowerPivot report on his or her local desktop and will likely be the sole consumer of it. All that is required for this is a local installation of Microsoft Office Excel 2010 and the PowerPivot add-in.

Organizational BI uses SQL Server Analysis Services and is solely managed by the IT staff. It is an Enterprise-ready solution that can handle major concerns like performance, high availability, and scalability. Organizational BI usually involves much more formal preparation and design processes. This method requires an installation of Analysis Services and Business Intelligence Development Studio.

Team BI refers to the previously described PowerPivot for SharePoint. The reports are designed by either IT staff or business users using Excel. The reports can then be shared and viewed through SharePoint. This technique requires the most set up. You must have Microsoft Office Excel 2010 and the PowerPivot add-in to develop and SharePoint with Analysis Services to manage the PowerPivot workbook data.

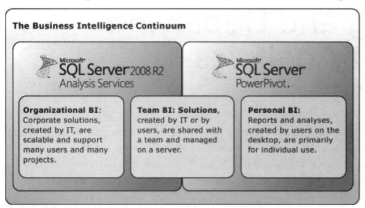

FIGURE 13-1

DEVELOPING A POWERPIVOT REPORT

Developing PowerPivot Reports is intended to be simple enough for a highly non-technical user to be able to provide significant value. After importing the desired data set into a PowerPivot workbook the user can design a pivot table and chart.

To get started you must install Microsoft Office Excel 2010 and then download and install the PowerPivot for Excel 2010 add-in at www.powerpivot.com. After installing all the necessary components open Excel 2010 and select the new PowerPivot tab in the Office ribbon. Click the PowerPivot Window button to open PowerPivot for Excel, shown in Figure 13-2.

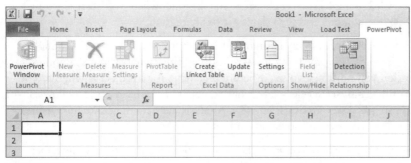

FIGURE 13-2

After the PowerPivot window opens you can select from many possible data source connections to import data into PowerPivot. By selecting the From Other Sources button you will see all the data source connections that are available in the native installation. After selecting a connection type you walk through a wizard that will import the data to report on. Figure 13-3 shows the configuration of a connection to SQL Server.

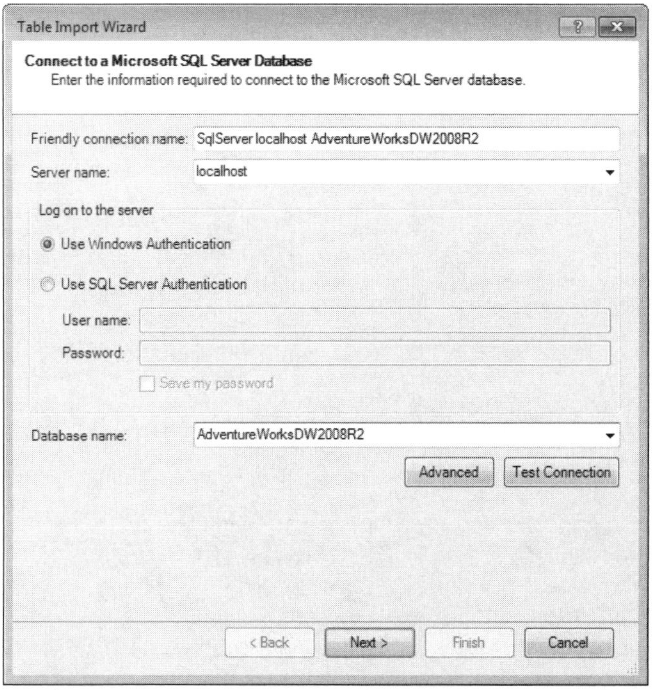

FIGURE 13-3

After confirming the connection properties you will be given the option to import the new data either by tables or views from SQL Server, or by query. If you decide to import by query you will be given a query window to write the statement to return the fields that will be used for your pivot table. If you choose to import by object you will be given a list to check off the objects to include. After selecting the objects you want, as shown in Figure 13-4, click Finish.

When you click Finish you will be able to see the objects being imported. When this completes, click Close to return to the PowerPivot window. Database relationships are carried over to PowerPivot, but if you need to make changes you can do this on the Design tab with the Manage Relationships button. Now that the data is imported you can create a report by clicking the PivotTable button on the Office ribbon. This returns you to Excel where you will be given the option to create a new worksheet or use an existing one for your report.

Next, use the PowerPivot Field List to select the fields that you want to display in your report. The items that are selected from this list are automatically added to the report in a PivotTable, PivotChart, or Slicers. Slicers are a new data visualization tool to Excel 2010 that allows the user to better see which records the report is being filtered on. Figure 13-5 shows the PowerPivot Field List and a completed report that uses a PivotTable, PivotChart, and Slicers.

FIGURE 13-4

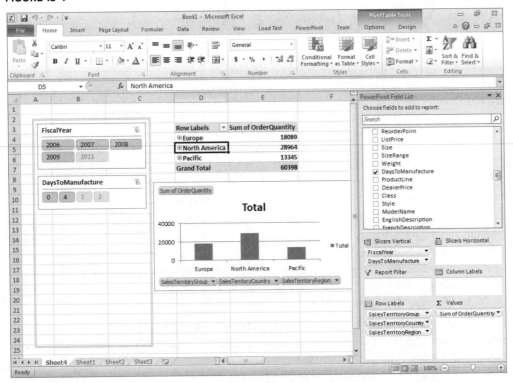

FIGURE 13-5

INTRODUCTION TO DATA ANALYSIS EXPRESSIONS (DAX)

Data Analysis Expressions (DAX) is what you will use to extend the capabilities of PowerPivot. DAX is similar to the Excel formula language, making it easier for current Excel users to learn. The newly provided DAX functions bring many of the SQL Server Analysis Service concepts to PowerPivot. For example, you can use the DAX function DATESYTD to calculate year-to-date figures of a measure.

You can write DAX functions in two places. The first place is in the PowerPivot window by using a Calculated Column. Calculated Columns are a way that you can add additional fields for the purposes of displaying in a report, creating relationships where they did not exist previously, or returning some quick analysis of the data. This would be comparable to a derived column in SQL Server. Figure 13-6 shows that Calculated Columns are written in the same place as typical Excel formulas. After scrolling to the farthest right point of the document you will see Add Column. Select this column and you will be able to write your expression and rename the column.

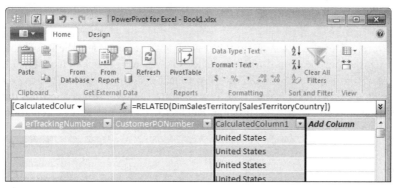

FIGURE 13-6

The Calculated Column Example shown in the following table provides many common DAX expressions used as Calculated Columns.

PROBLEM	EXPRESSION
Concatenate two fields	Calculated Column Expression: `= [FirstName] & " " & [LastName]` Expression Output Example: `Bill Gates`
Use a 2-digit date (for example: "03" for March instead of "3")	Calculated Column Expression: `=FORMAT(NOW(),"DD")` Expression Output Example: `03 (if the month is March)`
Replace blank (NULL) with another value	Calculated Column Expression: `=IF(TableName[ColumnName] ="","No Value","Valid Value")`

continues

(continued)

PROBLEM	EXPRESSION
Join tables in a many-to-one relationship and return a column (from the many table)	Calculated Column Expression: `=RELATED(TableName[ColumnName])`

Return a table from either direction (one-to-many or many-to one); must be used with another function because it returns an entire table	Calculated Column Expression:
	`=SUMX(RELATEDTABLE(TableName),TableName`
	`[ColumnName])`

Count related rows in other table	Calculated Column Expression: `=COUNTROWS(RELATEDTABLE(TableName))`

The second place DAX functions can be used is in Calculated Measures. These expressions are written not in the PowerPivot window, but instead in the PowerPivot Field List of a report. This would be comparable to an MDX calculation in Analysis Services.

To create a Calculated Measure, under the Home tab in the PowerPivot window select the PivotTable button and then PivotTable again from the drop-down box. Click OK when the Create PivotTable dialog box opens inside of Excel. Next, right-click in the PowerPivot Field List on the table in which you would like to create a Calculated Measure and select Add New Measure. In the Measure Settings dialog box name the measure and write the DAX formula shown in Figure 13-7 to complete the measure.

FIGURE 13-7

The Calculated Column Example shown in the following table provides many common DAX expressions used as Calculated Measures.

PROBLEM	EXPRESSION
Round a number to a specified number of digits	Calculated Measure Expression: `=ROUND(SUM(TableName[ColumnName]),2)`

Current Period Last Year	Calculated Measure Expression:
	`=CALCULATE(SUM(TableName[ColumnName]),DATEADD`
	`('DateTable'[DateColumn],-1,YEAR),All('DateTable'))`

PROBLEM	EXPRESSION
YTD Calculated Measure	Calculated Measure Expression: `=CALCULATE(SUM('TableName'[ColumnName]),DATESYTD('DateTable'[DateColumn]),All('DateTable'))`
QTD Calculated Measure	Calculated Measure Expression: `=CALCULATE(SUM('TableName'[ColumnName]),DATESQTD('DateTable'[DateColumn]),All('DateTable'))`
MTD Calculated Measure	Calculated Measure Expression: `=CALCULATE(SUM('TableName'[ColumnName]),DATESMTD('DateTable'[DateColumn]))`

CREATING AND DEPLOYING REPORTS TO A POWERPIVOT GALLERY

The PowerPivot Gallery is a SharePoint document library that can graphically preview each report to your end users before actually selecting them. In Lesson 8 you learned how to install and configure PowerPivot for SharePoint. If you have a standalone server install of PowerPivot for SharePoint, a PowerPivot Gallery is created for you upon the completion of the install. If the install was done to an existing SharePoint farm, you must create a PowerPivot Gallery manually. You can choose either to create a new PowerPivot site that includes a PowerPivot Gallery library or add the PowerPivot Gallery library to an existing site.

To create the PowerPivot site open your web browser and enter the URL `http://<YourServerName>` where SharePoint has been installed. Select the Site Actions drop-down box in the top left of the page and click New Site. Figure 13-8 shows the available template sites, from which you will select PowerPivot Site. Give the site a title and URL name and click Create. This site will automatically provide you with a PowerPivot Gallery so there is no need to manually add it.

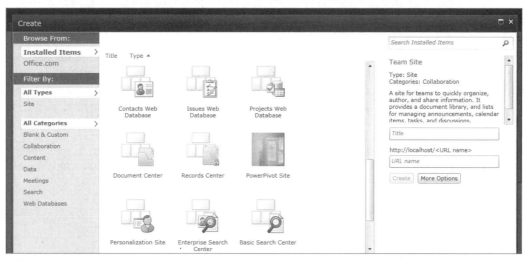

FIGURE 13-8

If you simply need to add the PowerPivot Gallery as a library to an existing site, select Site Actions in the top left of the page and click View All Site Content. After the All Site Content page opens click the Create button to create a new library. Figure 13-9 shows that by using the Library filter you can easily find the PowerPivot Gallery. Select the PowerPivot Gallery, give it a name, and click Create.

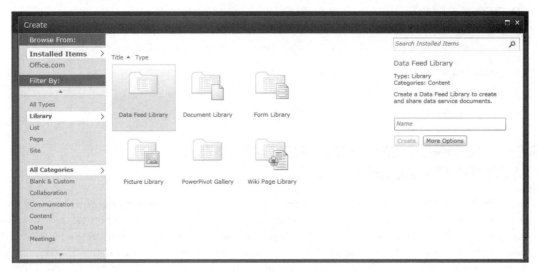

FIGURE 13-9

Now that you have a PowerPivot Gallery available for deployment open a PowerPivot workbook in Excel 2010. After the workbook you want to deploy opens click the File tab. Click Save & Send and select Save to SharePoint. Click Browse for a Location, which opens the Save As dialog box. In the file path box type `http://<YourServerName>` to connect to your SharePoint instance as shown in Figure 13-10. Open the PowerPivot Gallery and click Save. Before saving you can optionally click the Publish Options button to select which Excel sheets are deployed; by default the entire work-book is deployed, including blank sheets.

Once it has completed the deployment it will automatically open the document from SharePoint. If you would like to view all the documents in the PowerPivot Gallery navigate to the path where you just completed your deployment. By default the documents are shown in the Gallery view, but you can optionally change it to the popular Carousel view by clicking the Library tab at the top of the page and then selecting Carousel from the Current View drop-down box, as shown in Figure 13-11.

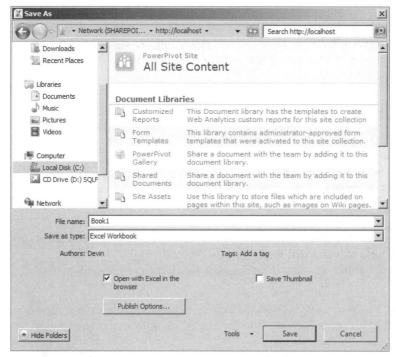

FIGURE 13-10

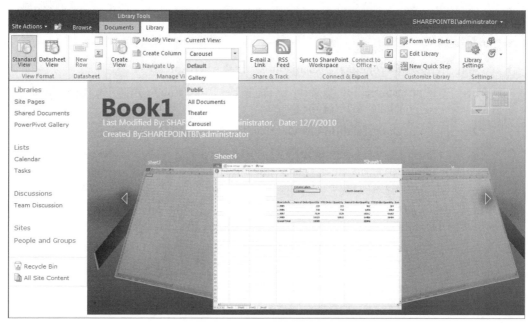

FIGURE 13-11

TRY IT

In this Try It you combine the three main topics of this lesson to complete your task. You first develop a basic PowerPivot report and then create a Calculated Measure using DAX. Finally, you deploy the result to a PowerPivot Gallery.

Lesson Requirements

To complete this lesson you need to have SharePoint 2010 already installed. If you have not done this yet, please refer to Lesson 8, which walks you through the installation steps. You must also have Excel 2010 with the PowerPivot add-in installed. The step-by-step example uses the AdventureWorks sample databases, which you can download from `www.codeplex.com`.

Hints

➤ Develop a PowerPivot workbook that uses the FactResellerSales table from the AdventureWorksDW2008R2 database. You should also select the related tables of FactResellerSales.

➤ Create a Calculated Measure on FactResellerSales that will allow you to do a comparison between the current SalesAmount column and the SalesAmount from the same period but from the previous year.

➤ Build a report that displays SalesAmount and the newly created measure.

➤ Create a PowerPivot site in SharePoint and deploy your report to the PowerPivot Gallery.

Step-by-Step

1. Go to Start ➪ All Programs ➪ Microsoft Office ➪ Microsoft Excel 2010.

2. After Excel opens select the PowerPivot tab in the Office ribbon and click PowerPivot Window to launch PowerPivot for Excel.

3. Click the From Database drop-down box and select From SQL Server.

4. In the Connect to a Microsoft SQL Server Database dialog box enter the server name property of the server on which you installed the AdventureWorks sample. Select AdventureWorksDW2008R2 from the Database Name drop-down box and click Next.

5. In the Choose How to Import the Data dialog box leave the default setting of "Select from a list of tables and views to choose the data to import" and click Next.

6. Select the FactResellerSales table and click the Select Related Tables button. Figure 13-12 shows you should have a total of seven tables selected. Click Finish.

7. The wizard next imports all the data into PowerPivot. When this completes, click Close.

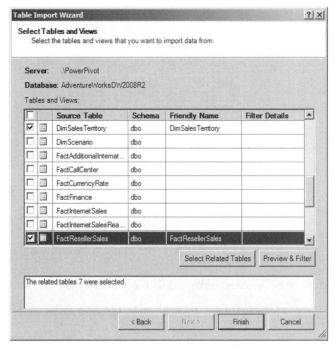

FIGURE 13-12

8. Each table is now imported into PowerPivot for Excel. To create a report click the PivotTable drop-down box on the Home tab and select Chart and Table (Horizontal). This returns you to Excel to create the report.

9. Click OK to create the PivotChart and PivotTable in a new worksheet.

10. In the PowerPivot Field List right-click the FactResellerSales table and click Add New Measure.

11. Name the measure **PriorYearSalesAmount** and type the following formula as shown in Figure 13-13:

```
=CALCULATE(SUM(FactResellerSales[SalesAmount]),DATEADD(DimDate[FullDateAlternateKey],
-1,YEAR),All(DimDate))
```

12. Verify the formula works by clicking the Check Formula button and click OK. After, the measure will automatically be added to the report.

13. The chart and table work independently from each other so select the object that did not get PriorYearSalesAmount automatically added to it, then check it in the PowerPivotFieldList to add it there as well. You may need to click Refresh in the field list to get the field added.

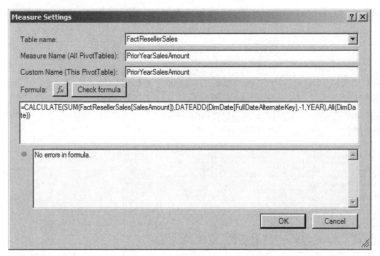

FIGURE 13-13

14. Add SalesAmount from FactResellerSales to the Values box of both the chart and table.

15. From the DimDate table select CalendarYear to be added to the Axis Fields of the chart and the Row Labels of the table.

16. From the DimSalesTerritory table add the SalesTerritoryCountry field to the Slicers Horizontal section. Your report and PowerPivot Field List selections should look similar to Figure 13-14.

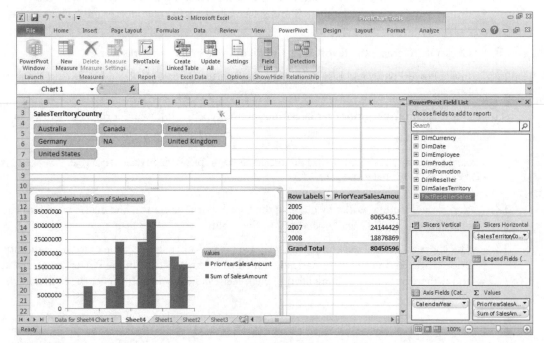

FIGURE 13-14

17. The last step is to deploy the report to a PowerPivot Gallery. Open a web browser and type in your SharePoint server: `http://<YourServerName>`.

18. Select Site Actions in the top left of the page and click New Site.

19. Choose the PowerPivot Site template and give it a title of **Lesson13**. Make the URL name also **Lesson13** and click Create.

20. Now that the PowerPivot site is created return to Excel to deploy the document to the PowerPivot Gallery.

21. Inside Excel select the File tab and choose Save & Send.

22. Click Save to SharePoint and select Browse for a Location. This opens the dialog box to save your document.

23. In the file path box type in your SharePoint server name: `http://<YourServerName>`.

24. Navigate to the Lesson13 PowerPivot site that was just created and open the PowerPivot Gallery document library.

25. Change the File Name to **Lesson13CompletedStepByStep** and click Save.

26. Once the deployment has completed the document will automatically be opened in SharePoint. Navigate to the Lesson13 PowerPivot site in your web browser and open the PowerPivot Gallery to view the reports. The PowerPivot Gallery should look like Figure 13-15.

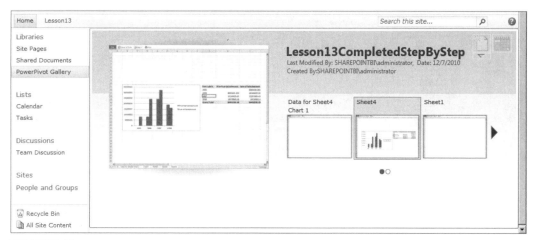

FIGURE 13-15

Congratulations! You have just created a PowerPivot report and deployed it to a PowerPivot Gallery in SharePoint.

 Please select Lesson 13 on the DVD to view the video that accompanies this lesson.

14

Developing and Deploying Visio Services Analytics Applications

Visio Services provides a seamless integration between Visio 2010 diagrams and SharePoint 2010. Diagrams originally created on the Visio desktop application can now be shared and viewed in the SharePoint web application. Visio has been a more widely accepted tool for Business Intelligence since Visio 2007 when the ability to bind data to Visio shapes was added. This gives users an easy-to-understand view of their data.

When publishing to SharePoint, Visio Services takes the .vsd files that are created in Visio and converts them into a new .vdw format, which is how SharePoint stores the diagrams until viewing. When a request is made for a diagram through SharePoint, Visio Services again converts the .vdw file into a Silverlight file so it can properly be viewed in a web browser. When deploying to SharePoint the developer simply saves the file as a .vdw file and then SharePoint does the rest of the heavy lifting behind the scenes, requiring little additional work by the person deploying the diagram or the person attempting to view it in SharePoint.

In Lesson 7 you learned how to configure and create the Visio Services application. You also learned how to handle different security measures that are necessary when working with Visio Services. This lesson is devoted to creating and publishing content in Visio 2010, which can then be deployed to SharePoint 2010.

Two key features of Visio Services are discussed in this lesson: data binding and interactivity. Having a data binding diagram can allow users to visualize live data through any diagram created. Interactivity is what gives a diagram life. This allows users to interact with a diagram by clicking elements that have been activated by the diagram creator. This lesson also shows you how you can deploy your finished product to SharePoint 2010.

CREATING A DIAGRAM WITH DATA CONNECTIVITY

Getting data connected to diagrams is the key element in how you will make Visio a relevant part of your Business Intelligence solution. Data can be connected to Visio diagram shapes from a variety of data sources including Excel, Access, SQL Server, SharePoint lists, or any

OLE DB or ODBC source. A wizard walks you through the steps of making a connection, which creates an .odc file similar to how Excel does when connecting to a data source. It is important to note that if you intend to automate the data refresh of your Web Drawing in SharePoint that the .odc file must also be located on the same SharePoint site, which the connection wizard will inform you as shown in Figure 14-1.

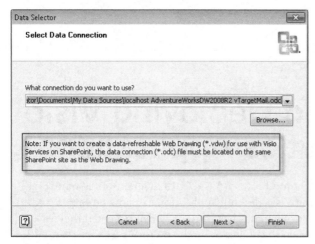

FIGURE 14-1

Depending on the type of diagram template selected, you will find that displaying your data can be rather simple. Some templates allow for Visio to aggregate source data, whereas others only permit displaying data as it appears in the source. This means you may have to do some data preparation if you chose a template that does not allow Visio to perform aggregations. For example, if your source is SQL Server, you may create an SQL Server View to display the data exactly how it is needed in the diagram you are creating.

To get started, open Visio 2010 and on the File tab select New. Here you can either create a blank diagram on your own or select a template. The fastest way to get started is by using the PivotDiagram under the Business category, which will use your data to automate the process of creating hierarchies in your data. The PivotDiagram also allows you to aggregate data directly inside Visio, unlike many other templates that strictly display data as it appears in the data source.

Immediately after selecting the PivotDiagram a wizard opens that walks you through the steps to connect to your source data. Figure 14-2 shows the selection screen for the data source that will be used in the diagram. Notice that Analysis Services can be used as a data source when using the PivotDiagram, but cannot be used when connecting to shapes in other templates.

After selecting the desired data source click Next to provide the connection information for the selected source. For example, if you select SQL Server you will provide the server where the source database is located. After providing this information you will be able to select the database and tables that you will use for the diagram. You can choose specific tables or bring in all tables from the database and then click Next. Click Finish to finalize the PivotDiagram wizard. This will create the .odc file that stores the connection string information. Now that the connection file is created you will have the option to select the file just created or another one created previously. Click Finish. When you click Finish if you had not previously selected the table you want to use in this connection, you must select it at this point. This is another reason why you may choose to create SQL Server Views for Visio because you must select only one table here.

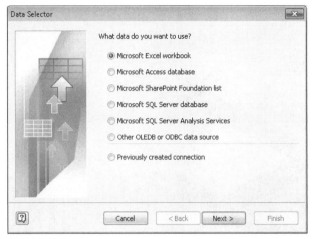

FIGURE 14-2

This will provide you with an empty diagram where you can select Add Category or Add Total to begin creating the diagram. Items from the Add Category section will add hierarchy levels and items from the Add Total section will add aggregations. Figure 14-3 shows a completed PivotDiagram.

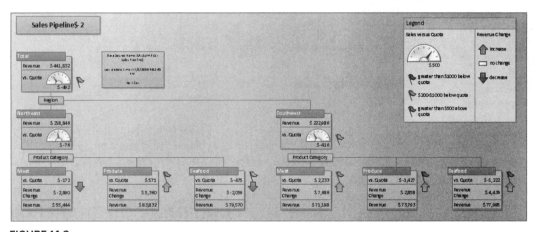

FIGURE 14-3

As previously mentioned, a PivotDiagram is the fastest way to display data in Visio, but data can also be linked to diagrams that had no previous data linkage. For example, you could even have Directional Map diagram and still connect data to it. With the diagram open you can select the Data tab and click the Link Data to Shapes button, which takes you through a similar connection wizard that you had for creating the PivotDiagram. After completing this connection wizard you can link specific rows of data from your source to explicit shapes on your diagram by clicking and dragging the row from the External Data window to the object you want to link. This automatically adds data fields to the diagram. Figure 14-4 shows a Directional Map template designed to display sales for two competing local stores. Optionally, you can change how the data is displayed by right-clicking the diagram data and selecting Edit Data Graphic under the Data section. This allows you to represent the data as text, a data bar, an icon, or color. Figure 14-4 shows data as text and a data bar.

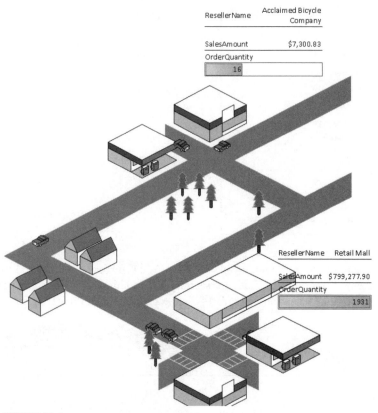

FIGURE 14-4

The Data tab also has a feature called Automatically Link, which takes shape fields that exist in your diagram and attempts to automatically map them to a data set that you have imported. This can speed up the process of mapping data to a diagram and prevent you from having to drag each row of data to the appropriate shape.

DEVELOPING AN INTERACTIVE VISIO DIAGRAM FOR SHAREPOINT

Having the ability to see data in a Visio diagram is great, but wouldn't it be better if consumers of the diagram could take action on what they see? If users see something unusual about a store's sales, they would likely want to see more details about that store. You can give them the ability to click shapes in a diagram that can link to any of the following:

➤ Another page or shape in the current drawing

➤ A page or shape in another drawing

➤ A document other than a Visio drawing

➤ A website, FTP site, or e-mail address

This effect can be created by right-clicking any shape and selecting Hyperlink. You can select the URL or document to link to under the Address property. You can also select a page of another diagram under the Sub-address property. For example, take the diagram shown in Figure 14-4 of the directional map and make the stores clickable. If you right-click the store called Acclaimed Bicycle Company and select Hyperlink, you can begin the diagram link. Click Browse next to the Sub-address property and select the diagram to link. There is already a store diagram created on a second page to link to. After selecting that page from the drop-down box click OK twice to return to the diagram. You can now test the link in Full Screen mode. When you click the shape it takes you to the store diagram shown in Figure 14-5.

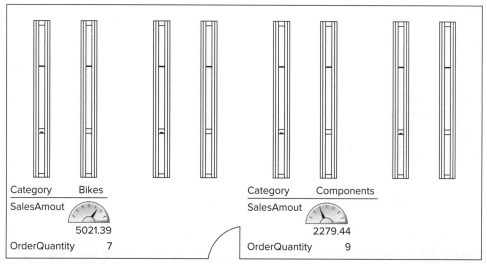

FIGURE 14-5

DEPLOYING A VISIO DIAGRAM

The deployment process is very simple once you are ready to deploy the Visio diagram that you have developed. After choosing a SharePoint site that you would like to save the diagrams to you will need to either select an existing document library or create a new one that you would like to save the .vdw Web Drawings file to. Inside the Visio 2010 desktop application where you have developed your diagram go to the File tab and select Save & Send. This provides the option to Save to SharePoint where you can then browse to the desired document library on your SharePoint server for deployment. Note that Figure 14-6 shows Save As Type changed to Web Drawing (*vdw), which is necessary to make the diagram interactive in SharePoint. If you save the file to SharePoint as a regular .vsd file, you will only be able to manage it as a file without viewing it in the web browser. After clicking Save, the document is deployed and once it completes it immediately opens in your web browser showing the completed deployment.

You can also test that the deployment worked successfully by navigating to the SharePoint document library that you just deployed to and open the diagrams. Figure 14-7 shows the deployed diagram now viewable from the Web. It is important to note that if data links have been established to shapes in your diagram and you would like your data to refresh from the Web that the .odc files must also be deployed. Otherwise the data in your diagrams will be static. The setup and security of these files were discussed in Lesson 7.

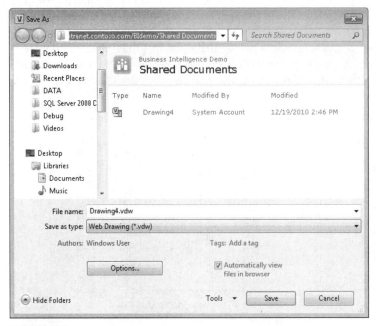

FIGURE 14-6

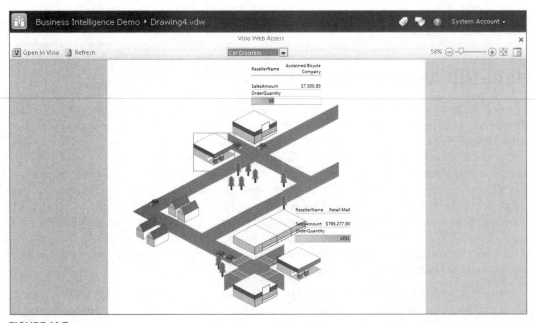

FIGURE 14-7

TRY IT

In this Try It you create a PivotDiagram that connects to customer data to visualize customer demographics.

Lesson Requirements

To complete this lesson you will be required to have SharePoint 2010 as well as Visio 2010 already installed. The step-by-step example uses the AdventureWorks sample databases, which you can download from www.codeplex.com.

Hints

➤ Develop a Visio diagram using the PivotDiagram template.

➤ Use the vTargetMail view from the AdventureWorksDW2008R2 database for the source data.

➤ Deploy the completed diagram to SharePoint 2010.

Step-by-Step

1. Go to Start ⇨ All Programs ⇨ Microsoft Office ⇨ Microsoft Visio 2010.

2. After Visio opens select New under the File tab.

3. Double-click the Business template category, then select the PivotDiagram and click Create, as shown in Figure 14-8.

4. The Data Selector Wizard automatically opens after you click Create. Choose Microsoft SQL Server Database and click Next.

5. This opens another wizard called the Data Connection Wizard. This wizard creates the .odc file used for pulling in data. In the Server Name property type the SQL Server that you installed the Adventure Works samples on and then click Next, as shown in Figure 14-9.

6. Select the AdventureWorksDW2008R2 database from the "Select the database that contains the data you want" drop-down box.

7. Choose the vTargetMail view from the list that is populated after selecting the database and then click Next.

8. The last screen of the Data Connection Wizard asks you where you would like to save the .odc file that is created. Select a path you can easily find later and click Finish.

9. This returns you to the Data Selector Wizard where you select the .odc file that was just created. Click Next.

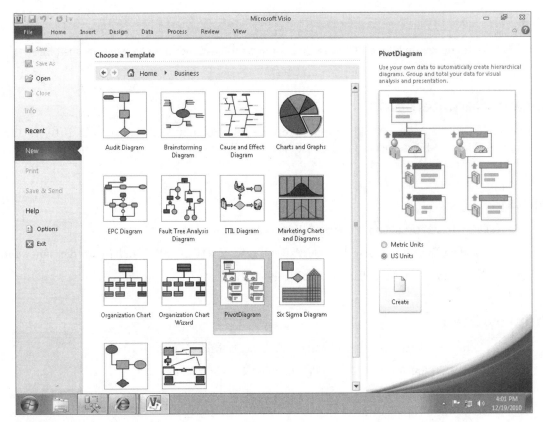

FIGURE 14-8

FIGURE 14-9

If you want to create a data-refreshable Web Drawing (*.vdw) for use with Visio Services on SharePoint, the data connection (*.odc) file must be located on the same SharePoint site as the Web Drawing.

10. By default all columns and all rows are brought into the diagram but you can optionally remove any columns or rows that you do not need. Leave the default (All Columns) and (All Data) selected and click Next.

11. Click Finish to complete the Data Selector Wizard. This will open the designer for Visio with a PivotDiagram pane open to begin selecting the fields you would like to display in the diagram. Figure 14-10 shows the design surface.

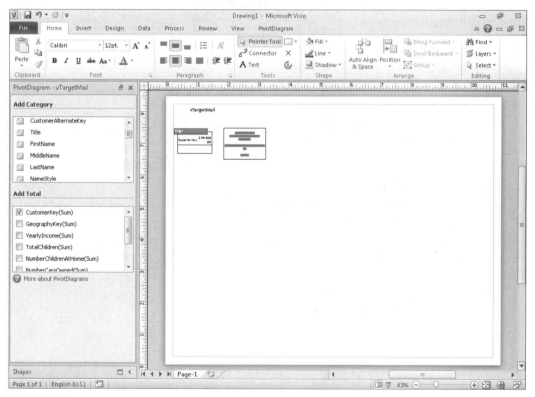

FIGURE 14-10

12. In the bottom-right corner of the designer you can zoom in and out to get a closer look at what the diagram displays. Right now it shows the CustomerKey summarized.

13. This is not a number that you would typically summarize. You would more likely like to see this number aggregated using a Count. Conveniently, a Count of all the rows in the data set is already provided. To change this to a Count aggregation uncheck CustomerKey(Sum) in the Add Total section of the PivotDiagram pane, then check Count at the bottom of the list of fields to select, as shown in Figure 14-11.

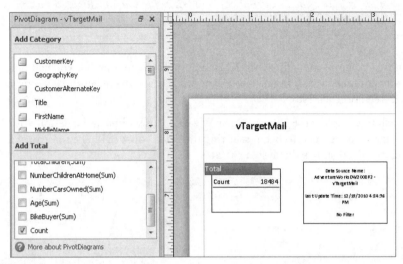

FIGURE 14-11

14. From the Add Total list add the YearlyIncome(Sum) field but change it to an average by right-clicking it and selecting Avg.

15. Do the same for the Age(Sum) field so you have both average age and average yearly income on your diagram.

16. You can adjust the diagram so all fields can easily be read by selecting the shape and expand it by grabbing its edges.

17. Change the YearlyIncome(Avg) field on the diagram to be represented by a data bar by right-clicking the field inside the diagram and selecting Data ⇨ Edit Data Graphic. Figure 14-12 shows the selection.

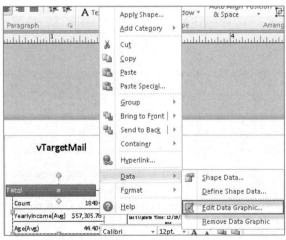

FIGURE 14-12

18. This opens the Edit Data Graphic: Data Graphic dialog. Select YearlyIncome(Avg) and click Edit Item.

19. In the Edit Item box change the Displayed As property to Data Bar. Also, change the Maximum Value property under the Details section to 100000 and click OK. Figure 14-13 shows these changes completed.

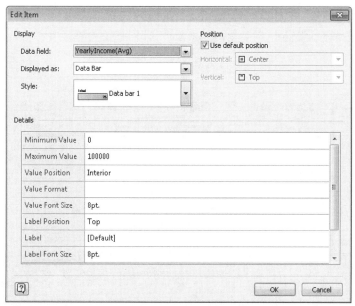

FIGURE 14-13

20. Click OK again when you return to the Edit Data Graphic: Data Graphic dialog.

21. Now to add a few more categories. From the Add Category section of the PivotDiagram pane click Gender and Region in that order.

22. The diagram design is now complete and is ready to be deployed to SharePoint. Go to the File tab and select Save & Send.

23. Choose the Save to SharePoint option and then click Browse for a location.

24. In the file path box in the top of the Save As window type your SharePoint server URL: http://<YourServerName>.

25. Select any document library from any SharePoint site (this can be any site created in previous lessons too). Change the Save As Type to Web Drawing (*.vdw) and name the file Lesson14.vdw before clicking Save. Figure 14-14 shows the completed diagram deployed to the SharePoint library.

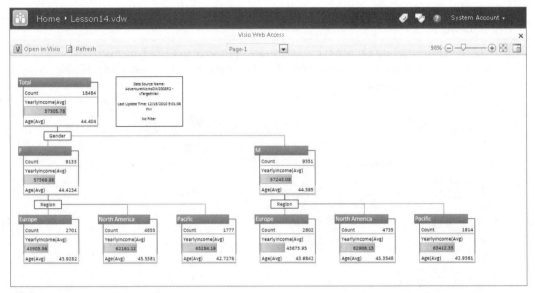

FIGURE 14-14

Congratulations! You have created a Visio diagram and deployed it to a SharePoint document library.

 Please select Lesson 14 on the DVD to view the video that accompanies this lesson.

SECTION IV
Creating Advanced Analytics in SharePoint

▶ **LESSON 15:** Implementing Data Refresh in Excel Services and PowerPivot

▶ **LESSON 16:** Developing and Deploying PerformancePoint Analytic Reports

▶ **LESSON 17:** Developing and Deploying PerformancePoint Scorecards

▶ **LESSON 18:** Creating and Deploying PerformancePoint Dashboards

▶ **LESSON 19:** Developing and Deploying PerformancePoint and SharePoint Filters

▶ **LESSON 20:** Strategy Mapping with Visio and PerformancePoint

▶ **LESSON 21:** Developing and Deploying Reporting Services Reports to SharePoint

15

Implementing Data Refresh in Excel Services and PowerPivot

In Lessons 12 and 13 you learned how to deploy Excel and PowerPivot reports you have created to SharePoint. This was great because it gave everyone in your company easier access to reports that were created from the report designer's desktop. Though this is helpful, it provides only a static view of the data set represented in the report. Implementing a scheduled data refresh of these reports can help give consumers of the report the most up-to-date data.

When you begin the process of scheduling a data refresh you should always ask yourself these questions:

➤ Does this data actually need to be refreshed?

➤ How often will this report be viewed?

➤ How often is my source data updated?

It seems obvious that you would want data to be refreshed, but depending on the circumstances that is not always the case. For example, maybe you would prefer that someone review the data prior to it being published. You could have frequently changing business rules that would prevent you from assuming that what was right on Monday is also right on Wednesday. In this case you want someone who is very familiar with the business rules to review the report prior to publishing it on SharePoint.

Generally the person who develops the report will also provide the frequency at which the data should be updated. Your business may have many reports that are viewed only weekly or maybe even monthly. For example, you may have several month-end reports that are viewed only the first week after a completed month. There is no need to view these any other time of the month so they can be scheduled to update only on the last day of every month.

Another important consideration is how often the source data changes. The business users may need the report data refreshed hourly, but the source data only changes nightly.

For example, your PowerPivot data source is a data warehouse that only gets updated nightly. If that is the case, it is not necessary to update your PowerPivot data more than once a day.

These are important questions to ask yourself before going through the process of implementing either Excel or PowerPivot data refreshes.

IMPLEMENTING AN EXCEL SERVICES DATA REFRESH

In Lesson 5 you learned how to configure Excel Services by ensuring that your files are in a trusted location and by setting up a Target Service Application so a user account does not have to be used when viewing Excel workbooks. By making these changes on the Central Administration site you will be ready for the discussion in this lesson. If you have not already reviewed Lesson 5, please do so to have an understanding of the setup required.

Data refreshes can be done in three ways in Excel Services. The user can manually select to refresh the connection, the developer can set the connection to automatically refresh when the workbook is open, or you can set up a periodic refresh, which will refresh based on a frequency the report author defines.

The manual refresh is done from inside SharePoint. Navigate and open the report you want to manually refresh. Once the report is open select the Data drop-down box and click Refresh All Connections to refresh all data in the current workbook. Figure 15-1 shows the manual refresh option. This method is very simple and front facing so users can execute the refresh.

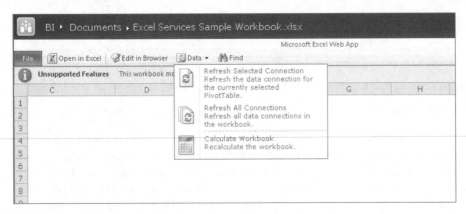

FIGURE 15-1

The next two methods are done from inside of Excel. To create a periodic refresh you must open the workbook for which you want to create the refresh plan and on the Data tab select Connections. This will show you the list of connections that are being used in this workbook, as shown in Figure 15-2.

Select the connection you want to configure and then click Properties. The Connection Properties screen allows you to define a periodic refresh by checking the property that is set by default to Refresh Every 60 Minutes. You can manipulate this to fit your needs, so if you need the data refreshed every 15 minutes you can change the time.

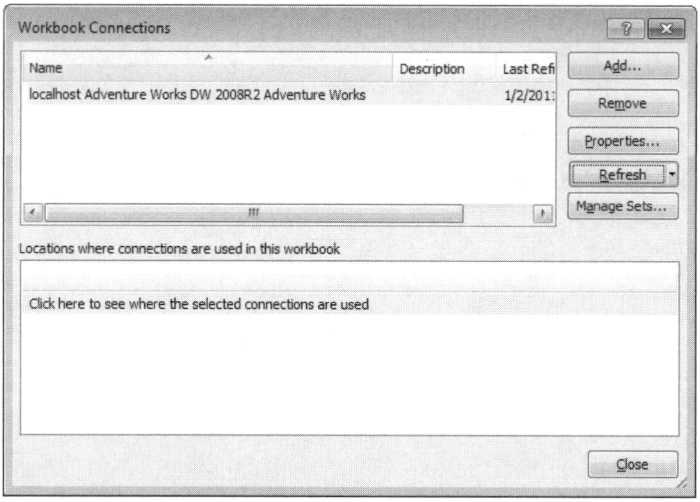

FIGURE 15-2

You can also set the data refresh to occur when the file is opened from this screen. By checking the Refresh Data When Opening the File property your data is automatically updated every time the file is opened. Figure 15-3 shows both the periodic refresh and the refresh when the file is opened options.

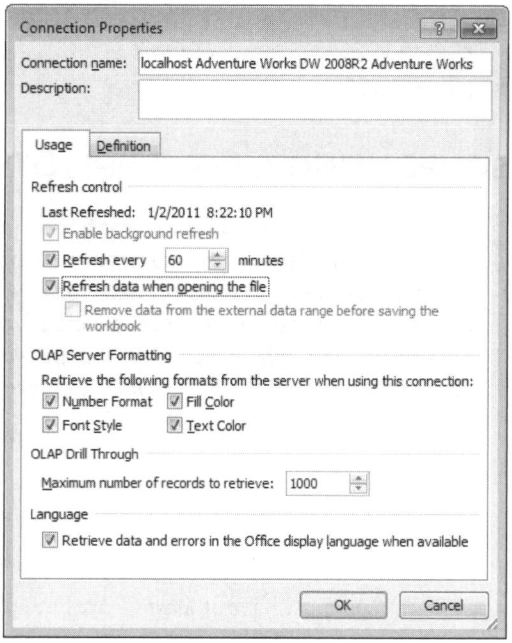

One last item to note from the Connection Properties screen is on the Definition tab. If you have the credentials that you would like used for a data source saved in the Secure Store Service, which was detailed in Lesson 5, you can use this Definition tab to point the connection to that account. By selecting Authentication Settings next to the Excel Services property you can select SSS, which will then ask you for your SSS ID or Target Application ID that you created while inside SharePoint. The benefit of doing this is that your users do not have to have access to the data source. They can use the credentials set up in the Secure Store Service for viewing or creating a report. Figure 15-4 shows both the Definition tab and the Excel Services Authentication Settings.

FIGURE 15-3

You must ensure now that not only the Excel workbook is deployed to SharePoint but also the Office Data Connection (ODC) file. This file stores the settings and connection string used for refreshing the data used in the workbook.

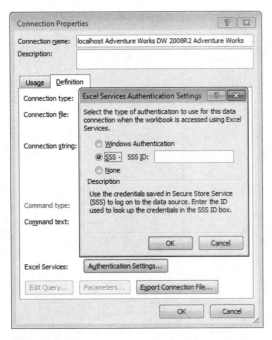

FIGURE 15-4

SCHEDULING A POWERPIVOT DATA REFRESH

In Lesson 8 you learned how to configure and install PowerPivot for SharePoint. It is critical that you follow that lesson very closely to now have the ability to schedule a data refresh. As a review, the major points in that lesson were the proper installation of both SharePoint and SQL Server as part of either a standalone or an existing farm and setting up a Target Service Application using an unattended data refresh account. Though you did quickly schedule a data refresh in Lesson 8 to test your configuration, this lesson focuses more on the details of that scheduling process.

Here are a couple caveats you must know about before configuring a data refresh on a PowerPivot workbook:

➤ Only one data refresh schedule can be created for each PowerPivot workbook.

➤ The workbook must be checked in at the time the refresh is set to occur.

➤ You must have at least Contribute permissions or greater on the workbook.

➤ The data source cannot be an Office document or Access database because those connection types are not supported in .odc (Office Data Connection) files.

To enable and schedule a data refresh navigate to the library that contains the PowerPivot workbook that you have previously deployed. When the library opens click Manage Data Refresh on the workbook you want to configure. Figure 15-5 shows the Manage Data Refresh button in a PowerPivot Gallery. This opens the Manage Data Refresh page, which allows you to define the frequency of the data refresh on the selected report.

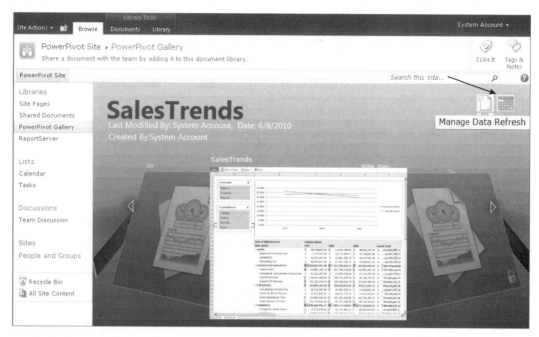

FIGURE 15-5

To turn on the data refresh on this workbook click the Enable checkbox. In the Schedule Details section define the frequency of the data refresh. This allows you to refresh your workbook daily, weekly, monthly, or even have a one-time-only refresh. You can then specify the earliest start time, which defines when a refresh request can be processed. You can force it to process only during non-business hours or specify a time. Business hours are defined in the Central Administration site under the PowerPivot Configure Service Application settings. Next, you may choose to provide an e-mail address for who you would like to notify if an error occurs during processing. You have three options for the credentials that can be used for the data refresh:

CREDENTIAL	DESCRIPTION
Use the data refresh account configured by the administrator	Processes the data refresh using the PowerPivot unattended data refresh account.
Connect using the following Windows user credentials	Enter a user name and password of your choosing that will process the data refresh.
Connect using the credentials saved in Secure Store Service (SSS) to log on to the data source. Enter the ID used to loop up the credentials in the SSS ID box.	The process of creating a Secure Store Services is described in Lesson 8. This option allows you to use the stored credentials that are contained in the target application.

All of these settings are shown in Figure 15-6.

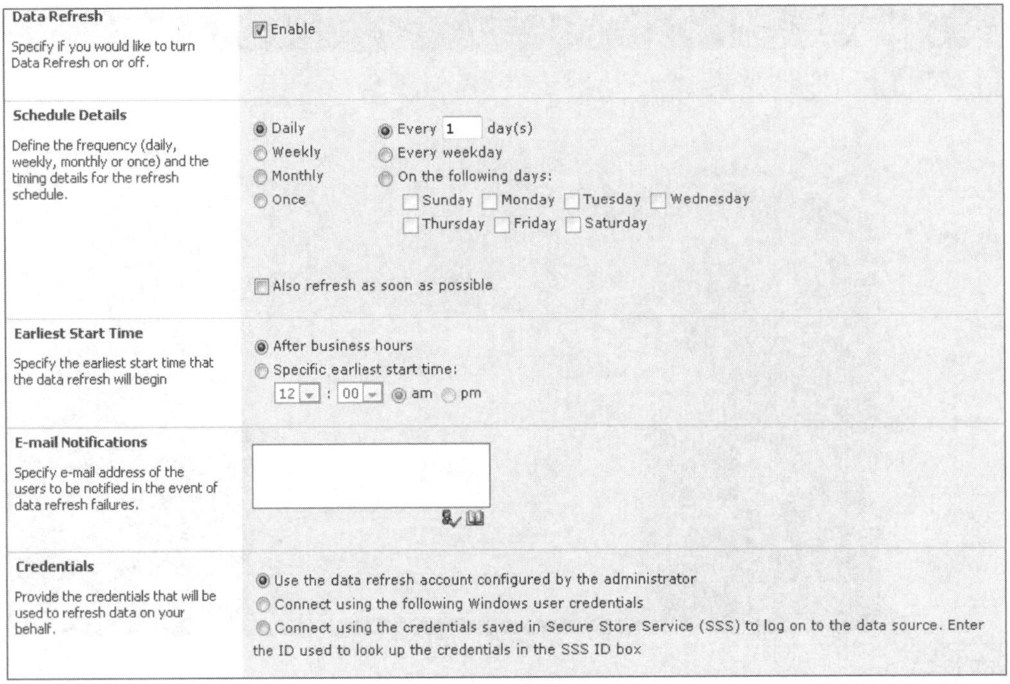

FIGURE 15-6

MONITORING DATA REFRESH FAILURES

SharePoint 2010 has evolved in helping you track data refresh problems that occur with PowerPivot. The PowerPivot Management Dashboard is designed to show you not only when there is a data refresh failure but it also provides server wellness information and workbook activity. To view the PowerPivot Management Dashboard open SharePoint 2010 Central Administration and select PowerPivot Management Dashboard under the General Application Settings heading.

The information on this dashboard is extremely valuable in understanding how PowerPivot is running on your current server setup. This can be used to determine when it is a good time to scale out to multiple PowerPivot servers by providing information like the number of queries run against your workbooks and how many users accessed those workbooks. You can also find information specific to server usage. For example, Figure 15-7 shows you can also view several charts that depict your server health.

Although this information is valuable, the main focus of this lesson is data refresh. On the bottom of the PowerPivot Management Dashboard is a grid view titled Data Refresh—Recent Activity. This provides a list of the workbooks, time of execution, and any failures that occur. Figure 15-8 shows this section of the dashboard. Though having this dashboard is nice, you would likely want to set up notification on the data refresh itself if a failure occurs, which you saw earlier in this lesson.

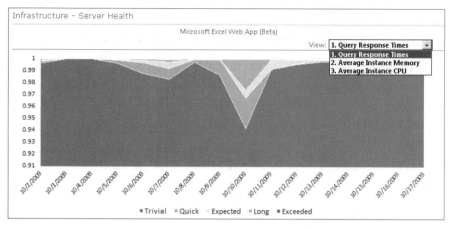

FIGURE 15-7

Data Refresh - Recent Activity

Workbook	End Time	Duration (seconds)
OperationsForecast.xlsx	5/24/2010 4:01:23 AM	1
AsiaForecast.xlsx	5/24/2010 4:01:23 AM	0
DanJumpForecasts.xlsx	5/24/2010 4:01:23 AM	0
industrybikesAccess.xlsx	5/24/2010 4:01:23 AM	0
SalesTerritoryAnalysis.xlsx	5/24/2010 4:01:23 AM	0
industrybikesAccess.xlsx	4/8/2010 10:44:27 ...	0

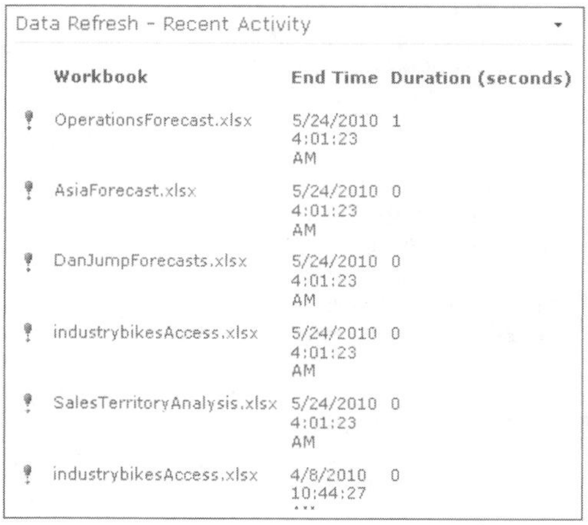

FIGURE 15-8

TRY IT

In this Try It you use the PowerPivot workbook that was created in the Try It section of Lesson 13 to schedule a data refresh on the connection that the workbook uses.

Lesson Requirements

To complete this lesson you will be required to have SharePoint 2010 already installed and configured for use with PowerPivot. The step-by-step example uses the completed results of the Lesson 13 Try It section. If you have not completed that lesson you can find the results of that Try It section at `www.wrox.com`.

Hints

➤ Ensure that the completed Lesson 13 Try It section is deployed to a PowerPivot Gallery.

➤ Schedule a data refresh to occur daily but not during business hours.

Step-by-Step

1. If you have not already deployed the completed Lesson 13, go to www.wrox.com and download this completed Try It section.

2. After completing the download open the PowerPivot workbook in Excel 2010.

3. On the File tab select Save & Send and select Save to SharePoint.

4. Click Browse for a location and type the URL for your SharePoint site on the top navigation.

5. Navigate to the PowerPivot site you created in Lesson 13 and save the PowerPivot workbook to the PowerPivot Gallery on that site. Figure 15-9 shows the saving screen.

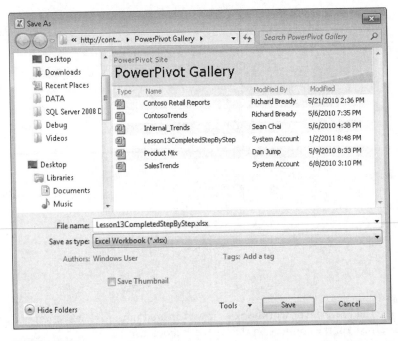

FIGURE 15-9

6. When the save completes your PowerPivot workbook will automatically be opened in a web browser to show that it is now on SharePoint but can still be fully interacted with.

7. From your web browser navigate to the PowerPivot Gallery that you just deployed the workbook to.

8. Find the workbook that you just deployed and click Manage Data Refresh. This is the Calendar button on the top right, as shown in Figure 15-10.

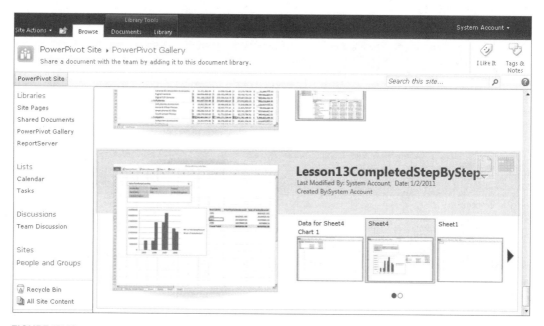

FIGURE 15-10

9. This will open the configuration of this workbook's data refresh. To enable the data refresh check Enable.

10. In the Schedule Details section leave the default of Daily and Every 1 day(s).

11. In the Earliest Start Time section leave the default of After Business Hours.

12. Under Credentials choose Connect Using the Following Windows User Credentials and type in your user name and password. Generally, you will choose either the data refresh account or the Secure Store Service but those two properties were configured in Lesson 8. The reason you should opt for one of those two options is because then you have an account set up that is devoted to PowerPivot and you do not have to retype your password every time you want to use it.

13. Ensure all data sources are selected and click OK. Figure 15-11 shows the completed set up of the data refresh.

14. This will schedule the data refresh to occur daily. If any errors occur when scheduling the data refresh, this is likely because of the account that you chose to automate the data refresh. Ensure this account has all the necessary privileges, then try again.

FIGURE 15-11

Congratulations! You have completed the process of scheduling a data refresh of your PowerPivot workbook.

Please select Lesson 15 on the DVD to view the video that accompanies this lesson.

16

Developing and Deploying PerformancePoint Analytic Reports

Reporting and visualization of an organization's data is the only way to turn that data into information. Information is the actionable form of data, turning it from bits and bytes into something the business can use to make decisions and spur action. PerformancePoint delivers a number of very dynamic ways to report on your data. With the capabilities in this product, you can create a variety of different types of reports.

This lesson focuses on one primary type, the analytical report. You learn how to build, extend, and deploy these reports to make dynamic content for your dashboards or other SharePoint pages.

TYPES OF REPORTS

PerformancePoint offers many types of reports, ten to be exact.

Analytic Charts

Analytic charts are one of the most dynamic and interactive report formats that can be used on the Web. This level of interactivity enables unprecedented user control right from the web page. Users have the ability to change measures, alter the chart type, select different layouts, and then drill through and decompose the record in a targeted way (more on this later). See an example in Figure 16-1.

Analytic Grid

The analytic grid is similar to the analytic chart except the data is displayed in a grid format instead of graphically. This would be beneficial for things like actuals vs. targets, displaying

KPIs (Key Performance Indicators) alongside their metrics and other numeric data points. See an example in Figure 16-2.

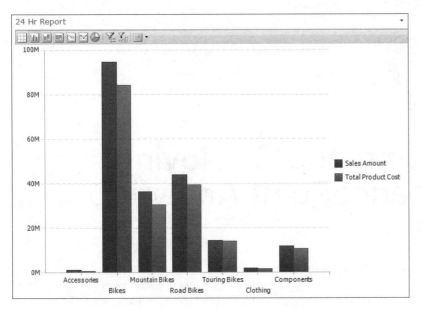

FIGURE 16-1

	⊞ Accessories	⊟ Bikes				⊞ Clothing	⊞ Components
Measures			⊞ Mountain Bikes	⊞ Road Bikes	⊞ Touring Bikes		
Internet Sales Amount	$700,759.96	$28,318,144.65	$9,952,759.56	$14,520,584.04	$3,844,801.05	$339,772.61	
Internet Standard Pr...	$262,085.39	$16,812,348.15	$5,439,135.46	$8,983,284.34	$2,389,928.35	$203,360.03	
Order Count	19,523	18,358	6,185	9,528	2,645	9,871	2,646

FIGURE 16-2

Decomposition Tree

This is a new version of a functionality that was available in ProClarity. It allows a user to quickly launch a report and then breakdown a piece of data into its components. This can be done right in the browser, enabling lots of functionality for the end user. See an example in Figure 16-3.

Show Details

This is the details report that loads from a Show Details action. This action loads from an analytic chart or grid. See an example of this in Figure 16-4.

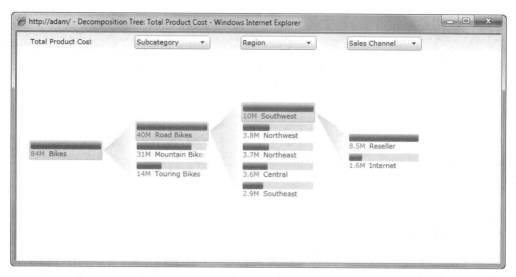

FIGURE 16-3

Order Quantity	Unit Price	Extended Amount	Standard Product Cost	Total Product Cost	Sales Amount	Tax Amount	Freight Cost	Carrier Tracking Numb
1	2024.994	2024.994	1898.0944	1898.0944	2024.994	161.9995	50.6249	4911-403C-98
3	2024.994	6074.982	1898.0944	5694.2832	6074.982	485.9986	151.8746	4911-403C-98
1	2024.994	2024.994	1898.0944	1898.0944	2024.994	161.9995	50.6249	4911-403C-98
1	2039.994	2039.994	1912.1544	1912.1544	2039.994	163.1995	50.9999	4911-403C-98
1	2039.994	2039.994	1912.1544	1912.1544	2039.994	163.1995	50.9999	4911-403C-98
2	2039.994	4079.988	1912.1544	3824.3088	4079.988	326.399	101.9997	4911-403C-98
1	2039.994	2039.994	1912.1544	1912.1544	2039.994	163.1995	50.9999	4911-403C-98
1	419.4589	419.4589	413.1463	413.1463	419.4589	33.5567	10.4865	6431-4D57-83
1	874.794	874.794	884.7083	884.7083	874.794	69.9835	21.8699	6431-4D57-83
3	2024.994	6074.982	1898.0944	5694.2832	6074.982	485.9986	151.8746	4E0A-4F89-AE
2	2024.994	4049.988	1898.0944	3796.1888	4049.988	323.999	101.2497	4E0A-4F89-AE
4	2024.994	8099.976	1898.0944	7592.3776	8099.976	647.9981	202.4994	4E0A-4F89-AE
2	2039.994	4079.988	1912.1544	3824.3088	4079.988	326.399	101.9997	4E0A-4F89-AE
2	2024.994	4049.988	1898.0944	3796.1888	4049.988	323.999	101.2497	4E0A-4F89-AE
3	419.4589	1258.3767	413.1463	1239.4389	1258.3767	100.6701	31.4594	2E53-4802-85

FIGURE 16-4

Excel Services

Excel workbooks that are deployed to SharePoint can be reused in part or whole as a PerformancePoint report part for a dashboard. The workbook needs to be deployed to a trusted SharePoint document library. Then a portion of it can be republished as a report in PerformancePoint.

KPI Details

KPI details reports allow you to display the detailed information about a scorecard item without taking up the real estate on the report. To display this information you just need to click a KPI and display details about it right from within the scorecard. The report that loads is the KPI details report.

ProClarity Analytics Server Page

This report was held over as a benefit for customers still running ProClarity Server. You should check out the decomposition report as it is replacing the ProClarity Analytics Server Page going forward.

Reporting Services

Reporting Services reports can be deployed directly to SharePoint, but they can also be used as part of a dashboard solution. These reports are great to display pre-canned content that will tie directly to a report that may be distributed via other channels to make sure there is continuity between the different methods of displaying data.

Strategy Map

Strategy maps are covered in more detail later in the book. For now you should know that a strategy map is a diagram created in Visio that is then overlaid with KPIs to provide a look at performance across different business processes.

Web Page

This is less of a report and more of a standard web part, but nonetheless is important. Some organizations have important information displayed on ASP.NET or static web pages throughout the organization. This information can be included in your PerformancePoint environment as a type of report in your dashboard.

CREATING YOUR FIRST REPORT

This lesson highlights the Analytic chart reports and then extends them with show details and decomposition reports. In Lesson 9, you learned how to configure your site for business intelligence. In the business intelligence site template you have a button to launch PerformancePoint Dashboard Designer. You don't need any previous configuration other than having that site template selected.

First you need to open Dashboard Designer and create a data source. You will use your Analysis Services cube from AdventureWorks2008R2. See an example of this data source in Figure 16-5.

New Data Source

Connection Settings	
● Use Standard Connection	
Server:	localhost
Database:	Adventure Works DW 2008R2
Roles:	
○ Use the following connection	
Connection String:	
Cube:	Adventure Works

Data Source Settings	
Authentication:	○ Unattended Service Account
	All users connect using the Unattended Service Account.
	○ Unattended Service Account and add authenticated user name in connection string
	All users connect using the Unattended Service Account. The authenticated user name is provided as the value of the "CustomData" connection string property.
	● Per-user Identity
Formatting Dimension:	Σ Measures
Cache Lifetime:	10 minutes

FIGURE 16-5

Next, right-click the PerformancePoint content menu item on the left and select New Report. Choose Analytic Chart Report. See this in Figures 16-6 and 16-7.

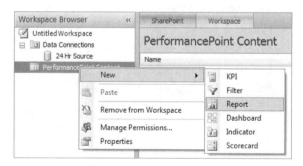

FIGURE 16-6

Now you can begin building out the report. Select your new data source in the windows and click Finish. You should see a layout like the one in Figure 16-8.

To build your report, find the measures that you want in the Details pane on the right and drag them into the Series box at the bottom of the report. In Figure 16-9 we chose Sales Amount and Total Product cost. Next, drag in a named set of your core products that will lay out the report automatically. The basic report is shown in Figure 16-9.

You can now deploy your report to SharePoint and see what it looks like. Because Dashboard Designer is connected to the server, once you save your report it's already deployed! Pretty cool! Go to your SharePoint site and take a look at what you can do with it in SharePoint in the next section. Spoiler alert: you will also see two other report types — Show Details and Decomposition — in the next section.

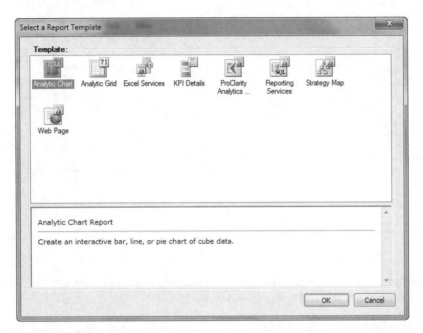

FIGURE 16-7

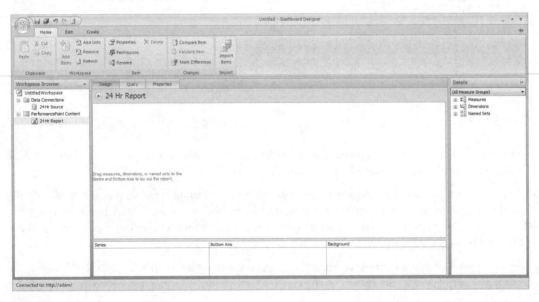

FIGURE 16-8

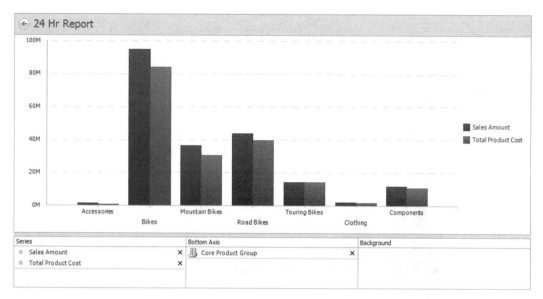

FIGURE 16-9

EXTENDING THE REPORT

When you open the SharePoint site and go to PerformancePoint Content on the navigation menu on the left you see your new report. You can drop down the arrow to the right and select Display Report to see it in the browser as shown in Figure 16-10.

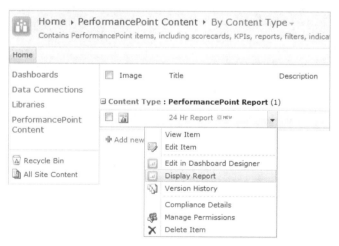

FIGURE 16-10

Once you have the report open it should look like Figure 16-11.

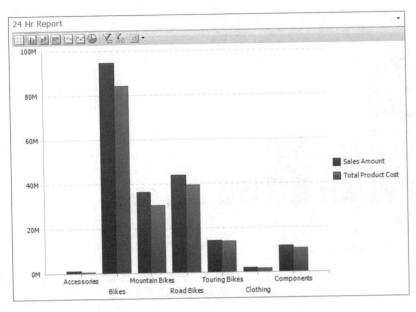

FIGURE 16-11

In Figure 16-12 you see the options available on the report when you right-click the content.

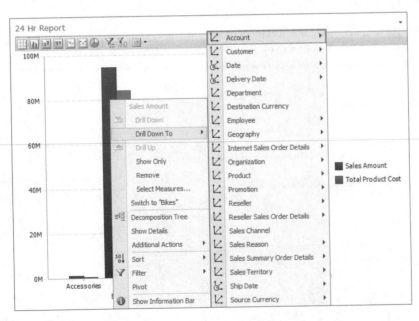

FIGURE 16-12

You can drill down across your data source, you can change which measures you are displaying, or you can drill through or view the decomposition tree, which breaks down the data into categories. Show details report functionality is shown in Figure 16-13.

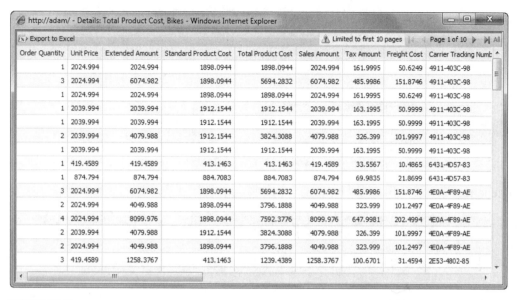

FIGURE 16-13

This functionality provides the ability to drill through to detail-level data, and then export directly to Excel from the button in the upper left if you want to. In Figure 16-14 you can see the decomposition tree and how you can click through to analyze your data.

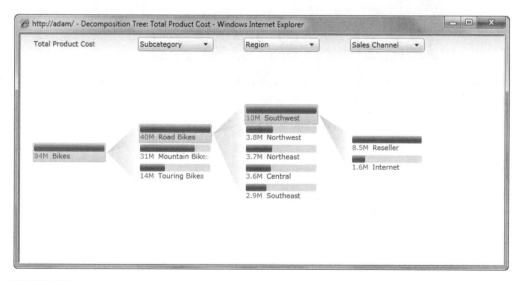

FIGURE 16-14

These items can then be converted to other content right from that screen. Drop down Region and convert it to a chart that then has all the functionality of your original report. Pretty powerful stuff. Check out this behavior in Figures 16-15 and 16-16.

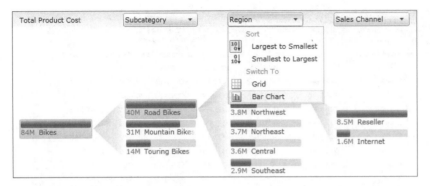

FIGURE 16-15

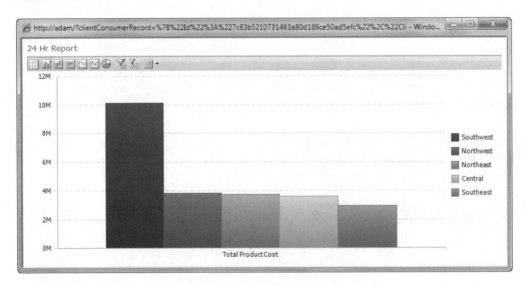

FIGURE 16-16

Now that's a report you can be proud of. You build one in the Try It.

TRY IT

In this Try It you build a chart report and then walk through the decomposition tree to dig even deeper. You create a cost analysis report to see what types of additional costs are figuring into your overall product cost the most.

Lesson Requirements

In this Try It you need to have a few things configured:

➤ AdventureWorks 2008R2 sample cube deployed

➤ SharePoint 2010 installed and PerformancePoint Service Application enabled

You'll be using these together to build the solution in this lesson's Try It.

Hints

➤ Make sure to use the Analysis Services database for AdventureWorks2008R2 for your data source.

➤ Remember to right-click the bars in the chart to find the decomposition tree.

➤ The options to convert the decomposition tree items to a chart or grid are in the drop-down headers in the decomposition report.

Step-by-Step

1. Open Dashboard Designer from your start menu or from your SharePoint site.

2. Create a new data source for the Adventure Works 2008R2 cube in Analysis Services.

3. Once the data source is created you are ready to create your report. Right-click the PerformancePoint Content menu item and select New ➪ Report.

4. Choose Analytic Chart, click Next, and select your newly created data source.

5. Once you have your empty report up, find the following measures in the Details pane on the right and drag them into the Series box:

   ➤ Reseller Total Product Cost

   ➤ Standard Product Cost

   ➤ Total Product Cost

6. Drag Core Product group from the named sets into the Bottom Axis group. This should lay out the report nicely.

7. Save the report and it will deploy to your SharePoint site.

8. Display the report in SharePoint and right-click the bars.

9. Select the decomposition tree report from the context menu.

10. Click the Road Bike item in the Subcategory column and choose your items to drill down through the data. Take some time and explore the products contributing to the cost, the sales channels, and other groupings of data.

Congratulations! You just built your first PerformancePoint Analytic Report and are well on your way to building dynamic content your users will love using. Keep going through the next lessons and you'll build on this new knowledge.

 Please select Lesson 16 on the DVD to view the video that accompanies this lesson.

17

Developing and Deploying PerformancePoint Scorecards

This lesson discusses the different components of scorecards, and how to build them up into a cohesive whole. By the end of this lesson you will be able to create an interactive visualization to compare values against target values or the previous year, with drill-down capability.

TERMINOLOGY

There is often confusion about the different terms used in Business Intelligence, but they are relatively simple, each item building upon the previous. In PerformancePoint terms, each of these terms also has specific functionality.

➤ **Metric** — Often called a measure. This is simply a value such as Sales Amount.

➤ **Actual** — A type of metric, the actual is a value achieved

➤ **Target** — Another type of metric, a target is an intended value. In PerformancePoint, targets also have specific indicators set.

➤ **KPI. Key Performance Indicator** — A KPI is an actual, measured against a target, typically with a graphical indicator. In PerformancePoint a single KPI can have multiple actuals and targets.

➤ **KPA. Key Performance Area** — In business terms, a Key Performance Area is an area of concern in the business, made of similar KPIs. In PerformancePoint, these terms have been replaced with "Leaf" KPIs and "Non-Leaf" KPIs — Leaf and Non-leaf KPIs are created in the same way, and are simply used differently in a scorecard.

➤ **Objectives** — At a top level, disparate KPAs roll up into Objectives — for instance, Finance, Customers, Learning, and Internal Business Process are all disparate objectives. These are implemented in Performance Point as a specialized form of KPI.

➤ **Scorecard** — A *scorecard* is composed of KPIs (as well as KPAs and Objectives), put together along with dimension drill-downs.

➤ **Report** — *Reports* in PerformancePoint can be various types of reports, including Analytic Charts & Grids, and Reporting Services Reports.

➤ **Filter** — A *filter* is a selector, be it a calendar or a drop-down, used to slice the data in other components.

➤ **Dashboard** — A *dashboard* is a combination of all these elements, linked together to build an interactive analytics portal.

CREATING KPIS

You can create KPIs in two ways. The first is letting PerformancePoint generate them from Analysis Services KPIs automatically when creating a scorecard, and the second is creating them manually. In both cases, you need to create a data source first.

Analysis Services data sources are the most feature-rich data sources, and are the best sources to start with. To set up an Analysis Services Data Source, follow these steps:

1. Open Dashboard designer. You can do this by browsing to the Data Connections folder and editing one of the existing items, or in an unedited Business Intelligence site, click on Start using PerformancePoint Services, and then Run Dashboard Designer.

2. In Dashboard Designer, right-click on Data Connections in the workspace browser, and select New Data Source.

3. Choose Analysis Services.

4. Set up the data source by inputting the server name, choosing a database, and choosing a cube, as shown in Figure 17-1.

5. Finally, choose a name and save the data source.

 Saving the data source is important, because some parts of the Dashboard Designer use only the saved version.

To create a KPI manually:

1. Right-click PerformancePoint Content in the workspace browser and select New ➪ KPI.

2. Select Blank KPI and click OK.

3. The Name field is selected showing New KPI, so add your KPI name now. See Figure 17-2 for a blank KPI prior to setting the data source mapping.

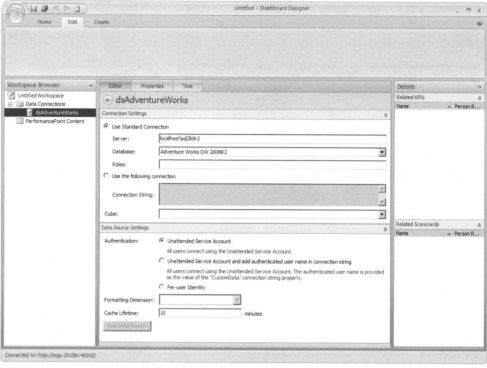

FIGURE 17-1

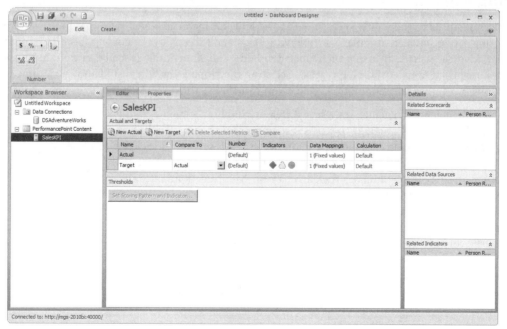

FIGURE 17-2

4. For both Actuals and Targets, to set the KPI to use the data source, click 1 (Fixed Values) and change the mapping from Fixed Source to the data source created earlier, as shown in Figure 17-3.

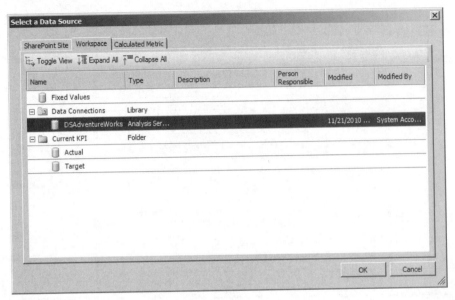

FIGURE 17-3

Filtering KPIs

It is often required to show only specific data for a KPI, for instance when there is a dimension for separating actual, budget, and plan, or to have actuals and targets for the current month and year. You can filter the metrics by using the Dimension Filter and Time Intelligence Filter options on the Dimensional Data Source Mapping screen. Selecting the Dimension Filter and choosing a dimension shows a member selection option, where you can choose the dimension members to filter by.

The Time Intelligence (TI) Filter is slightly different, and uses a language called the Simple Time Protocol (STP). For this language to work, it requires that the time dimension be mapped in the data source. This mapping is covered in detail in the Try It section. If the cube has multiple time dimensions, the mapped dimension is used. The syntax is simple. In the most basic format, a level is denominated, so Year denominates the current year, Month denominates the current month, and Day denominates the current day. In addition, you can specify offsets — Year-1 denominates last year, Month-1 denominates last month, and so on. STP provides an additional construct to get the first member in a hierarchy; for example, Month.FirstDay will give the first day of a month. Finally, you can use the colon (:) as a range operator; for example, use the formula Month.FirstDay : Month.Day to get the Month-to-Date value. These elements can be combined to form complex formulae — for instance, Year.FirstMonth.FirstDay : Year.Month.Day will give a Year-to-Date value, and (Year-1). FirstMonth.FirstDay : (Year-1).Month.Day will give the Year-to-Date for last year.

Figure 17-4 shows the Sales Amount measure filtered to show only values for the Sales Territory Europe for the Month-to-Date.

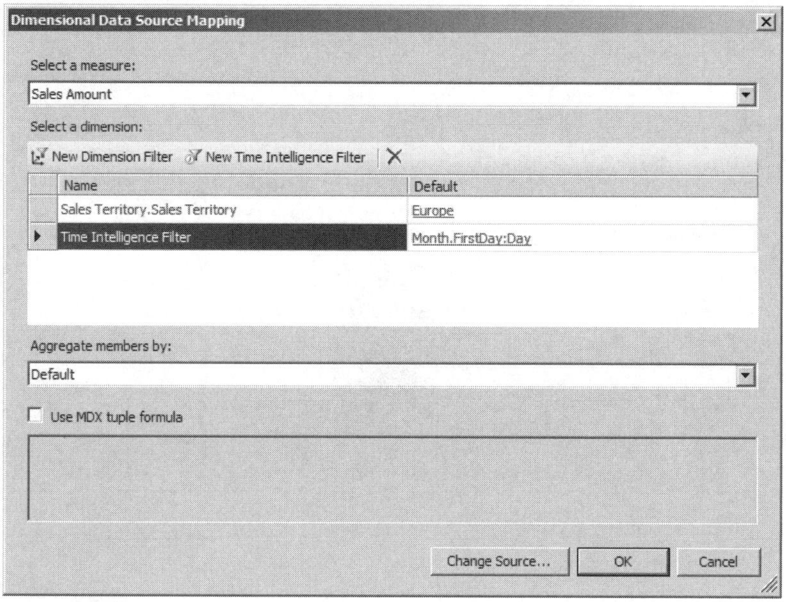

FIGURE 17-4

USING DIFFERENT SOURCES FOR SCORECARDS

Although Analysis Services provides the richest functionality, there is great utility in connecting PerformancePoint directly to SharePoint lists, SQL tables, and Excel worksheets stored in Excel Services. Excel worksheets can also be imported directly, but a much better approach is to upload the worksheet into a SharePoint list and connect to that list.

The restrictions when connecting to non-SSAS data sources start with the fact that, rather than mapping to a single SQL server or SharePoint site, a new data source needs to be mapped for each table or list. In addition, many of the advantages of an OLAP environment are lost, such as the multilevel hierarchies that are defined in the cube.

These restrictions are by no means overwhelming, and a trick to make your non-OLAP data source hierarchies dynamic (that is, they will refresh when new members are added) is highlighted in the following section.

Creating a connection to a SharePoint list or SQL table is almost identical, but a couple of key differences exist from OLAP sources. In a flat source, no dimensions exist, and these will need to be mapped — each column will need to be set to a key (a unique identifier), a dimension column (there is a specialist time dimension option), or a Fact column. The Fact column needs to have its aggregation set, that is, whether it rolls up by sum, average, and so on. Figure 17-5 shows a typical mapping.

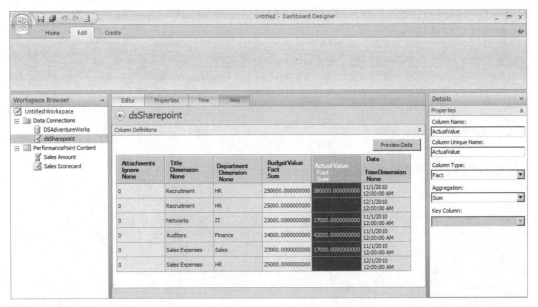

FIGURE 17-5

CREATING AND FORMATTING A SCORECARD

In its simplest incarnation, a scorecard is a collection of KPIs, and keeping this in mind will let you navigate the scorecard creation wizard much more easily. Using any template other than Blank Scorecard will create KPIs, and the wizard will set the options in exactly the same manner as doing so manually.

If the KPIs exist already, or you will be combining KPIs from multiple data sources, it is often easiest to create a blank scorecard, and start from there.

The scorecard design surface has two primary elements: the central editor, where items are added, and a Details tab on the right, as shown in Figure 17-6.

The Details tab is context-sensitive, and updates according to what is displayed on the design surface. In addition, when multiple data sources are used, you can use the drop-down at the bottom to filter which items are shown. The first item in the Details tab is a list of KPIs, organized by list and folder. To add a KPI to the scorecard, drag it from here to the design surface, on either of the Drop Items Here boxes. In both cases, the metrics will be aligned along the top, but the KPI itself will either be on top or down the left. Stacking KPIs along the left is the most common, and using the top bar is reserved for when the metrics on the KPIs are named dissimilarly. This is important because PerformancePoint assigns values to the cells in the grid according to the intersection of the KPI and the metric name, and even a slight difference in the metric name, such as a trailing space, can cause the cell to remain empty.

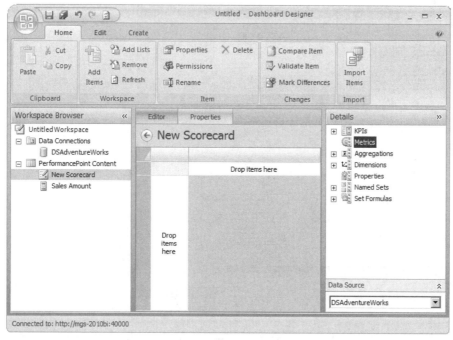

FIGURE 17-6

Adding a KPI automatically adds the metrics associated with that KPI to the scorecard; however, adding additional KPIs does not add metrics not already on the scorecard — they will now appear in the Metrics list and can be added manually to the columns.

Once the KPIs have been added to the scorecard, you can add additional drilldowns. This process differs slightly between Analysis Services and other sources.

To add a dimension drilldown, drag the dimension over from the Dimensions section on the Details tab to the design surface. A dimension member selection box will then be presented as shown in Figure 17-7. You have the option to select members individually, select all the children, or use the auto-select options. Auto-select means that the members chosen will update automatically when the dimension is updated in Analysis Services.

Now for adding dimensions from a non-SSAS source. You have two ways to add the dimension to the scorecard: using the Dimensions section or using Named Sets. The Dimension section enables you to select individual items, but the items will not update automatically when the list changes. Using Named Sets, on the other hand, will allow the scorecard to automatically update when the list changes, as shown in Figure 17-8.

 Named Sets on a flat source will automatically update when the list or table changes.

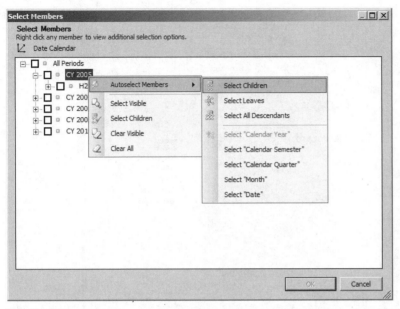

FIGURE 17-7

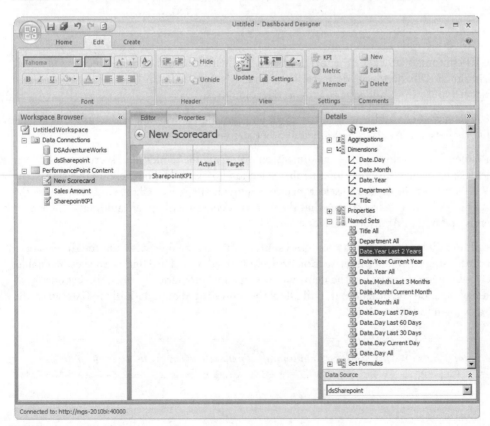

FIGURE 17-8

Once the KPIs, metrics, and dimensions are all added to the scorecard, additional formatting options are available by right-clicking on the design surface. Clicking anywhere on the design surface shows the View Settings option — the most common option used within this option is Filter Empty Rows. This option hides rows that have no data, as shown in Figure 17-9.

FIGURE 17-9

These rows will show in the designer in red, and not be shown when the scorecard is deployed.

Right-clicking the KPI itself shows the KPI Settings option — the only settings here are the display name of the KPI and a weighting. This weighting is used when rolling up to a non-leaf KPI or objective.

Finally, right-clicking a target metric and clicking on Metric Settings shows Figure 17-10. This setting allows for a large amount of control over how the target is displayed, including displaying the actual. This is useful when space is at a premium, and showing a variance is not necessary.

TRY IT

In this Try It, you create a scorecard using Analysis Services as a data source, with additional actual and target columns that are filtered by time intelligence.

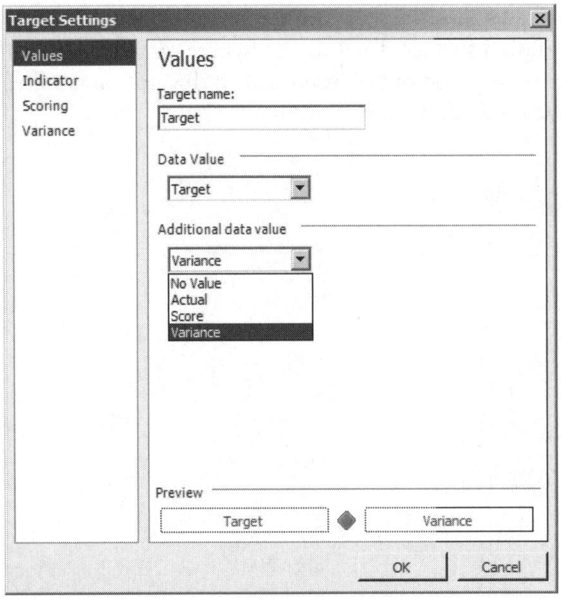

FIGURE 17-10

Lesson Requirements

Using the Adventure Works 2008 R2 cube, create a single KPI, with all actuals based on the Sales Amount measure, and targets based on Sales Amount Quota, or Sales Amount. Three actual metrics in total are required: the first one is named Actual, and contains no TI filters. The other two are called MTDLY and YTDLY, with TI filters based on Month-to-Date for last year and Year-to-Date for last year calculations. Three target metrics in total are required: the first is called Target, and uses Sales Amount Quota as the measure. The other two targets are MTD and YTD, and use Sales Amount as the measure, with Month-to-Date and Year-to-Date as the TI filters. These metrics are used to compare year-on-year performance. This KPI is to be embedded on a scorecard, with Sales Territory as the drilldown dimension and Sales Territory as the hierarchy within that dimension. Auto-select all Region members by selecting children of the All member.

The table below lists all the settings to be used for the metrics.

Metrics

METRIC TYPE	MEASURE NAME	TI FILTER	COMPARE TO
Actual	Actual		
Target	Target		Actual
Actual	MTDLY	Last Year Month-to-date	

METRIC TYPE	MEASURE NAME	TI FILTER	COMPARE TO
Target	MTD	Month-to-date	MTDLY
Actual	YTDLY	Last Year Year-to-date	
Target	YTD	Year-to-date	YTDLY

Hints

➤ Choosing the current value (MTD and YTD) as the targets with the previous year's value as the actual (MTDLY and YTDLY) may seem counterintuitive, but doing it this way works correctly when calculating the normalized distance from worst as the variance, because you can use 0 rather than an arbitrary higher value as the worst.

➤ Because the Adventure Works cube is static, and Time Intelligence is dynamic, map to 2007 as the current year.

The table below is a cheat sheet of all time intelligence formulae.

STP Formulae

FORMULA	NAME
Month.FirstDay:Month.Day	Month-to-date
(Year-1).Month.FirstDay:(Year-1).Month.Day	Last Year Month-to-date
Year.FirstMonth.FirstDay:Month.Day	Year-to-date
(Year-1).FirstMonth.FirstDay:(Year-1).Month.Day	Last Year Year-to-date

Step-by-Step

1. Create a new Analysis Services data source, and name it **dsAdventureWorks**.

2. Enter the server name, typically **localhost** in a development environment. Choose Adventure Works 2008 R2 for the database and Adventure Works for the cube. Leave authentication on Unattended Service Account.

3. Click the Time tab at the top — see Figure 17-11 for all the settings.

4. Select Date.Date.Calendar for the Time Dimension.

5. Select 1 January 2007 for the current date by clicking the Browse button.

6. Choose Day for the Hierarchy Level.

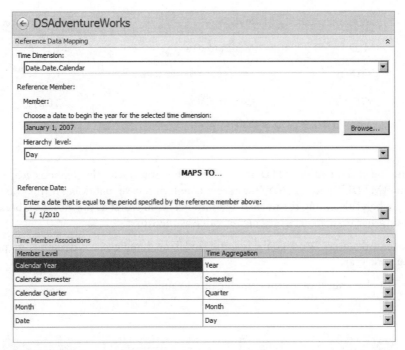

FIGURE 17-11

7. Choose 1 January 2011 (or the current year) for the Reference Date.

8. Map Calendar Year to Year.

9. Map Calendar Semester to Semester.

10. Map Calendar Quarter to Quarter.

11. Map Month to Month.

12. Map Date to Day.

13. Save the data source.

14. Create a new blank KPI named `Sales Amount`.

15. Change the source for the actual to dsAdventureWorks, as shown in Figure 17-12.

16. Change the measure to Sales Amount.

17. Change the source for Target to dsAdventureWorks, then click OK.

18. Change the measure for Target to Sales Amount Quota, then click OK.

19. Add a new Actual and name it MTDLY.

20. Change the data source mapping for MTDLY to dsAdventureWorks.

21. Change the measure for MTDLY to Sales Amount.

22. Click New Time Intelligence Filter.

FIGURE 17-12

23. Add the formula (Year-1).Month.FirstDay: (Year-1).Month.Day, then click OK and click OK again.

24. Add a new Actual and name it YTDLY.

25. Change the data source mapping for YTDLY to dsAdventureWorks.

26. Change the measure for YTDLY to Sales Amount.

27. Click New Time Intelligence Filter.

28. Add the formula (Year-1).FirstMonth.FirstDay:(Year-1).Month.Day.

29. Add a new Target and name it MTD.

30. Change the data source mapping for MTD to dsAdventureWorks.

31. Change the measure for MTD to Sales Amount.

32. Click New Time Intelligence Filter.

33. Add the formula Year.Month.FirstDay: Year.Month.Day.

34. Change the Compare To field to MTDLY.

35. Change the Scoring pattern thresholds to 120% (Best), 101% (Threshold 2), 99% (Threshold 1), and 0% (Worst). See Figure 17-13.

36. Add a new Target, YTD.

37. Change the data source mapping for YTD to dsAdventureWorks.

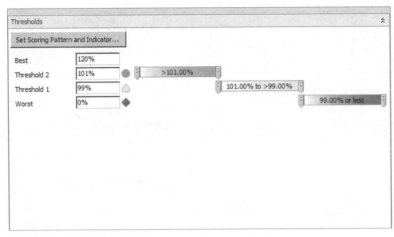

FIGURE 17-13

38. Change the measure for YTD to Sales Amount.

39. Click New Time Intelligence Filter.

40. Add the formula Year.FirstMonth.FirstDay: Year.Month.Day.

41. Change the Compare To field to YTDLY.

42. Change the Scoring pattern thresholds to 120% (Best), 101% (Threshold 2), 99% (Threshold 1), and 0% (Worst).

43. Create a new blank scorecard named `Sales Scorecard` by right-clicking on PerformancePoint Content in the workspace browser, then New > Scorecard. Select Standard from the list on the right, choose the Blank Scorecard and click OK.

44. Drag the Sales Amount KPI to the rows on the scorecard (on the left).

45. Delete the Actual, Target, MTDLY, and YTDLY columns.

46. Right-click the MTD column, and choose Metric Settings.

47. Change the Additional Data Value to Actual.

48. Change the Target Name from MTD to MTD vs MTDLY.

49. Right-click the YTD column, and choose Metric Settings.

50. Change the Additional Data Value to Actual.

51. Change the Target Name from YTD to YTD vs YTDLY.

52. Expand Dimensions in the Details tab, expand the Sales Territory, and drag the Sales Territory hierarchy onto the scorecard, as the Last Child of the Sales Amount KPI.

53. In the Select Members window, right-click All Sales Territories, and select Autoselect Members ⇨ Select Children as shown in Figure 17-14.

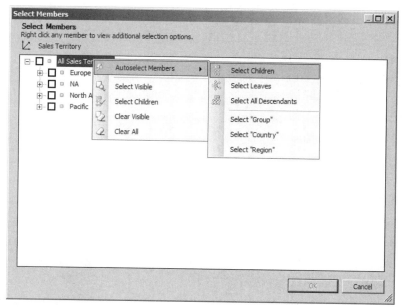

FIGURE 17-14

54. Click Update in the Edit tab of the ribbon.

55. Right-click any of the cells, and select View Settings.

56. Select the Filter tab, and check the Filter Empty Rows box.

57. Click Update in the Edit tab of the ribbon to see a scorecard similar to that in Figure 17-15. Your figures may vary as the scorecard dynamically adjusts according to the current date.

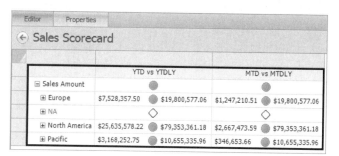

FIGURE 17-15

 Please select Lesson 17 on the DVD to view the video that accompanies this lesson.

18

Creating and Deploying PerformancePoint Dashboards

Creating a dashboard is about understanding what information is required for a particular audience to do their jobs efficiently, and presenting it in the most effective way possible. In some cases, this will be a very simple set of five to seven indicators, and in other cases, these indicators serve as a springboard to a sophisticated analysis. In this lesson, you learn how to add components to your dashboards to enable these functions.

DASHBOARDS VS. WEB PART PAGES

Designing a dashboard with PerformancePoint Dashboard Designer creates a dashboard layout in the PerformancePoint content library, with multiple pages within the layout. Deploying this dashboard to SharePoint creates the Web Part pages, with Web Part linked to the PerformancePoint components (scorecards, reports, and filters) built into the dashboard.

This web part page becomes a native SharePoint page, and can be edited through the SharePoint web-based page editor. Deploying the dashboard again will overwrite these changes, and this means that dashboards created through Dashboard Designer are effectively limited to PerformancePoint components.

Leveraging the rest of SharePoint's functionality, and enabling collaboration within your dashboards requires building a SharePoint page using SharePoint tools, and adding PerformancePoint components to that page.

BUILDING A PERFORMANCEPOINT DASHBOARD

This section covers "native" PerformancePoint dashboards first, because many of the concepts carry over from here to SharePoint.

A dashboard consists of multiple zones (a web part zone in a SharePoint page), each of which contains a PerformancePoint component (a web part in SharePoint). Once placed on a dashboard, these components can either send or receive parameters. Filters can send parameters, reports can receive them, and scorecards can both send and receive them. These parameters are called *connections*. You can see these components in the dashboard design screen in Figure 18-1.

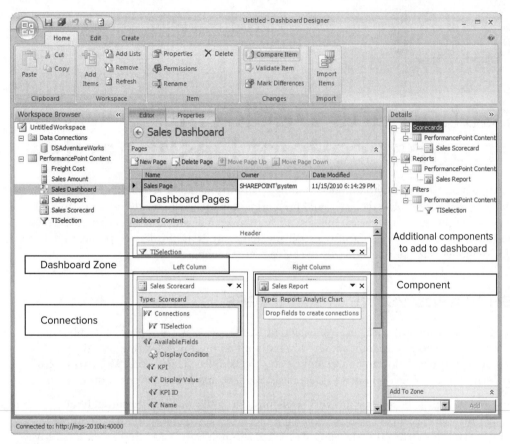

FIGURE 18-1

Each page within the dashboard has its own set of zones to add components to, which you do by dragging a component from the Details pane to the appropriate zone. Once components are added, you add connections by clicking a field on a component, and dragging it over to another component. Doing this brings up the screen in Figure 18-2.

The drop-downs list items within the component that can be linked up — for instance, a scorecard can send the member from the dimension linked to its row, or the one linked to its columns, as well as custom properties. A report can receive values for any dimension or member linked in its bottom axis, series, or the background.

Once all these steps have been completed, the dashboard is complete, and can be deployed to SharePoint by right-clicking the dashboard name in the Workspace section and selecting Deploy to SharePoint.

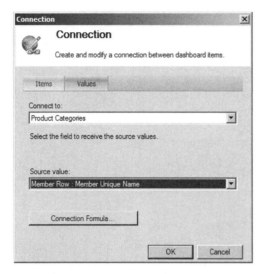

FIGURE 18-2

 Member Unique Name is the most typical source when sending values from Filters.

Building a dashboard in SharePoint involves the same conceptual steps: create a dashboard, choose a layout, add components, and link them up — but the steps themselves are performed differently.

Create the new page by opening the Site Actions menu at the top left of every SharePoint page, and choose More Options. From the window that opens, choose to create a Web Part Page, and in the next window, set the location to be your dashboard page and choose a layout.

Adding components to a SharePoint page is a little more complex, because it is not only PerformancePoint components that can be added. Start by clicking Add a Web Part, then choosing PerformancePoint in the Categories selector. Then choose the type of PerformancePoint component and click Add.

This adds a Web Part to the page, which still needs to be configured to render the component you created earlier in Dashboard Designer. Click Here to Open the Tool Pane, will, as it says, open the tool pane. The tool pane, as shown in Figure 18-3, allows you to set the title, the size of the web part, and whether or not to display the title and border in Chrome. By clicking the box next to the Location text box, you can browse to the component you want to add. Click Apply to preview your changes.

 Choose a Chrome Type of None for all filter parts.

Once you have done this for all your components, you need to add the connections between components. To do so, click the arrow opposite the name of the component, and choose Connections ⇨ Send PerformancePoint Values To and then choose the specific component, as shown in Figure 18-4.

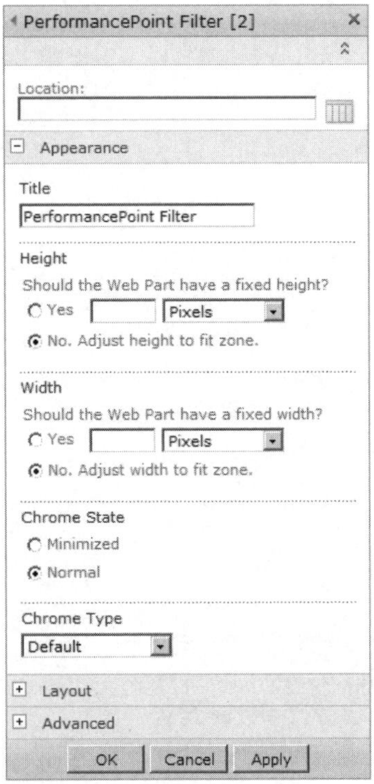

FIGURE 18-3

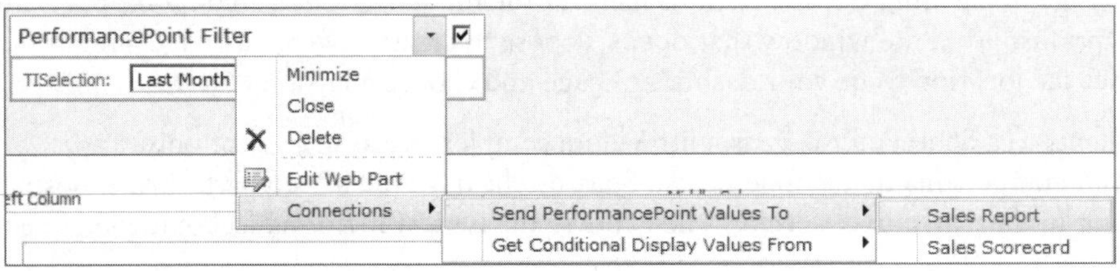

FIGURE 18-4

A pop-up window appears, asking for a connection type, because SharePoint supports several. Because both components are PerformancePoint components, choose Get PerformancePoint Values From and click Configure.

The Edit Connections tab is the equivalent of the Connections window in Dashboard Designer. Click Add Connection, and select the appropriate properties under both Source Value and Connect To to set up the connection, as shown in Figure 18-5. Lesson 19 covers more details on the options on this tab.

Finally, click Stop Editing in the ribbon to view the page in its final form.

FIGURE 18-5

ADDING INTERACTIVITY TO YOUR DASHBOARD

Analytic charts and reports already provide a great level of interactivity to PerformancePoint dashboards, but by adding custom properties to KPIs, and adding Reporting Services (SSRS) reports and SharePoint collaboration features to your page, your dashboard becomes much more than just a collection of charts and KPIs.

First, add a custom property to a KPI to enable dynamic measure changing of an analytic chart. In Dashboard Designer, open up your KPI, and change to the properties page. Add a new text property called MeasureName and add the MDX for your KPIs measure as its value, for example [Measures].[Sales Amount]. It's important to get this right, because when it is sent to another component, it will be issued as a query exactly as specified here. The reason the measure name is not picked up automatically is that it is possible to have multiple actuals with different underlying measures.

This approach can also be used to pass dimension members.

See Figure 18-6 for an example.

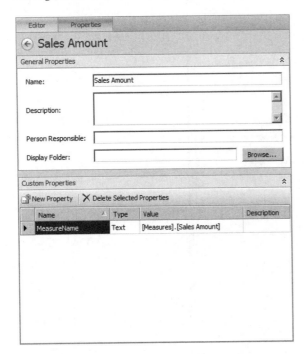

FIGURE 18-6

In your dashboard (either through Dashboard Designer or the SharePoint web interface), add a connection from the scorecard to the analytic report. Choose Connections ➪ Send Filter Value To ➪ the report that you need to send values to.

Figure 18-7 shows a SharePoint connection.

Once this has been set up for multiple KPIs on a scorecard, clicking a KPI in the scorecard changes the measure used in the report.

 This only works for clicking directly on a KPI, not clicking on a dimension below it.

Dynamic measures can be set up in SSRS reports, which can then be linked in the same manner. SSRS reports are added either by adding an SQL Server Reporting web part in SharePoint, or adding a report of type Reporting Services in Dashboard Designer. Adding connections is the same for these reports.

 PerformancePoint SSRS reports update asynchronously without requiring a page refresh, whereas SQL Server Reporting web parts require a page refresh.

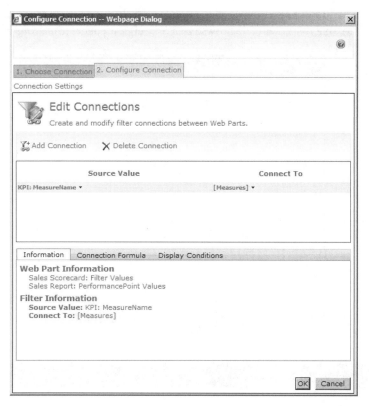

FIGURE 18-7

Collaborating on the figures presented in the dashboard is an important part of enabling actionable intelligence in a dashboard, and two mechanisms are available to do this. The first is adding comments, also called annotations, directly to the cube using the scorecard. To do this, simply right-click a value in the scorecard and click Comments. This enables you to view previous comments and add new ones, as shown in Figure 18-8.

Although exceptionally useful, this approach has several limitations. The first is that the data source behind the scorecard needs to be an Analysis Services cube, and the second is that the value itself needs to be a specific tuple in the cube — in other words, where a named set such as a Year-To-Date set is used to filter the value, these comments can't be used.

The second approach is to add a Note Board to the page that the reports are on. This is accomplished by adding another web part, the Note Board web part under the Social Collaboration category, as shown in Figure 18-9.

Once a Note Board has been added to the page, users with the Contribute security right to the site can add notes to communicate with other viewers of the page.

The final feature you may want to add to your dashboard is integrating a way for users to get to help topics, FAQs, and documentation on how metrics are calculated. Linking to this content is achieved by adding a web part to your dashboard — the web part is called Summary Links, and is under the Content Rollup category. After adding the web part, click New Link to bring up the window in Figure 18-10. You can add a link to an external site, or browse to a SharePoint page within your site.

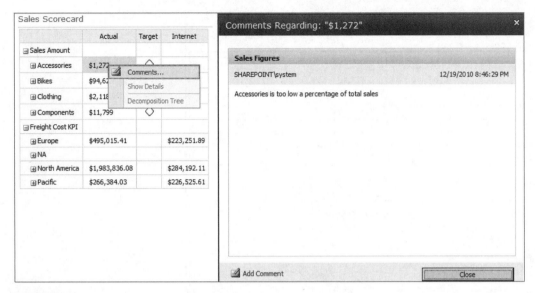

FIGURE 18-8

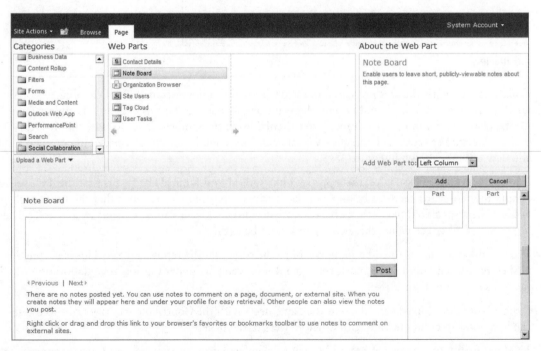

FIGURE 18-9

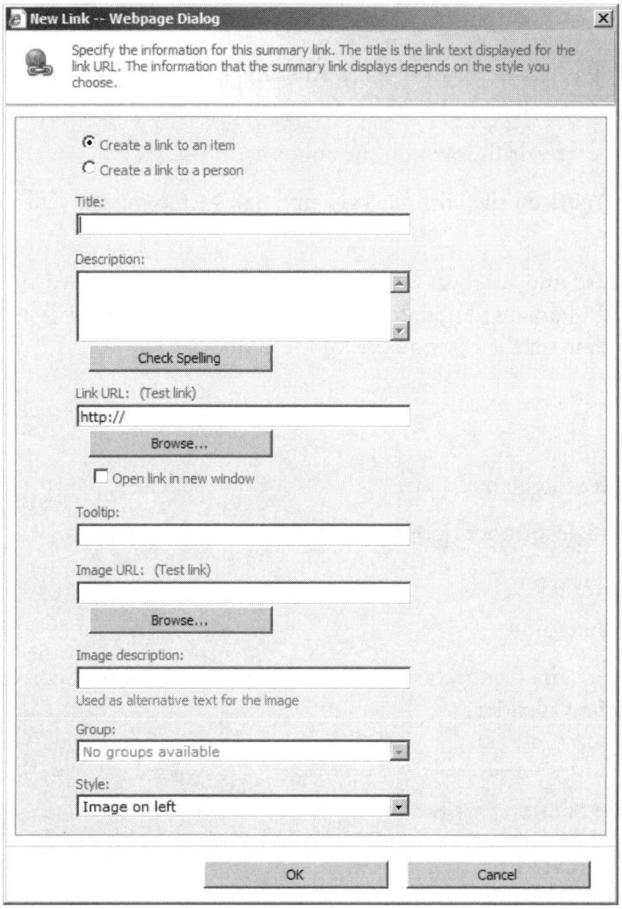

FIGURE 18-10

Many options are available, including groups and style sheets, to customize the look of your links.

> *SharePoint Wiki Libraries are a great place to store FAQs and end user documentation.*

TRY IT

In this Try It, you create a dashboard that contains a scorecard and an Analysis Services report, link them together, and then add a note board to the same page.

Lesson Requirements

Create Two KPIs, one using Sales Amount as the Actual and Sales Amount Quota as the target, and the second KPI with Freight Cost as the Actual, and no target.

Add both KPIs to a scorecard. Use Years as the drill-down on the columns.

Create an Analysis Services Report with Years on the bottom Axis, and Sales Amount and Sales Amount Quota on the series.

Create a SharePoint page with the scorecard and Analysis Services report, and link these two components in such a way that clicking the KPI name will update both the series items, and clicking on the date in the scorecard will update the date on the bottom axis of the chart.

Hints

➤ Create a new custom property, MeasureName.

➤ Set Sales Amount to {[Measures].[Sales Amount],[Measures].[Sales Amount Quota]}.

➤ Set Freight Cost [Measures].[Freight Cost].

➤ Use Date.Calendar for the Date dimension.

➤ Use <<UniqueName>>.Children for the Connection formula when connecting the Scorecard column member to the reports Date.Calendar.

 It is always a good idea to choose the same measures for the default measures on the report as are on your first KPI.

Step-by-Step

1. Open the Sales Amount KPI created in the previous chapter.

2. Change to the Properties tab.

3. Add a new custom property. Choose the text type.

4. Set the value to {[Measures].[Sales Amount], [Measures].[Sales Amount Quota]}.

5. Set the name to MeasureName, as shown in Figure 18-11.

6. Change to the Editor tab.

7. Click on the link under Number Format on the Actual line.

8. Choose Currency from the dropdown, and set the multiplier to 0.001 and click OK.

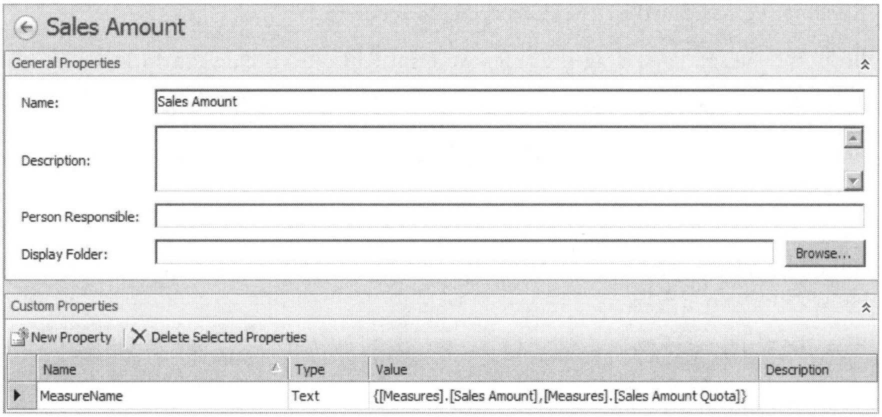

FIGURE 18-11

9. Click on the link under Number Format on the Target line.

10. Choose Currency from the dropdown, and set the multiplier to 0.001 and click OK. Save the KPI.

11. Right-click PerformancePoint Content and create a new KPI.

12. Name the KPI **Freight Cost**.

13. Delete the Target metric.

14. Click 1 (Fixed Values) under Data Mappings.

15. Click Change Source, and choose the dsAdventureWorks data source.

16. Select the Freight Cost measure and click OK.

17. Click the link under Number Format.

18. Choose Currency, and set the multiplier to 0.001 and click OK.

19. Change to the Properties tab.

20. Add a new custom property. Choose the text type.

21. Set the value to [Measures].[Freight Cost].

22. Set the name to MeasureName.

23. Save the KPI.

24. Right-click PerformancePoint Content and create a new scorecard.

25. Select Blank Scorecard under the Standard tab.

26. Rename the scorecard to **Interactive Scorecard**.

27. From the Design Pane drag the Sales Amount KPI onto the design surface.

28. Drag the Freight Cost KPI onto the design surface directly below Sales Amount.

29. From the Dimensions list drag Date.Calendar to above Actual on the scorecard. Select All Periods.

30. Drag Date.Calendar to above Target on the scorecard. Select All Periods, as shown in Figure 18-12.

31. Save the scorecard.

32. Create a new report by right-clicking PerformancePoint Content.

33. Choose Analytic Chart and click OK.

34. Choose dsAdventureWorks as the data source and click Finish.

FIGURE 18-12

35. Call the report **Interactive Report**.

36. Change the drop-down directly under the Details pane to Sales Summary to filter the measures.

37. Expand Measures and Drag Sales Amount to the Series box.

38. Change the drop-down directly under Details to Sales Targets to filter the measures.

39. Drag Sales Amount to the Series box.

40. Drag Sales Amount Quota to the Series box.

41. Drag Date.Calendar to the Bottom Axis.

42. Click the arrow next to Date.Calendar.

43. Deselect the default member, right-click All Periods, and select Children. This brings up the chart, as shown in Figure 18-13.

44. Save the report.

45. Go to SharePoint and select Site Actions ⇨ More Options.

46. Select Web Part Page and click Create.

47. Call the web part page **All Periods Analysis**, as shown in Figure 18-14.

48. Change the document library to Dashboards and click Create.

49. Click the left-most web part zone: Add a Web Part.

50. Choose the PerformancePoint category, PerformancePoint Scorecard web part, and click OK, as shown in Figure 18-15.

51. Click the Click Here to Open the Tool Pane link.

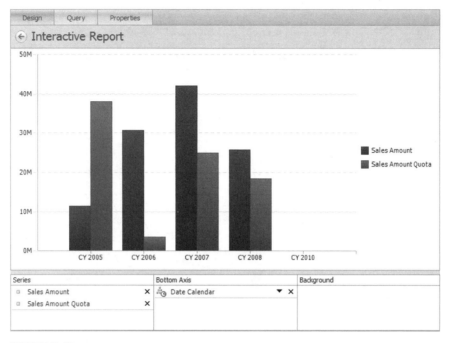

FIGURE 18-13

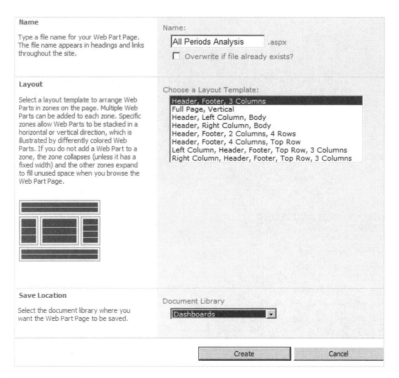

FIGURE 18-14

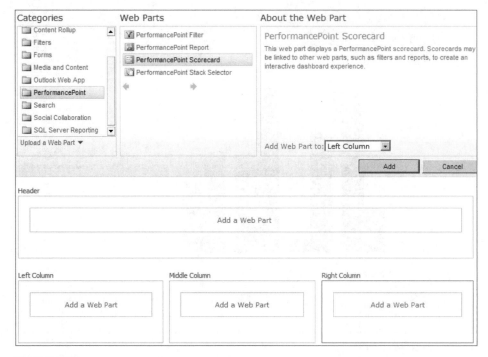

FIGURE 18-15

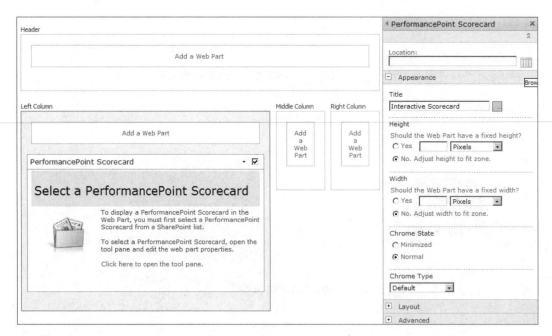

FIGURE 18-16

52. Set the title to **Interactive Scorecard**, as shown in Figure 18-16.

53. Click the button next to the Location text box, browse to the Interactive Scorecard you created previously, and select it by double-clicking.

54. Click OK.

55. Click Add a Web Part in the middle column.

56. Choose the PerformancePoint category and PerformancePoint Report web part, and click OK.

57. Click the Click Here to Open the Tool Pane link.

58. Set the title to **Interactive Report**.

59. Click the Yes radio button for height, and set the textbox to 300 pixels.

60. Click the Yes radio button for width, and set the textbox to 400 pixels.

61. Click the button next to the Location text box, browse to the Interactive Report you created previously, and select it by double-clicking. The settings are shown in Figure 18-17.

62. Click OK.

63. Click the arrow next to Interactive Scorecard, and select Connections ➪ Send Filter Values To ➪ Interactive Report.

64. Choose Get PerformancePoint Values from the drop-down and click Configure, as shown in Figure 18-18.

65. Click Add Connection and select KPI:MeasureName for the Source Value, and [Measures] for Connect To.

66. Click Add Connection and select Column Member ➪ Member Unique Name for the Source Value, and [Date. [Calendar] for Connect To.

67. Click the Connection Formula tab at the bottom to bring up the editor in Figure 18-19.

68. Type **<<UniqueName>>.Children** and click OK.

69. Your dashboard is now interactive — test it by clicking the KPIs, and expanding the date drill down and clicking the values.

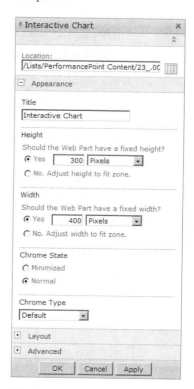

FIGURE 18-17

70. To add a Note Board part, click Add a Web Part above Interactive Scorecard.

71. Choose the Social Collaboration category, select Note Board, and click OK.

72. Click the web part bar next to the Note Board heading, and drag the whole web part below the scorecard.

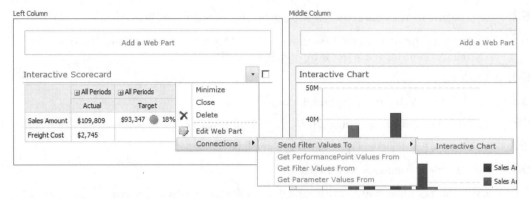

FIGURE 18-18

FIGURE 18-19

73. Click Stop Editing.

74. You can now add some notes, as shown in Figure 18-20.

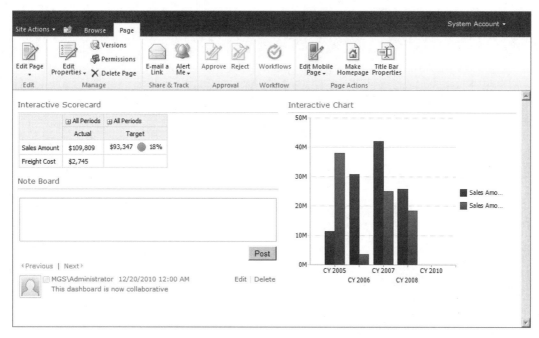

FIGURE 18-20

 Please select Lesson 18 on the DVD to view the video that accompanies this lesson.

19

Developing and Deploying PerformancePoint and SharePoint Filters

Filters enable a greater level of interactivity for users, and can be used to filter multiple charts, scorecards, and reports at once. In this lesson you learn about the most important filters, how to create them, and how to link them to both PerformancePoint components and SharePoint components.

PERFORMANCEPOINT FILTERS VS. SHAREPOINT FILTERS

Both PerformancePoint and SharePoint provide different filter controls, and each has advantages and disadvantages. PerformancePoint filters generally have much more richly featured UIs, whereas SharePoint filters are more interactive with the SharePoint platform, providing capabilities such as being able to accept defaults from other filters or receiving values from the URL.

Of course different capabilities exist within the different types of filters — SharePoint provides only a dimension filter for SSAS sources, whereas PerformancePoint provides multiple filter types. The Current User and Query String filter types are provided only by SharePoint.

In addition, PerformancePoint filters have the ability to add formulae to connections from the filter to the component — for example, a date picker control could filter a chart by the full month rather than just the day. In Figure 19-1, we've added a formula to return all the children of the current member.

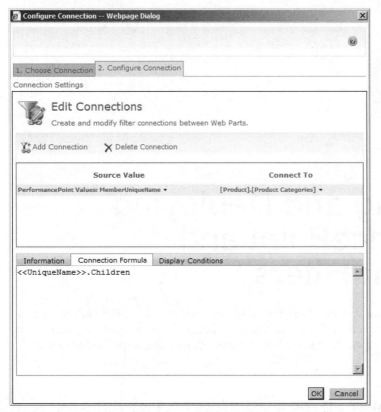

FIGURE 19-1

These formulae can use many of the standard MDX functions, using `<<UniqueName>>` or
`<<SourceName>>` as a placeholder for the currently selected value.

COMMON FILTERS

Filters can either be added to PerformancePoint Dashboards through Dashboard Designer, or
to SharePoint pages. The set of steps to add filters is very similar in both, and has been covered
in the previous lesson on dashboards. The only addition is the use of connection formulae to
modify the values sent from the filter to the component. This section goes through a subset of the
PerformancePoint filters, and two of the SharePoint filters. The PerformancePoint filters are listed in
Figure 19-2, and SharePoint filters in Figure 19-3.

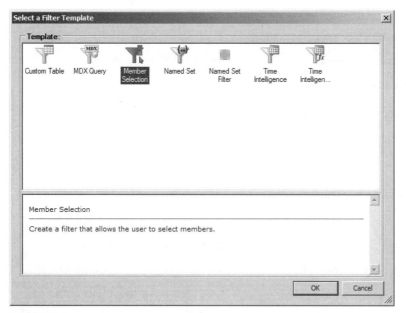

FIGURE 19-2

FIGURE 19-3

Time Intelligence Filters

Time Intelligence or TI filters come in two varieties. A Time Intelligence Post Connection Formula filter is a calendar control that passes a date range related to the date picked in the calendar — the calendar defaults to the current date.

A Time Intelligence filter is a drop-down filter with each entry being a formula related to the current data.

The formulae used are built up from the following items, called Simple Time Period (STP) Specification:

```
Structure: [(]<Period>[Offset>[)][ <Function>[<Offset>]]]
```

The following table provides a reference for all the elements of the STP specification.

STP - Simple Time Period Reference Sheet

TO DISPLAY	FORMULA	DISPLAY
Today	Day	Displays the current date
Yesterday	day-1	Displays the day before the current date
Tomorrow	day+1	Displays the day after the current date
Last Month and today	(Month-1), day	Displays values for last month and today
Last 10 days	day:day-9	Displays the last 10 days, including today
Last 10 days (excluding today)	day-1:day-10	Displays the last 10 days, excluding today
Same day last year	(year-1).day	Goes back a year and displays the equivalent day
Same month last year	(year-1).month	Goes back a year and displays the equivalent month; bear in mind that this will be a full month (see MTD last year)
Month to date	Month.FirstDay : Month.Day	Shows values for Month to Date
Month to date last year	(Year-1).Month. FirstDay:(Year-1). Month.Day	Shows values for Month to Date last year
Same range of months to date for last year	(year-1).firstmonth: (year-1).month	Shows months to date for last year
Year to date	yeartodate	Year to date values
Year to date (by month)	yeartodate. fullmonth	Year to date at month level, useful especially for showing months on charts
Year to date (by day)	yeartodate.fullday	Year to date at day level — accurate data to the day

In Figure 19-4, you can see the two filter types next to each other.

Creating a Time Intelligence Connection Formula is very simple, because the only parameter to set is the data source to be used — select Time Intelligence Connection Formula. However, when linking it to a PerformancePoint component (also called adding a connection) an additional step of adding a formula can also be done. See Figure 19-5 for an example of adding a formula for all the months of this year prior to the current month in Dashboard Designer.

FIGURE 19-4

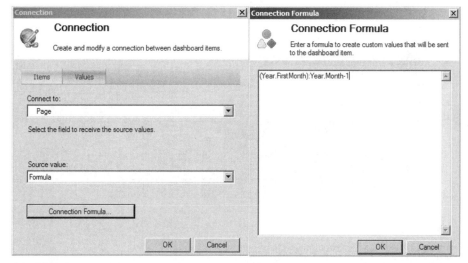

FIGURE 19-5

Note that Source Value could either be Formula or Member Unique Name. If connecting to a Reporting Services Report, it must be Member Unique Name, because the report will not be able to parse the formula.

You have some additional steps when creating the drop-down version. Start by creating a new Time Intelligence filter and selecting the data source. In the next screen, enter the formulae and display names for the entries you require in the drop-down, as in Figure 19-6.

You can also preview the formula generated to ensure that it is correct by clicking the Preview button, as shown in Figure 19-7.

Because there is no hierarchy, choose List for the display method.

Time Intelligence formulae don't work with fiscal calendars that have a different month end. In addition, the dimension members need to exist for the formula to be generated.

Because the formulae are entered and used from the drop-down box, no connection formula will be specified when connecting a filter.

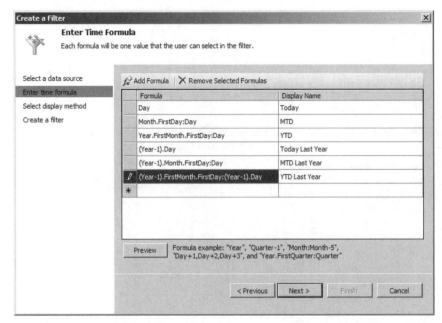

FIGURE 19-6

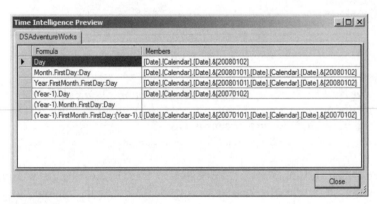

FIGURE 19-7

Member Selection Filter

A Member Selection filter allows you to include specific members of a dimension, as well as set the filter to dynamically update as more members are added to the dimension.

Start by creating a new Member Selection filter, and choosing a data source.

In the next step, select a dimension and the appropriate members, as in Figure 19-8.

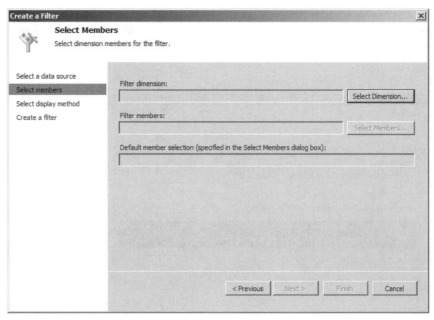

FIGURE 19-8

After selecting a dimension, select the members as well as set the default by clicking Select Members. Unlike the scorecard, only members you select will appear in the drop-down. Use the Autoselect option to dynamically select members as they're added to the dimension. Right-click and select Set as Default Selection, as in Figure 19-9.

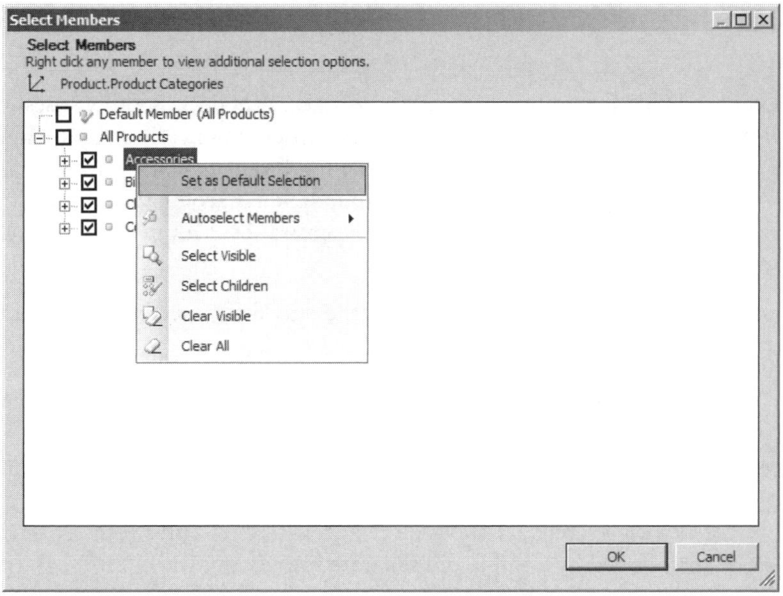

FIGURE 19-9

Depending on whether you want to allow multiple selections, you can choose either Tree or Multi-Select tree, as shown in Figure 19-10. If you have members from multiple dimension levels, List is likely to be confusing.

Click Finish to create the filter.

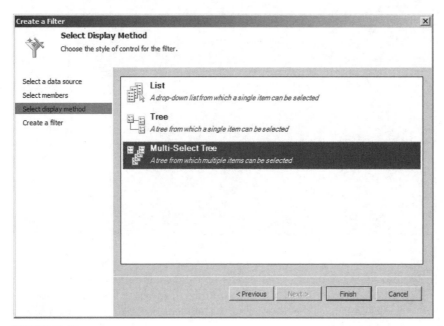

FIGURE 19-10

Named Set Filter

A Named Set is a collection of individual members in analysis services. A Named Set filter uses the individual members of this set as items to choose from in the drop-down selection. To use an Adventure Works Named Set as an example, choosing Top 25 Selling Products would give you a drop-down list of all the 25 products, and allow you to select an individual product from these 25 products. However, what it will not allow you to do, is use the entire set as a filter — i.e., send *all* 25 members across as a filter.

Setting up a Named Set filter is similar to the other filters, with the only difference being the Named Set selection screen shown in Figure 19-11.

Custom MDX Filter

A Custom MDX filter gives a very similar capability to the Named Set filter, except that the members of the set are defined in PerformancePoint rather than in Analysis Services. After choosing a data source, you will be presented with a screen, as shown in Figure 19-12, to enter your set — this follows standard set syntax — surrounded by { and }, and separated by commas.

Notice how the names of the members are displayed in Figure 19-13.

Note that filtering individual members, for example, ([Product].[Product Categories].[Subcategory].&[30]*[Date].[Calendar].[Calendar Year].&[2010]*) is not supported.*

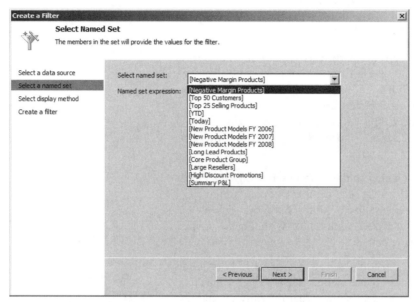

FIGURE 19-11

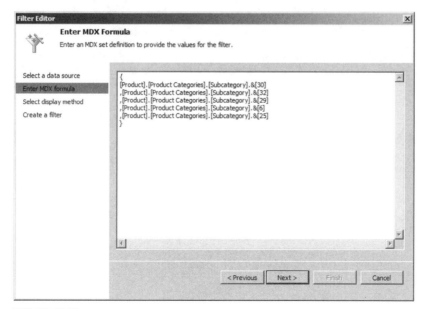

FIGURE 19-12

SQL Server Analysis Services Filter

The SQL Server Analysis Services filter is the only SharePoint filter you will use often - all the filters you have used so far this lesson have been PerformancePoint filters. Unlike all of the previous filters, you create this one in the SharePoint web pages, rather than in Dashboard Designer. To do so, add it as a Web Part under the Filters Category, and then edit it to set it up, as shown in Figure 19-14.

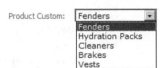

FIGURE 19-13

The most common setup for this filter is to browse to an Office Data Connection file in a Data Connection library — this data connection will need to have been set up previously, for example, using Excel. Lesson 12 covers creating an .ODC file for data connections. After selecting a data source, a dimension and hierarchy need to be selected. Figure 19-15 shows the filter on a page.

Clicking the Filter button next to the drop-down brings up another drop-down that allows for selecting members — very similar in functionality to the Member Selection filter, but more limited. The real reason to use this filter is in combination with a query string parameter filter, to set the default.

Click Add a Web Part, then add a Query String (URL) Filter under the Filter Category. Configure the web part using the settings in the following table. Figure 19-16 shows what the fully set up Filter should look like.

FIGURE 19-14

Query String Filter Settings

FIELD	VALUE
Filter Name	qsProductCategory
Query String Parameter Name	qsProductCategory
Default Value	[Product].[Product Categories].[Category].&[4]
Title	qsProductCategory

This will set the default to the Accessories member. The Query String Parameter Name is the name to be used in the URL later. Next, connect the Query String Parameter filter to the SQL Server Analysis Services filter, as in Figure 19-17. This means that when no query string parameter is supplied in the URL, the Query String Parameter filter will default to the Accessories member.

To send this default value, you will need to either set up a Summary Links web part, or create a navigation item. You are going to test the filter by manually editing the URL. Stop editing the page, delete everything after `.aspx` (including the question mark) in the URL, and add the following to the URL at the end: `?qsProductCategory = [Product].[Product Categories].[Category].%26[1]`. This will now set the default for the selection box to Bikes, while still letting the user override the value by selecting a different one.

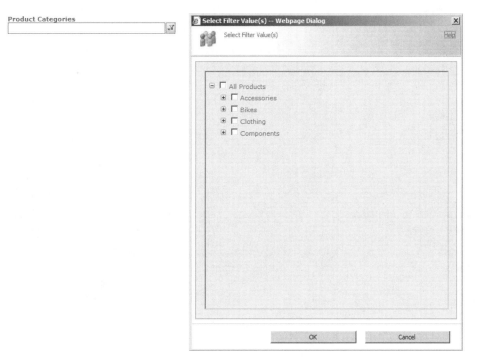

FIGURE 19-15

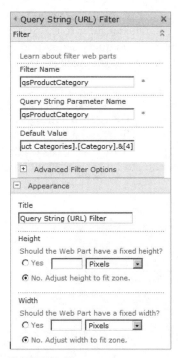

FIGURE 19-16

FIGURE 19-17

 The & (ampersand) needs to be replaced with %26 — also known as URL encoding it — to work correctly.

TRY IT

In this Try It, you add a Time Intelligence filter to the All Periods Analysis Page created in Lesson 18, as well as a Product Category filter.

Lesson Requirements

Create a Time Intelligence filter called **TIFilter**, using YTD at month level, YTD Last Year at Month Level, MTD at day level, MTD Last Year at day level, last 10 days, and last 10 days Last Year as the formulae.

Create a Member Selection filter called **msProductCategory**, and auto-select all children of Accessories, Bikes, Clothing, and Components. Set Bikes to be the default, and include the All member.

Add both these filters to the All Periods Analysis Page, and connect TIFilter to the Interactive Scorecard columns, and to Interactive Report using Date.Calendar. Connect msProductCategory to only Interactive Scorecard, and use Page as the connector.

Hints

➤ Remember that the year to date figures must ignore values lower than day.

➤ You will need to remove the connection from the scorecard to the chart.

➤ Remember to map the first of January in this year to the first of January 2008 in your data source.

➤ The formulae you need for the six TI filter items are:

Formulae

FORMULA	DISPLAY NAME
Year.FirstMonth:Month	YTD
(Year-1).FirstMonth:(Year-1).Month	YTD LY
Month.FirstDay:Day	MTD
(Year-1).Month.FirstDay: (Year-1).Day	MTD LY
Day-9:Day	10 Days
(Year-1).Day-9: (Year-1).Day	10 Days LY

Step-by-Step

1. Open Dashboard Designer by opening up the content created in the previous lesson.
2. Right-click the PerformancePoint Content list, and create a new filter.
3. Choose Time Intelligence, and click OK.
4. Click Add Data Source, select the dsAdventureWorks data source created previously, and click Next.
5. Add the formulae defined in the hints, as in Figure 19-18.
6. Click Next.
7. Choose Tree from the Display Methods and click Finish.

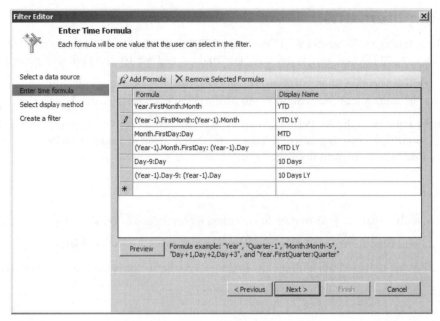

FIGURE 19-18

8. Name the filter **TIFilter**, right-click it, and save.

9. Right-click the PerformancePoint Content list, and create a new filter.

10. Choose Member Selection and click OK.

11. Select the dsAdventureWorks data source.

12. Click Select Dimension and choose Product.ProductCategories.

13. Click Select Members to bring up the screen in Figure 19-19.

14. Select All Products, Accessories, Bikes, Clothing, and Components.

15. Right-click Accessories and Autoselect Members ⇨ Select Children.

16. Right-click Bikes and Autoselect Members ⇨ Select Children.

17. Right-click Clothing and Autoselect Members ⇨ Select Children.

18. Right-click Components and Autoselect Members ⇨ Select Children.

19. Right-click Bikes and Set as Default Selection.

20. Click OK to see the completed screen in Figure 19-20.

21. Click Next.

22. Choose Multi-Select Tree and click Finish.

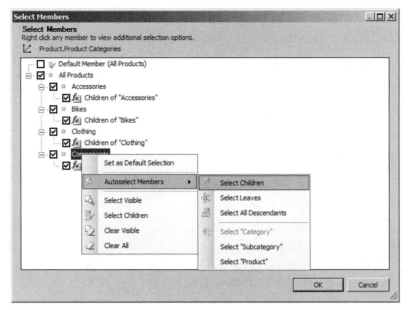

FIGURE 19-19

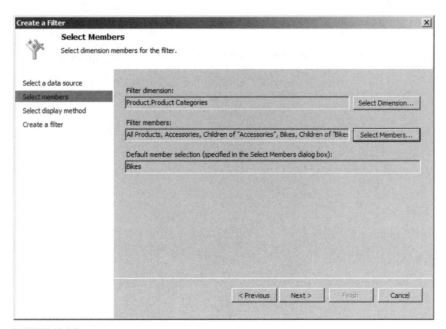

FIGURE 19-20

23. Name the filter **msProductCategories**, right-click, and save it.

24. Go to SharePoint and open the All Periods Analysis page.

25. Click Site Action, and click Edit Page.

26. Click Add a Web Part in the top web part zone.

27. Choose PerformancePoint in Categories, select PerformancePoint Filter, and click Add.

28. Click Click Here to Open the Tool Pane to bring up the configuration screen.

29. Click the orange button next to the Location textbox, and browse to the TIFilter.

30. Change the Title to **TI Filter**, and the Chrome Type to None, and click OK, as in Figure 19-21.

31. Click the down arrow to the right of the words TI Filter, and choose Connections ⇨ Send PerformancePoint Values To ⇨ Interactive Scorecard, as in Figure 19-22.

32. Select Get PerformancePoint Values from the Connection type and click Configure.

33. Click Add Connection.

34. Select Member Unique Name for Source Value.

FIGURE 19-21

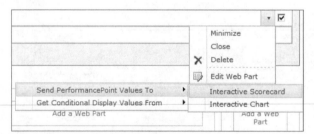

FIGURE 19-22

35. Select Endpoint_Column.

36. Click OK.

37. Click the down arrow to the right of the words TI Interactive Report, and choose Connections ⇨ Get PerformancePoint Values From ⇨ Interactive Scorecard (it will already be ticked).

38. Select the row that has Column Member:MemberUniqueName as the source, as in Figure 19-23.

39. Click Delete Connection, then click OK.

40. Click the down arrow to the right of the words TI Filter, and choose Connections ⇨ Send PerformancePoint Values To ⇨ Interactive Report.

FIGURE 19-23

41. Select Get PerformancePoint Values from the Connection type and click Configure.

42. Click Add Connection.

43. Select Member Unique Name for Source Value.

44. Select [Date].[Calendar] for Connect To, and click OK.

45. Click Add a Web Part in the left column above the Interactive Scorecard.

46. Choose PerformancePoint in Categories, select PerformancePoint Filter, and click Add.

47. Click Click Here to Open the Tool Pane to bring up the configuration screen.

48. Click the orange button next to the Location textbox, and browse to the ProductCategories.

49. Change the Title to Product Categories, and the Chrome Type to None, and click OK.

50. Click the down arrow to the right of the words Product Categories, and choose Connections ➪ Send PerformancePoint Values To ➪ Interactive Scorecard.

51. Select Get PerformancePoint Values from the Connection type and click Configure.

52. Click Add Connection.

53. Select Member Unique Name for Source Value.

54. Select Endpoint_Page to filter all the values.

55. Note how the time filter changes both the controls, but the product categories filter only changes the scorecard values, as in Figure 19-24. Also note how the interactivity is lost on the drill-downs on the columns, being overridden on the filter.

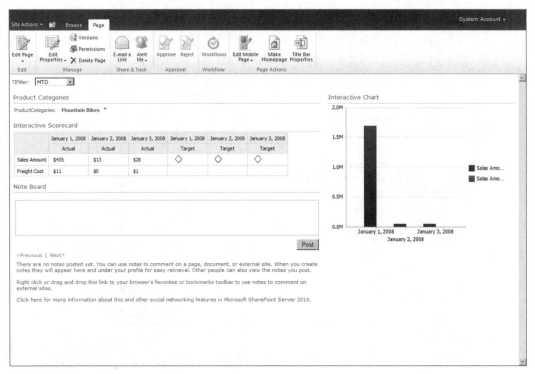

FIGURE 19-24

The dashboard you have just created is an example of the utility to be found in mixing business intelligence and collaboration content using the SharePoint environment, but it is just an introduction — experiment by adding other collaboration web parts to your dashboards.

 Please select Lesson 19 on the DVD to view the video that accompanies this lesson.

20

Strategy Mapping with Visio and PerformancePoint

In SharePoint 2010 you have the ability to create relationships between key performance indicators (KPIs) and a shapes Visio diagram. This relationship is called a *strategy map*. Typically, in a PerformancePoint Dashboard you will see a scorecard coupled with a strategy map, as shown in Figure 20-1.

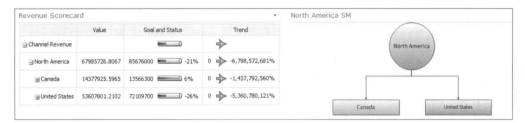

FIGURE 20-1

When creating strategy maps, you are not limited to the one shown in the figure. You can use any Visio diagram to create a strategy map. However, when designing your diagram, care should be taken when choosing shapes. If you want the shapes and colors to automatically update, avoid using complex shapes such as those that include groupings or sets of other shapes. In this lesson, you will learn how to leverage the contents of a scorecard to create a strategy map.

WHY DO WE MAP STRATEGY?

Strategy maps are created for various reasons. Typically, strategy maps are created to assist organizations in visualizing and uncovering strategic objectives. In addition, the mapping also illustrates cause-effect relationships among an organization or department objectives and strategies. For example, you could create a strategy map to show performance metrics across plants in a region. You could also create a strategy map that shows how individual branch offices are performing across the country. Regardless of your motive, the end results should reveal existing or potential bottlenecks that may hinder the success of your company.

CREATING A STRATEGY MAP

You can use PerformancePoint Dashboard Designer to create a strategy map inside of SharePoint 2010 that can be included on your dashboard. A scorecard will be used as the data source for the strategy map. Each shape is connected to a KPI in a scorecard when designing and configuring a strategy map. The color of the shape will correspond to the performance of the particular item.

To create a strategy map, start by creating a diagram in Visio and a scorecard in PerformancePoint. Before you create a strategy map report, make sure that you are using the 64-bit version of Microsoft Visio. Figure 20-2 is a simple Visio drawing, which is a simple strategy map that shows a country grouping at the top level and its corresponding countries below.

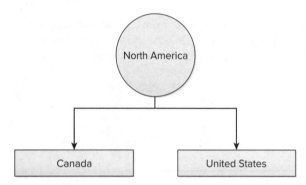

FIGURE 20-2

Once you have completed these steps, start the Dashboard Designer and locate the Workspace Browser pane. Then right-click the PerformancePoint Content item and select New ⇨ Report from the dialog box that appears. In the Select a Report Template window, shown in Figure 20-3, choose Strategy Map and click OK.

On the next screen select the scorecard that will serve as the data source for the strategy map. A blank report will be created. Now click the Edit Strategy Map icon in the top-left corner of the designer and the Strategy Map Editor will appear, as shown in Figure 20-4.

You can now either import an existing Visio file using the Import Visio File button or you can create a Visio diagram from scratch by clicking the Stencil button. Regardless of your selection, all the subsequent steps are the same. Select a shape from the diagram and click Connect in the menu bar. The Connect Shape dialog window appears, as shown in Figure 20-5.

Select a cell from the Goal and Status column in the scorecard, click the Connect button, and click Close. Repeat the steps for each shape on the diagram. Once you are finished, click the Apply button.

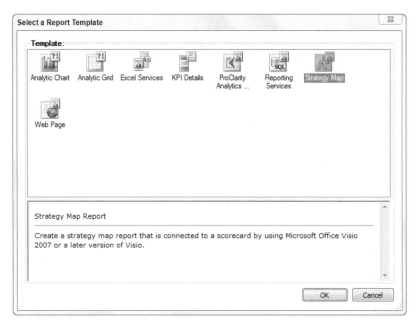

FIGURE 20-3

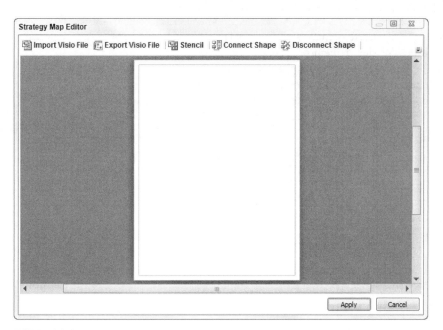

FIGURE 20-4

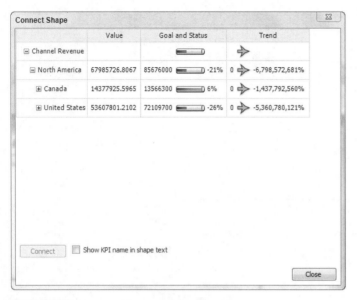

FIGURE 20-5

DEPLOYING AND TESTING A STRATEGY MAP

Now that you have created a strategy map, you will need to deploy and test it in SharePoint. The deployment process is very straightforward. To deploy your strategy map, ensure that it is selected in the Workspace Browser. Then click the save icon on the Dashboard Designer menu bar. Once you are done, open your SharePoint Business Intelligence site and click PerformancePoint Content, as shown in Figure 20-6.

FIGURE 20-6

Finally, to test your strategy map, hover over the item in the list and a drop-down arrow will appear. Click the arrow and select Display Report, as shown in Figure 20-7.

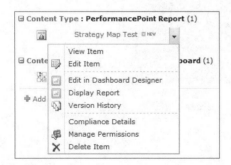

FIGURE 20-7

TRY IT

In this Try It, you learn to create a strategy map from a Visio diagram. You also learn how to deploy the completed strategy map to your SharePoint site.

Lesson Requirements

Use the Dashboard Designer to create a scorecard. Then create a strategy map that will use the aforementioned scorecard as the data source for each shape. You will need to download Lesson20VisioDiagram from the Wrox website. You will also need to download Visio Viewer, which is located here: `www.microsoft.com/downloads/en/details .aspx?FamilyID=f9ed50b0-c7df-4fb8-89f8-db2932e624f7`.

Hints

➤ Create a data source that connects to the Adventure Works 2008 R2 cube.

➤ Create a scorecard using the Dashboard Designer.

➤ Create a strategy map using the Dashboard Designer.

➤ Using the Dashboard Designer, save your strategy map to your SharePoint Business Intelligence site.

Step-by-Step

1. If you have not yet done so, deploy the completed Adventure Works cube that you receive when you download the sample databases from `www.codeplex.com`. You will find the sample files to deploy in the C:\Program Files\Microsoft SQL Server\100\Tools\Samples\ AdventureWorkes2008R2 Analysis Services Project directory.

2. Open the SharePoint site Knights24HourSharepoint. If you are starting first on this lesson, just create a new site using the Business Intelligence Center template.

3. Select PerformancePoint Content from the Navigation pane on the left.

4. Click Add New Item. This opens the PerformancePoint Dashboard Designer.

5. Right-click Data Connections and select New Data Source.

6. Choose Analysis Services as the template and click OK.

7. Rename the connection to **Adventure Works** and fill in the properties shown in Figure 20-8.

8. Right-click the PerformancePoint Content folder and select New ➪ Scorecard.

9. Select the Analysis Services template that will use an existing Analysis Services data source to create the scorecard and click OK.

10. Select the newly created data source and click Next.

11. Select Import SQL Server Analysis Services KPI and click Next.

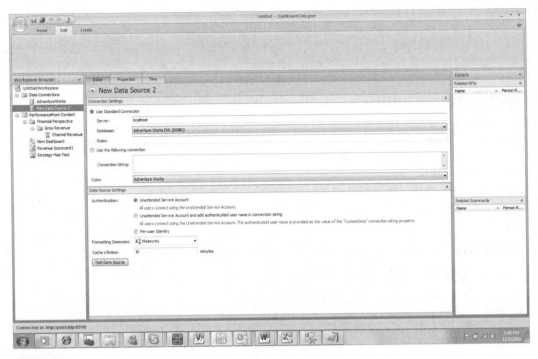

FIGURE 20-8

12. Check the Channel Revenue KPI and click Next, as shown in Figure 20-9.

13. Click Next to bypass the Add Measure Filters window without making any changes.

14. Click Next to bypass the Add Member Columns windows without making any changes. You can add measure filters and member columns at any time.

15. Click Finish to publish the KPI to the PerformancePoint Content folder.

16. Rename the new scorecard `Channel Revenue Scorecard` in the Workspace Browser.

17. With the scorecard open, drag the Sales Territory hierarchy from the Sales Territory dimension to the right of the words Channel Revenue. The words "Last child" should appear before you drop the hierarchy.

18. The Select Members dialog box will open. Expand All and check North America before you click OK.

If you expand any of the Groups, you will see the scorecard values, goals, status, and trends.

19. The scorecard is not complete. Right-click the PerformancePoint Content folder and select New ➪ Report.

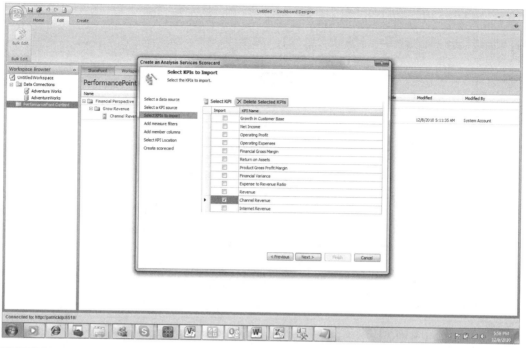

FIGURE 20-9

20. Select the Strategy Map option and click OK.

21. Choose the Channel Revenue Scorecard and click Finish.

22. Rename the report `United States Strategy Map`.

23. Click the Edit Strategy Map icon that is located under the Edit Tab on the ribbon, as shown in Figure 20-10.

24. Click Import Visio File In on the Strategy Map Editor menu.

25. Browse to the directory where you saved the downloaded Visio diagram, select it, and click Open.

26. Click the circle labeled North America and click the Connect Shape item in the menu bar.

FIGURE 20-10

27. On the Connect Shape dialog window, select the cell that is in the Goal and Status column on the North America Row, as shown in Figure 20-11.

28. Uncheck the Show KPI name in the shape text checkbox and click the buttons labeled Connect and Close.

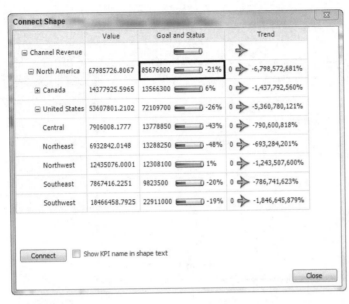

FIGURE 20-11

29. Repeat the steps for all of the remaining shapes. Ensure that you select the row that corresponds to the label in the shape.

30. When you are done, click Apply and your diagram should resemble Figure 20-12.

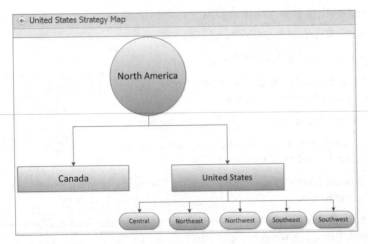

FIGURE 20-12

31. Click the Save All icon in the Dashboard Designer to deploy the scorecard and the strategy map.

32. Open your SharePoint Business Intelligence site and click PerformancePoint Content.

33. Hover over the United States Strategy Map and click the drop-down arrow that appears.

34. From the dialog box select Display Report and your strategy map will appear.

 Please select Lesson 20 on the DVD to view the video that accompanies this lesson.

21

Developing and Deploying Reporting Services Reports to SharePoint

In previous lessons you have learned how to develop BI solutions, which can then be deployed to SharePoint to be consumed by end users. This lesson focuses on deploying a major piece of the SQL Server Business Intelligence stack, Reporting Services, to SharePoint. Giving end users the ability to view Reporting Services reports from SharePoint completes the SharePoint Business Intelligence puzzle.

Reporting Services without integrating and deploying to SharePoint means end users must go to multiple interfaces to find everything they need for making decisions. With this non-integrated setup it's more likely that the users will choose only one or none of the platforms to view reports.

CREATING A REPORT USING BIDS

Two tools are primarily used for developing Reporting Services reports. The more forward-facing lighter development application is called Report Builder. This tool is not typically used by developers but is instead meant more for power users. Power users are generally people who know the business more than they know the technology but are computer savvy enough to figure out how to design a simple report. With Report Builder a power user can either create a new report or modify an existing one, and simply by clicking Save the report is pushed back to SharePoint.

Report Builder was designed with the end user in mind, so much of what you see with this tool will be to get the report author up-and-running as fast as possible. For example, SQL Server 2008 R2 provides a tool called Report Parts, which enables a report developer to save portions of his report to the server. Power users using Report Builder can then consume those Report Parts in their own design without having to understand the original author's source query or layout design.

You can open Report Builder from the SharePoint library that stores your reports. It is a client-side tool so if you have never used it before it will be automatically downloaded and installed after selecting the tool from SharePoint. The latest version of the tool is Report Builder 3.0, which has several other great features beyond the scope of this lesson. However, you will notice that Report Builder has the same look and feel as other Office products to make end users more comfortable using it, as shown in Figure 21-1.

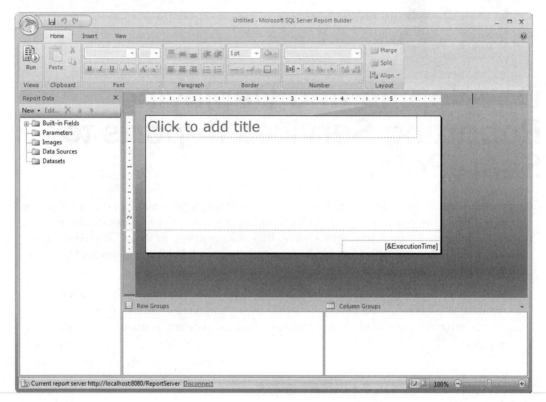

FIGURE 21-1

The other tool for authoring reports is called Business Intelligence Development Studio (BIDS), which is considered to be a tool for developers because it uses a Visual Studio shell and is more about the details of creating a report rather than quickly getting one up-and-running. BIDS is part of the toolset that can be optionally installed during the installation of SQL Server. Once the program is installed you will find it by navigating to Start ➪ All Programs ➪ Microsoft SQL Server 2008 R2 ➪ SQL Server Business Intelligence Development Studio.

To begin, you will need to create a solution and project by selecting File ➪ New ➪ Project. Figure 21-2 shows the New Project dialog box where you will define the project type, Report Server Project, for this lesson, and name both the solution and project. The solution organizes multiple projects together to make it easier to find all project-related items at once by opening a single file. Next, which was just mentioned, is a project. Projects are separated by the type of work you are doing. For example, if you are designing reports you will create a Report Server Project, whereas if you're developing a cube you would create an Analysis Services Project.

New Project

Project types:
- **Business Intelligence Projects**
- Other Project Types

Templates: .NET Framework 3.5

Visual Studio installed templates
- Analysis Services Project
- Integration Services Connections Proje...
- Report Server Project Wizard
- Report Server Project
- Import Analysis Services Database
- Integration Services Project
- Report Model Project

My Templates
- Search Online Templates...

Create an empty Report Server project.

Name: Report Project1

Location: C:\Class

Solution Name: Report Project1

☑ Create directory for solution

OK   Cancel

FIGURE 21-2

After the project and solution are created you are ready to focus on developing a report. To create a new report, open the Solution Explorer pane by pressing Ctrl+Alt+L. Figure 21-3 shows the Solution Explorer pane after it has been opened. Assuming you are using SQL Server 2008 R2, when you look at the contents of the Solution Explorer you will find the Project: Shared Data Sources, Shared Datasets, and Reports. We discuss each of these objects as we go through the creation of a report using the Report Wizard.

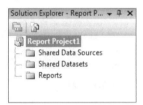

FIGURE 21-3

Start the Report Wizard by right-clicking the Reports folder in the Solution Explorer pane and selecting Add New Report. This lesson demonstrates the wizard, but you could optionally create a report without using a wizard by right-clicking the Reports folder and then selecting Add ⇨ New Item. Creating a report without the wizard gives you more flexibility with the initial design of the report, but it starts you off with an empty design surface.

After opening the Report Wizard click Next on the welcome screen, which will bring you to the Select the Data Source screen. Here you will define the connection name, type, and connection string. The name is simply how you would like this connection to be referred to within Reporting Services. The type refers to the type of connection you need for the report data. For example, if your source data for this report is Oracle, you can select it from the Type drop-down box. A connection string is where you will define the how and where you will access the connection type. To define a connection string, click the Edit button and typically, depending on the type of connection, you will provide a server name and database. The last feature of a data source, which is helpful when you have multiple reports that will require the same data source, is the checkbox labeled Make This a Shared Data Source. If you check this box the connection definition is available for reuse in multiple reports and is deployed to the server. Figure 21-4 shows the available properties when defining the data source. After preparing the data source, click Next to define the data set.

FIGURE 21-4

On the Design the Query screen you write a query that will return results that will be used in the report design. You can either manually type the query in the Query String box or click the Query Builder button, which will have a mouse-driven way of building a query. The Query Builder is useful when you do not know your source data very well because it provides a graphical way of joining objects and returning fields. The query you provide here must be written in an acceptable language for your data source type. For example, if you have an Analysis Services source type your query language would be MDX, but if you have a SQL Server source type the query language would be TSQL. After writing your query, click Next.

Next you must provide a report type. The two possible report types are Tabular and Matrix as shown in Figure 21-5. A Tabular report is generally a detail-level report, meaning it shows a very low granularity of the data. For example, you would use a Tabular report type to generate a list of all your sales by order. Tabular reports can have groupings but it can only be done on rows. A Matrix report, on the other hand, is intended for aggregating data. It is also different in that it can do grouping on both rows and columns. So a Matrix report may be used to shows product sales by year. The years would be grouped on columns and the products would be grouped on rows. The intersecting point would display the total sales for a particular year for a specific product. The report type you choose will depend on the data that you want to display. Once you have decided on a report type, click Next.

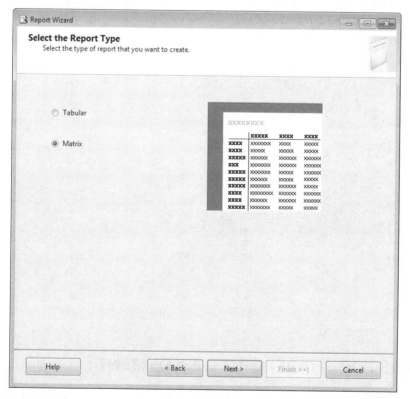

FIGURE 21-5

Depending on your selection of the report type the next screen will either say Design a Matrix or Design a Table. This section allows you to place the fields in any section of the report you would like. As you place the fields in the desired locations you will notice that it will highlight that section in a generic report preview. If you have selected a Matrix report type you will see a property on this page called Enable Drilldown in the bottom left of the wizard. Enable Drilldown will be editable only if you have more than one row grouping. When this checkbox is selected your report will automatically have the lowest level of the row grouping collapsed into the higher level. For example, when using the fields Product and Category, you can collapse the Product field into Category so that it is only visible when a user clicks a plus sign (+) next to the Category field value. This gives you a much cleaner report when it is initially rendered by the user. After adding these fields to the desired locations, click Next.

The final screens vary slightly depending on whether you select a Tabular or Matrix report. If you selected a Matrix report type you will provide a style and name for the report to complete the wizard. If you selected Tabular you will have one extra screen called Choose the Table Layout, which allows you to change some minor visualizations as well as adding subtotals or drilldowns. Before clicking Finish to create the report, ensure you have named it appropriately for the report topic area, then check Preview Report in the bottom. This is not the last time you can name the report, so if you need to rename it later simply right-click the report name in the Solution Explorer and select Rename. A final completed report may look like Figure 21-6. Everything done in this section walks you through using the wizard to create a report but you can easily make modifications to what the wizard has produced by changing to the Design tab in the report editor window.

Sales by Year

	2005	2006	2007	2008
⊞ Bike Racks			137	191
⊞ Bike Stands			119	130
⊞ Bottles and Cages			3273	4708
⊞ Caps			885	1305
⊞ Cleaners			383	525
⊞ Fenders			883	1238
⊞ Gloves			581	849
⊞ Helmets			2646	3794
⊞ Hydration Packs			305	428
⊞ Jerseys			1354	1978
⊞ Mountain Bikes	173	615	2088	2094
⊞ Road Bikes	840	2062	2797	2369
⊞ Shorts			435	584
⊞ Socks			248	320
⊞ Tires and Tubes			7279	10053
⊞ Touring Bikes			825	1342
⊞ Vests			205	357

FIGURE 21-6

CONFIGURING BIDS FOR SHAREPOINT DEPLOYMENT

Once the report is designed to your satisfaction you are ready to deploy it to SharePoint. If you have ever deployed Reporting Services reports to the more traditional native mode installation, you will find the configuration from BIDS is slightly different.

You can find the deployment configuration in the properties of the Report Server project. Open the Solution Explorer pane, right-click the Report Server Project, and select Properties. First, point the TargetServerURL property to the SharePoint URL. Then point the four properties labeled Target above this one to the appropriate library to which you wish to deploy as shown in Figure 21-7.

When you have the need to deploy to multiple instances, BIDS has some nice built-in functionality to make it easy to change which instance you are deploying to. As part of the Standard toolbar you will find a drop-down box that is set by default to Debug. You can create multiple settings here so that when you have it set to Debug it will deploy to your development environment, or when it is set to Release it deploys to production. The names of these settings can also be changed when you select Configuration Manager from the same drop-down box.

To use this functionality all you have to do is have the drop-down box set to Debug when you configure deployment to the development environment, then change it to Release and configure the project properties for production. After the configuration is done you can easily toggle back and forth on your deployment settings. Figure 21-8 shows the Debug toolbar.

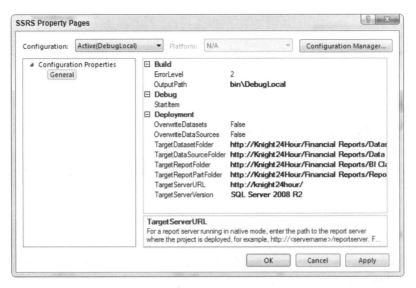

FIGURE 21-7

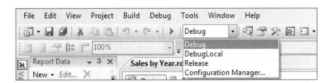

FIGURE 21-8

DEPLOYING A REPORT FROM BIDS TO SHAREPOINT

After configuring the deployment in the Report Server project properties, you are ready to deploy. You can choose to deploy either the entire project or just individual reports. If you decide to deploy individual reports, be aware that the data source must also be deployed for the report to work. When you deploy for the first time, it is best to just deploy the entire project so all shared data sources and shared data sets get deployed to SharePoint. To deploy the project, right-click the project name in the Solution Explorer and select Deploy. If you just want to deploy individual reports, right-click the report name again in the Solution Explorer and select Deploy.

By default, in the properties of the project, the shared data sources and shared data sets will not be overwritten if deployed multiple times. This is important to be aware of because when you make changes to a shared data set the new changes will not overwrite what is on the server by default. If you need to overwrite what has already been deployed previously, right-click the project name in the Solution Explorer and select Properties. Then change either of the properties OverwriteDatasets or OverwriteDataSource to True, which will then allow you to overwrite those objects during deployment.

TRY IT

In this Try It you design a Reporting Services report and then deploy it to a SharePoint library on an existing site.

Lesson Requirements

To complete this lesson you will be required to have SharePoint 2010 and SQL Server 2008 R2 already installed and configured with the Reporting Services add-in for SharePoint. Lesson 10 walks you through this configuration if you have not already completed it. You will also need the AdventureWorksDW2008R2 sample database from `www.codeplex.com` to follow the report design.

Hints

➤ Use the Report Wizard to design a report that displays the number of sales made on the Internet by product subcategory and year.

➤ After creating the report deploy it to an existing SharePoint library you have created from any of the previous lessons.

Step-by-Step

1. Open BIDS by navigating to Start ➪ All Programs ➪ Microsoft SQL Server 2008 R2 ➪ SQL Server Business Intelligence Development Studio.

2. Create a new Report Server project by selecting File ➪ New ➪ Project.

3. Select Report Server Project, name it **Lesson 21**, and click OK.

4. Open the Solution Explorer (Ctrl+Alt+L) and create a new report.

5. Right-click the Reports folder and select Add New Report to open the Report Wizard.

6. Click Next on the Welcome screen, which will take you to the Select the Data Source page.

7. Create a new data source by providing the name **AdventureWorksDW2008R2** and clicking Edit next to the Connection String box to define the connection. This will open the Connection Properties window.

8. Type the server name on which you have installed the AdventureWorksDW2008R2 sample database and then select the database from the drop-down list labeled Select or Enter a Database Name. Click OK.

9. Click the checkbox called Make This a Shared Data Source as shown in Figure 21-9. Click Next after these steps are completed.

10. You are now in the Design the Query page. You could either build a query yourself by selecting Query Builder to graphically write the query or type the TSQL query in the Query String box. Because this lesson is not intended to teach you TSQL you can just write the following query in the Query String box and click Next:

```
SELECT      DimProductSubcategory.EnglishProductSubcategoryName,
            DimDate.CalendarYear,
            SUM(FactInternetSales.OrderQuantity) AS OrderQuantity
FROM        FactInternetSales INNER JOIN
            DimDate ON FactInternetSales.OrderDateKey = DimDate.DateKey INNER JOIN
            DimProduct ON FactInternetSales.ProductKey = DimProduct.ProductKey
            INNER JOIN
            DimProductSubcategory ON DimProduct.ProductSubcategoryKey =
            DimProductSubcategory.ProductSubcategoryKey
GROUP BY    DimProductSubcategory.EnglishProductSubcategoryName,
            DimDate.CalendarYear
```

FIGURE 21-9

11. Select Matrix for the Report Type and click Next.

12. On the Design the Matrix page select EnglishProductSubcategoryName and drag it to the Rows section. Also, drag CalendarYear to Columns and OrderQuantity to Details. Figure 21-10 shows this step completed. Once all the available fields are placed click Next.

13. Leave the default of Slate for the Matrix Style and click Next again.

14. Name the report **Sales by Product** and click the Preview Report checkbox to immediately see the report results. Click Finish. The completed report should look like Figure 21-11.

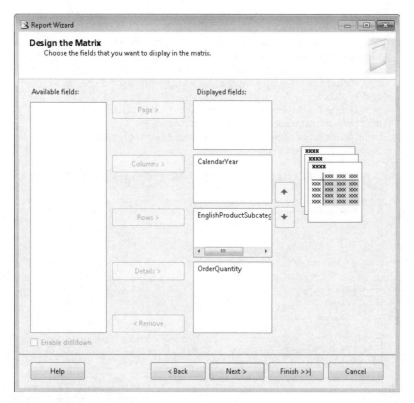

FIGURE 21-10

Sales By Product

	2005	2006	2007	2008
Bike Racks			137	191
Bike Stands			119	130
Bottles and Cages			3273	4708
Caps			885	1305
Cleaners			383	525
Fenders			883	1238
Gloves			581	849
Helmets			2646	3794
Hydration Packs			305	428
Jerseys			1354	1978
Mountain Bikes	173	615	2088	2094
Road Bikes	840	2062	2797	2369
Shorts			435	584
Socks			248	320
Tires and Tubes			7279	10053
Touring Bikes			825	1342
Vests			205	357

FIGURE 21-11

15. You are now ready to deploy the completed solution to SharePoint. Right-click the project name Lesson 21 in the Solution Explorer pane and click Properties.

16. Change the following information to deploy the reports to SharePoint and click OK:

PROPERTY	VALUE
TargetDatasetFolder	http://yourservername/sitename/libraryname/Datasets
TargetDataSourceFolder	http://yourservername/sitename/libraryname/Data Sources
TargetReportFolder	http://yourservername/sitename/libraryname/Reports
TargetReportPartFolder	http://yourservername/sitename/libraryname/Report Parts
TargetServerURL	http://yourservername/

17. Your report should now be deployed. Navigate to the SharePoint site that you just deployed to and see the reports on the server. If you had any issues review step 16 and compare it to the actual URL of the site as it appears in your web browser. Another potential issue that can occur is that the items get deployed but are not connected. If you select a deployed report to SharePoint you can manage the data source and reconnect it. Figure 21-12 shows the report viewable from SharePoint.

FIGURE 21-12

Congratulations! You have successfully developed and deployed a Reporting Services report to SharePoint.

 Please select Lesson 21 on the DVD to view the video that accompanies this lesson.

SECTION V
Branding and Managing Organizational Business Intelligence

▶ **LESSON 22:** Theming and Personalizing Your Business Intelligence Site

▶ **LESSON 23:** Using SharePoint Designer to Customize Master Pages

▶ **LESSON 24:** Controlling Your Reporting with Versioning, Auditing, and Content Expiration

▶ **LESSON 25:** Managing Report Approval with SharePoint Workflow

▶ **LESSON 26:** Setting Up SharePoint Search to Catalog Analytics and Reports

22

Theming and Personalizing Your Business Intelligence Site

In this lesson, you learn how to create a theme in SharePoint using PowerPoint, modify existing themes in the Theme Gallery, and customize the navigation to ease user navigation.

THEMES IN SHAREPOINT: AN INTRODUCTION

A theme in SharePoint is simply a set of colors assigned to specific property types. It doesn't affect the design of pages — to change the design, Page Layouts and Master Pages must be used. Where the use of themes becomes important is in creating themes based on a similar set of colors, but changing specific sets of colors to help users easily determine which subsite on a site collection they are navigating through. This is especially useful when various departments have similar site designs, and being able to tell if the page being shown is related to HR or IT would take more than a glance otherwise. Themes are all stored in the Theme Gallery, for ease of use later.

USING POWERPOINT TO CREATE SHAREPOINT THEMES

You can create themes either through the SharePoint website, or by using a PowerPoint theme, which allows for the easy reuse of corporate color schemes that are in PowerPoint templates.

To create a new theme for use in SharePoint, open up PowerPoint and select the Design tab. Click the Colors button and choose Create New Theme Colors, as shown in Figure 22-1.

This will present a screen where you can choose the colors to use for the theme, as shown in Figure 22-2.

By clicking the Fonts button underneath Colors, you can also set the fonts used in the theme, as shown in Figure 22-3.

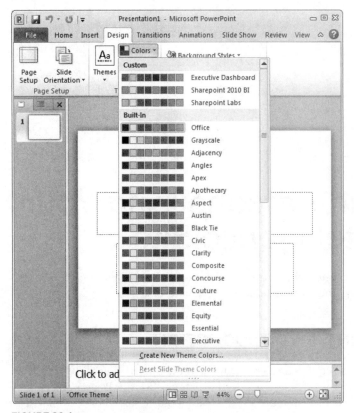

FIGURE 22-1

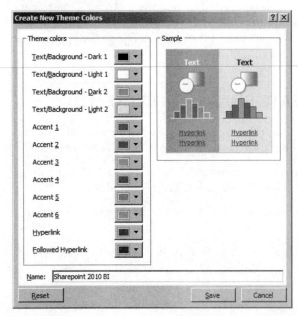

FIGURE 22-2

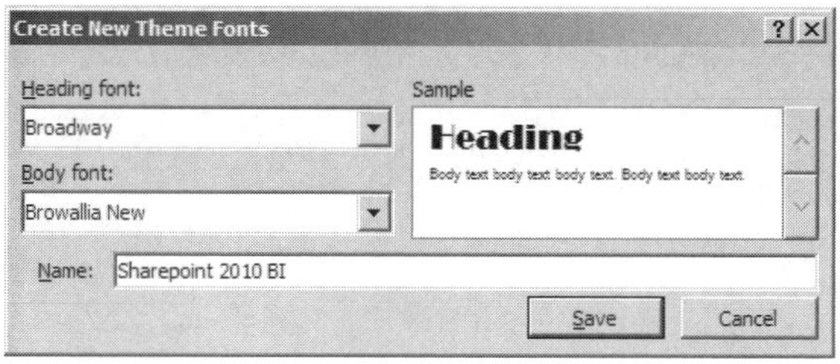

FIGURE 22-3

Now that you've created the theme, you need to save it to a theme file. Click the down arrow directly next to the Effects button, as shown in Figure 22-4.

FIGURE 22-4

Finally, click Save Current Theme and save the file.

Now that you have a theme, you need to apply it to SharePoint. In the site you want to apply the theme to, click Site Actions ➪ Site Settings, and then click Site Theme, as shown in Figure 22-5.

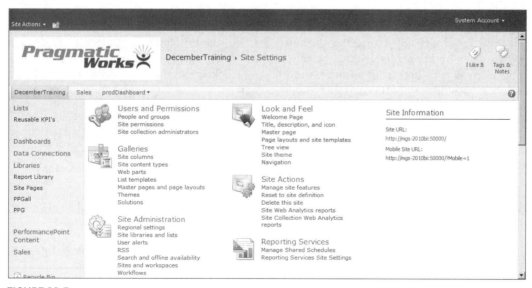

FIGURE 22-5

Click the Theme Gallery link in the ribbon to go to the Theme Gallery, as shown in Figure 22-6, and then upload the theme you've just created by clicking Upload Document in the Documents tab.

After uploading the theme, go back to the settings page and click Site Theme. Choose the theme you've just uploaded, as shown in Figure 22-7.

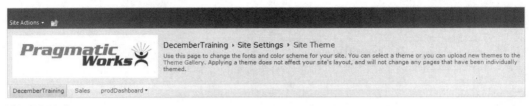

FIGURE 22-6

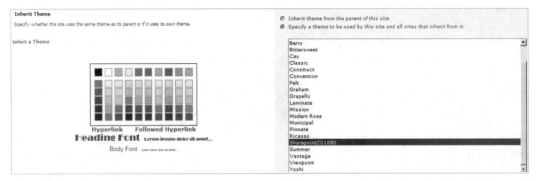

FIGURE 22-7

You can preview the theme, as well as change the individual colors. This is a great way to use a common color scheme across all the sites, and then customize a single element to distinguish the sites from each other.

The final step in the basic theming of a SharePoint site is changing the logo used by the site. You do this using the SharePoint settings website and it is a two-step process: First, the image needs to be uploaded to a library in SharePoint, and then the site image must be set to use that image. To upload an image, you must first create a library to store it in. Click Site Actions ➪ More Options, and create a document library — Image Gallery is a good name.

 If the Publishing Feature is activated, the image can be stored in the Images library, which you can find by clicking Site Actions ➪ View All Site Content.

Once the library is created, upload your logo image to the library. In the library, right-click the picture you just uploaded and choose Copy Shortcut, as shown in Figure 22-8.

Click Site Actions ➪ Site Settings again, and then click Title, Description, and Icon, as shown in Figure 22-9.

Now paste the URL you copied into the URL textbox, and click OK, as shown in Figure 22-10.

Click OK to finish changing the logo.

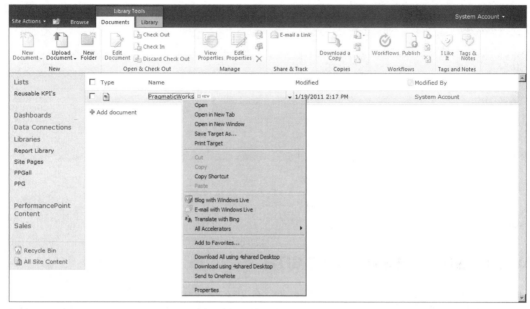

FIGURE 22-8

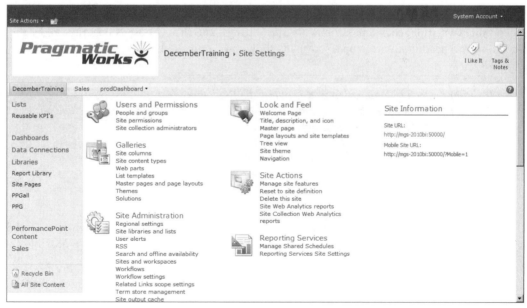

FIGURE 22-9

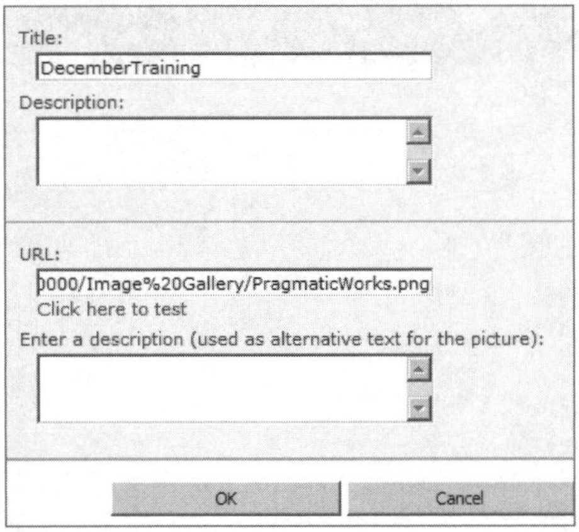

Title:

DecemberTraining

Description:

URL:

0000/Image%20Gallery/PragmaticWorks.png

Click here to test

Enter a description (used as alternative text for the picture):

OK   Cancel

FIGURE 22-10

NAVIGATING A SHAREPOINT SITE

Once a SharePoint site has been themed, you need to give some thought to how users will navigate around the site. By default, the navigation bar on top, called the Global Navigation, is used to navigate to sites within the site collection, and the navigation on the left-hand side, called Current Navigation, is used to navigate lists and libraries within the current site. Though this approach works fairly well for generic SharePoint sites, some customization may be required in a BI site.

To edit the navigation, click Site Actions ➪ Site Settings, and then choose Navigation under the Look and Feel heading to bring up a screen, as shown in Figure 22-11.

In order to find Navigation in this place, the Publishing feature must be activated — this is done by default when creating a site using the Business Intelligence Center site template, but not all templates activate this feature. In order to activate this feature, go to Site Actions ➪ Site Settings then under the Site Collection Administration section click on Site Collection Features. Now click the Activate button for the Office SharePoint Server Publishing Infrastructure feature.

The setting to display the same navigation items as the parent is available only when at a subsite level, and is grayed out when at the parent level. Only two levels of navigation are possible.

To create a new heading, click Add Heading to bring up the dialog box shown in Figure 22-12. You can restrict the navigation heading to be seen only by certain audiences by using the Audience selection.

In order to be usable by Touch-Screen interfaces, do not add a link to a drop-down menu.

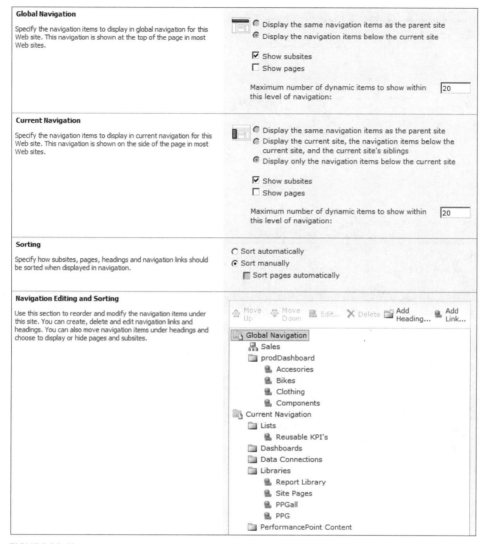

FIGURE 22-11

Click OK to create the heading. Next, click Add Link. This will bring up an almost identical screen — in fact the only difference is that the URL field is prepopulated with http://. Give your link a title and click Browse to add the link itself, setting the screen as shown in Figure 22-13.

Once you've added your links, reorganizing them is a matter of clicking the Move Up and Move Down buttons until the links are in the correct order, as shown in Figure 22-14. Click OK to apply the changes when you are done.

The final use of the navigation menu links is in combination with the Query String filters created in Lesson 19. To use this functionality, check the name of the Query String Parameter Name, as shown in Figure 22-15. You can copy this name to use when creating the navigation items.

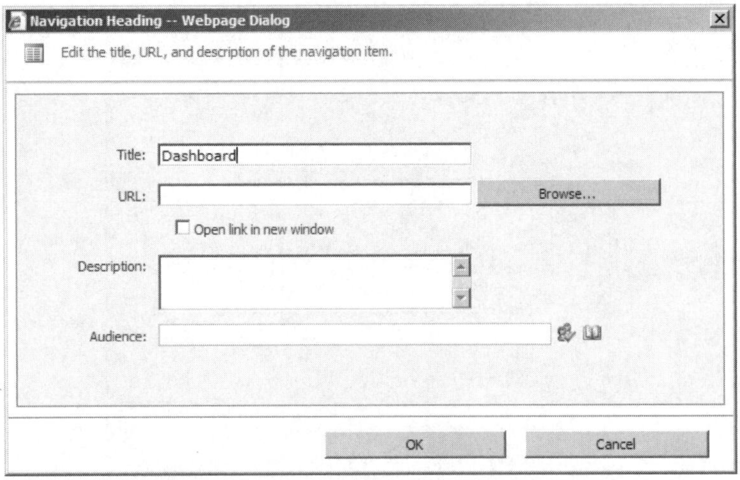

FIGURE 22-12

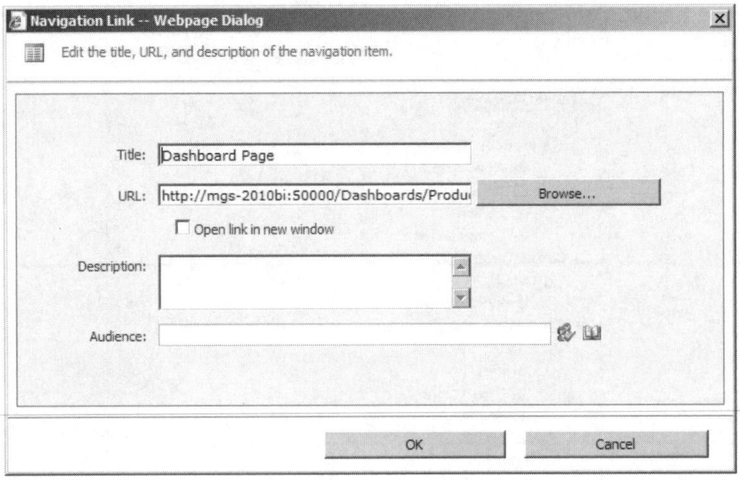

FIGURE 22-13

Now, on the link that was created in the navigation, add a question mark, the parameter name that you copied in the previous step, an equals sign, and the value of the member. Replace any ampersands in the member name with %26.

For example, if the page is ProductSales in the Dashboards library, the link for the Bikes member in the Products Category will be `/Dashboards/ProductSales.aspx?QSProductCategory=[Product].[Product Categories].[Category].%26[1]`.

In this link is the name of the page, the `/Dashboards/ProductSales.aspx`, `?` denotes that the following text is a parameter, `QSProductCategory` is the name of the Query String Parameter that will be receiving the value, and `[Product].[Product Categories].[Category].%26[1]` is the actual value being passed to the page.

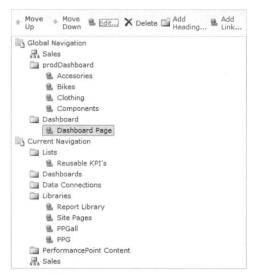

FIGURE 22-14

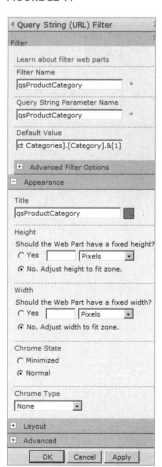

FIGURE 22-15

Replacing & with %26 is known as URL Encoding. This is necessary because multiple parameters in a URL are separated by &.

To get the MDX member, browse the cube in SSMS (SQL Server Management Studio) and drag the member to the query window and copy it.

TRY IT

In this Try It, you create a new Theme in PowerPoint and upload it to the Theme Gallery. You also create a new link to a page within your site.

Lesson Requirements

Create a theme in PowerPoint, using the standard fonts, and change the following colors in the theme colors:

➤ **Text/Background** — Dark 1 : Blue, Hyperlink, Lighter 40%

➤ **Text/Background** — Dark 2 : Olive Green, Accent 3, Lighter 60%

➤ **Hyperlink** — Orange, Accent 6, Darker 25%

Add a Global Navigation heading called Lab Pages.

Add a Global Navigation link to the All Periods Analysis page created in Lesson 18.

Hints

➤ Call your theme SharePoint Labs.

➤ Add the navigation to Global Navigation.

Step-by-Step

1. Open PowerPoint.

2. Click the Design tab.

3. Click Colors.

4. Click Create New Theme Colors.

5. Set the Theme Colors, as shown in Figure 22-16.

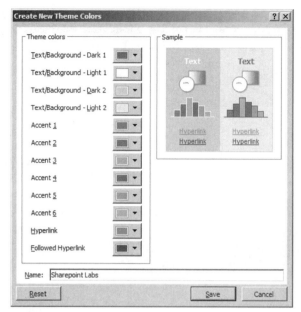

FIGURE 22-16

6. Click Save.

7. Click the bottom arrow next to the design ribbon, highlighted in Figure 22-17.

FIGURE 22-17

8. Click Save Current Theme.

9. Browse to a convenient location, and save the theme as **SharePointLabs**. The .thmx extension will be added automatically.

10. Open the SharePoint site, click Site Actions ⇨ Site Settings, and then choose Site Theme under Look and Feel to load the page shown in Figure 22-18.

11. Click Theme Gallery, then click Upload Document, as shown in Figure 22-19.

12. Browse to the .thmx file you saved earlier, and upload it.

13. Choose Theme Gallery for the content type, and click Save.

14. Click Site Actions ⇨ Site Settings, then choose Site Theme under Look and Feel.

15. Choose the SharePointLabs theme.

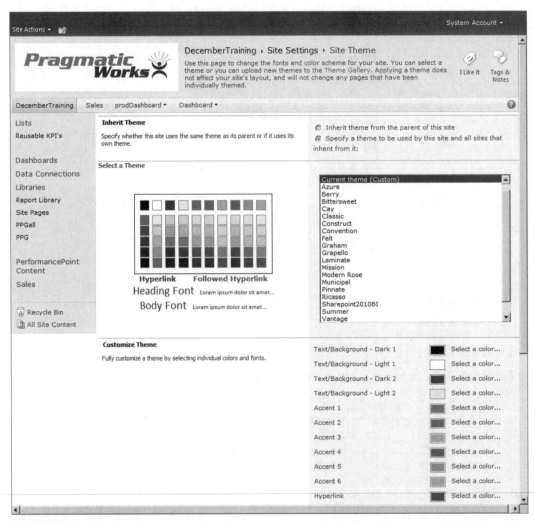

FIGURE 22-18

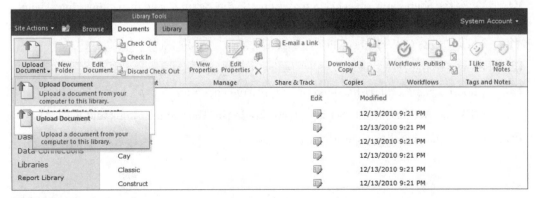

FIGURE 22-19

16. Click the Preview button to see Figure 22-20.

FIGURE 22-20

17. Close the preview and click OK.

18. Click Navigation under Look and Feel.

19. Click Global Navigation in the Navigation Editing and Sorting tab, as shown in Figure 22-21.

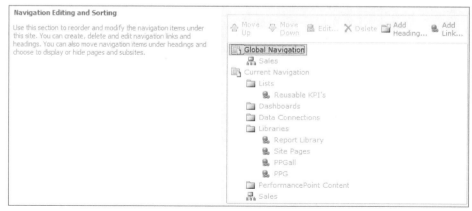

FIGURE 22-21

20. Click Add Heading, set the title to **Lab Pages**, and click OK.

21. Click Lab Pages, and click Add Link.

22. Set the title to **All Periods Analysis**.

23. Click the Browse button, and browse to the All Periods Analysis page created in Lesson 18, as shown in Figure 22-22.

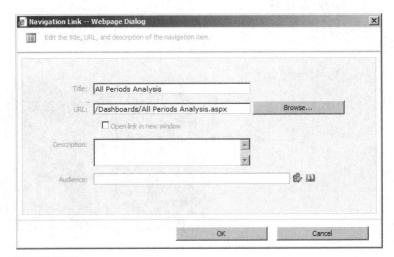

FIGURE 22-22

24. Click OK to finish, and view a top navigation similar to Figure 22-23.

FIGURE 22-23

 Please select Lesson 22 on the DVD to view the video that accompanies this lesson.

23

Using SharePoint Designer to Customize Master Pages

In this lesson, you learn how to use SharePoint Designer to customize the layout of all the pages in your SharePoint site by using Master Pages. This lesson does not delve deeply into CSS or JavaScript, which are both HTML technologies that can be used in Master Pages, but it does touch on where they are used. An understanding of HTML and XML is a requirement.

INTRODUCTION TO SHAREPOINT DESIGNER

SharePoint Designer is used for customizations that aren't possible using SharePoint settings. It is designed for use by power users who aren't developers, and thus sits between using SharePoint web settings and Visual Studio in both complexity and capability. SharePoint Designer works only when connected to a SharePoint site — once a site is opened, the screen in Figure 23-1 is displayed.

The design surface is split into a navigation bar showing the site objects down the left, a context-sensitive ribbon on the top, with the remainder of the screen reserved for editing. The site settings are displayed on the opening screen.

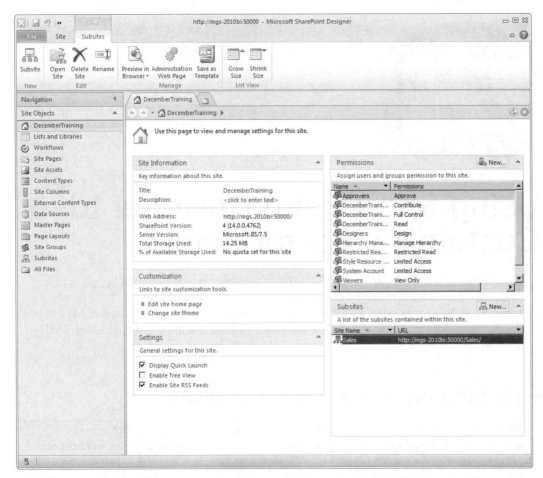

FIGURE 23-1

Clicking the Master Pages link brings up a list of Master Pages, as shown in Figure 23-2.

Because all SharePoint content, including the Master Pages, is stored in SharePoint lists, the version control and document approval features are all enabled. In addition, in order to change the master page, it is necessary to click Edit File in Advanced Mode rather than just opening it.

For all SharePoint default content, such as the four Master Pages shown in Figure 23-2, it is always better to copy the master page and change the site settings to use it rather than editing the SharePoint content.

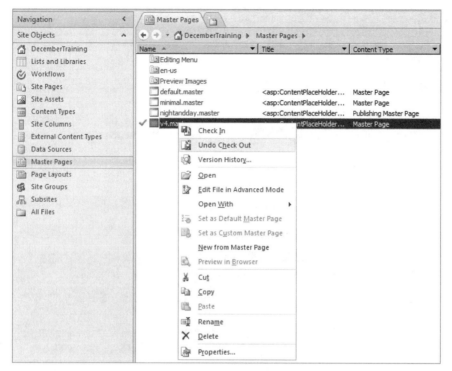

FIGURE 23-2

MASTER PAGE CONCEPTS

On a SharePoint site, just like on a website, some elements will be common to all pages, such as the navigation bar and ribbon on top, and the navigation bar on the left. However, these elements, despite being common, will be represented differently according to the specific page — for instance, some pages will hide the left navigation bar. This is where Master Pages come in — a master page includes zones that will be set according to the specific page, allowing for relative repositioning of different content without the page needing to be changed. Pages can also activate different zones, or update different zones. In Figure 23-3, where the Development.master master page is open in split view, the PlaceholderSiteName is used to show a dynamic site name. In this view, the title is set to December Training, but when a page is browsed it is updated to the familiar breadcrumb.

Other placeholders are in place for the main content, the navigation, and even the ribbon. These placeholders will be processed into final content in combination with the page content, as well as the current security settings, to produce each page that the users see.

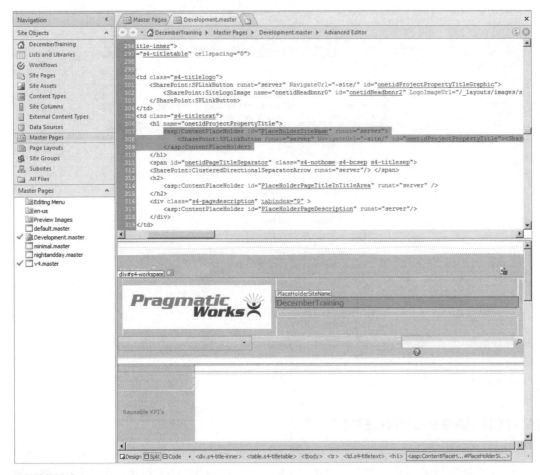

FIGURE 23-3

MASTER PAGES IN SHAREPOINT

> *Editing in SharePoint Designer is best accomplished using a split view to see both the code and the preview. To activate this view, click on View ➤ Split in the ribbon.*

Several areas within the master page are important in SharePoint Master Pages. Most of these areas are not places that you will change, but rather are pieces of content you will need to include when you are creating your own master page. Before changing them in any way, copy the v4 master page to `Development.master`.

In SharePoint's default Master Pages, the areas (mostly HTML tags) listed within the content placeholders table are mostly contained within `<div>` tags, which are linked to CSS classes — this is a good model to follow when building your own Master Pages: creating your site structure; and styling using `<div>` tags. The areas contained within these tags can be content placeholders — sections that will be replaced when the page is rendered, either from SharePoint content or from page content. They can also be native tags such as the image tag used for the help link. Finally, there are XML tags specific to SharePoint: all of these will open the tag with `SharePoint:` and the tag name.

Changing the CSS class that is used is covered in a later section of this lesson.

The following table lists all the content placeholders.

CONTENT PLACEHOLDERS

PLACEHOLDER CONTROL	DESCRIPTION
`<asp:ContentPlaceHolder id="PlaceHolderQuickLaunchTop" runat="server">`	The top of the Quick Launch menu.
`<asp:ContentPlaceHolder id="PlaceHolderQuickLaunchBottom" runat="server">`	The bottom of the Quick Launch menu.
`<asp:ContentPlaceHolder id="PlaceHolderPageTitle" runat="server"/>`	The title of the site.
`<asp:ContentPlaceHolder id="PlaceHolderAdditionalPageHead" runat="server"/>`	A placeholder in the head section of the page used to add extra components such as ECMAScript (JavaScript, JScript) and cascading style sheets (CSS) to the page.
`<asp:ContentPlaceHolder id="PlaceHolderBodyAreaClass" runat="server"/>`	The class of the body area.
`<asp:ContentPlaceHolder ID="SPNavigation" runat="server">`	A control used for additional page editing controls.
`<asp:ContentPlaceHolder id="PlaceHolderSiteName" runat="server">`	The name of the site where the current page resides.
`<asp:ContentPlaceHolder id="PlaceHolderPageTitleInTitleArea" runat="server" />`	The title of the page, which appears in the title area on the page.

continues

(continued)

PLACEHOLDER CONTROL	DESCRIPTION
`<asp:ContentPlaceHolder id="PlaceHolderPageDescription" runat="server"/>`	The description of the current page.
`<asp:ContentPlaceHolder id="PlaceHolderSearchArea" runat="server">`	The section of the page for the search controls.
`<asp:ContentPlaceHolder id=" PlaceHolderGlobalNavigation" runat="server">`	The breadcrumb control on the page.
`<asp:ContentPlaceHolder id="PlaceHolderTitleBreadcrumb" runat="server">`	The breadcrumb text for the breadcrumb control.
`<asp:ContentPlaceHolder id="Pl aceHolderGlobalNavigationSite Map" runat="server">`	The list of subsites and sibling sites in the global navigation on the page.
`<asp:ContentPlaceHolder id="PlaceHolderTopNavBar" runat="server">`	The container used to hold the top navigation bar.
`<asp:ContentPlaceHolder id="PlaceHolderHorizontalNav" runat="server">`	The navigation menu that is inside the top navigation bar.
`<asp:ContentPlaceHolder id="Pl aceHolderLeftNavBarDataSource" runat="server" />`	The placement of the data source used to populate the left navigation bar.
`<asp:ContentPlaceHolder id="P laceHolderCalendarNavigator" runat="server" />`	The date picker used when a calendar is visible on the page.
`<asp:ContentPlaceHolder id="PlaceHolderLeftNavBarTop" runat="server"/>`	The top section of the left navigation bar.
`<asp:ContentPlaceHolder id="PlaceHolderLeftNavBar" runat="server">`	The Quick Launch bar.
`<asp:ContentPlaceHolder id="PlaceHolderLeftActions" runat="server">`	The additional objects above the Quick Launch bar.

PLACEHOLDER CONTROL	DESCRIPTION
`<asp:ContentPlaceHolder id="PlaceHolderMain" runat="server">`	The main content of the page.
`<asp:ContentPlaceHolder id="PlaceHolderFormDigest" runat="server">`	The container where the Page Form digest control is stored.
`<asp:ContentPlaceHolder id="PlaceHolderUtilityContent" runat="server"/>`	The additional content at the bottom of the page. This is outside of the form tag.
`<asp:ContentPlaceHolder id="PlaceHolderTitleAreaClass" runat="server"/>`	The class for the title area. This is now in the head tag. Any customizations that add a WebPartZone in a content tag to this placeholder will cause an error on the page.
`<asp:ContentPlaceHolder id="PlaceHolderPageImage" runat="server"/>`	This placeholder does not appear as part of the UI and must be present for backward compatibility.
`<asp:ContentPlaceHolder id="PlaceHolderTitleLeftBorder" runat="server">`	This placeholder does not appear as part of the UI and must be present for backward compatibility.
`<asp:ContentPlaceHolder id="PlaceHolderMiniConsole" runat="server"/>`	This placeholder does not appear as part of the UI and must be present for backward compatibility.
`<asp:ContentPlaceHolder id="PlaceHolderTitleRightMargin" runat="server"/>`	This placeholder does not appear as part of the UI and must be present for backward compatibility.
`<asp:ContentPlaceHolder id="PlaceHolderTitleAreaSeparator" runat="server"/>`	This placeholder does not appear as part of the UI and must be present for backward compatibility.
`<asp:ContentPlaceHolder id="PlaceHolderNavSpacer" runat="server">`	This placeholder does not appear as part of the UI and must be present for backward compatibility.
`<asp:ContentPlaceHolder id="PlaceHolderLeftNavBarBorder" runat="server">`	This placeholder does not appear as part of the UI and must be present for backward compatibility.
`<asp:ContentPlaceHolder id="PlaceHolderBodyLeftBorder" runat="server">`	This placeholder does not appear as part of the UI and must be present for backward compatibility.

The first area to be aware of is contained within the `SharePoint:SPRibbon` tag, as shown in Figure 23-4.

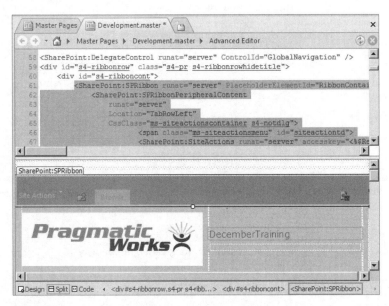

FIGURE 23-4

The items contained within the SharePoint ribbon include the styling of the ribbon and the items within the Site Actions menu, as well as the context-sensitive menu. The only change that is advised within the ribbon is changing the CSS class to style the ribbon.

The second area is the content contained within the tag `<asp:ContentPlaceHolder id="PlaceHolderSiteName" runat="server">`.

This is the placeholder for the site title, as shown in Figure 23-5.

Right below this is the tag `<asp:ContentPlaceHolder id="PlaceHolderPageTitleInTitleArea" runat="server" />` — this tag is the breadcrumb, and though it is often associated with the site title, it by no means has to be, so feel free to move it around.

The next area of interest is the tag `<asp:ContentPlaceHolder id="PlaceHolderTopNavBar" runat="server">` — the contents of this tag mark where the global navigation goes. Generally speaking, don't touch the contents of this tag — some settings might be changed for truly advanced customizations, but they are few and far between. Typically, you would change only the CSS class and move this tag around your page. See Figure 23-6.

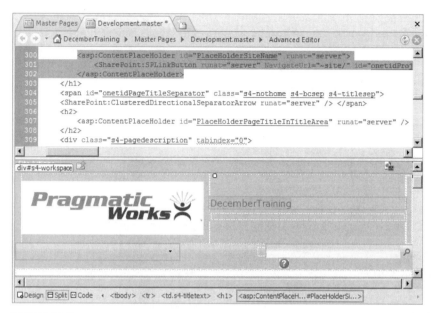

FIGURE 23-5

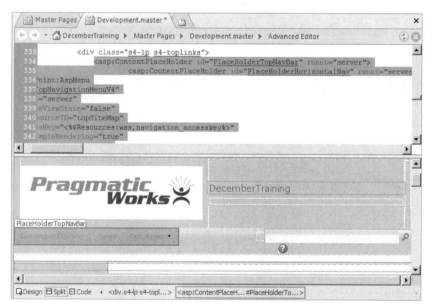

FIGURE 23-6

The `<asp:ContentPlaceHolder id="PlaceHolderSearchArea" runat="server">` tag is for the search area — in this case, only move the tag around, as shown in Figure 23-7, it doesn't even have a CSS class set here.

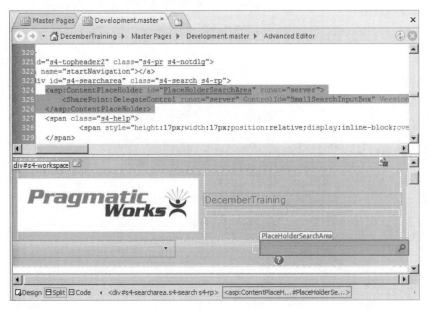

FIGURE 23-7

As shown in Figure 23-8, the help icon is a single image tag: `<img src="/_layouts/images/ fgimg.png" alt="<%$Resources:wss,multipages_helplinkalt_text%>" style="left:-0px !important;top:-309px !important;position:absolute;" align="absmiddle" border="0" runat="server" />`.

The next set of areas are grouped together under the `<div id="s4-leftpanel" class="s4-notdlg">` tag in the `V4.master` page. Several of these placeholders are not typically used in a Business Intelligence center. The tag containing the main areas for the left-hand navigation is the `<asp:ContentPlaceHolder id="PlaceHolderLeftNavBar" runat="server">` tag, as shown in Figure 23-9.

As you can see, all the items currently shown in the nav also show here in design mode, but they will update automatically as the site changes. It should be noted that nav is an often used shortening of navigation. It's also worth noting that within this particular tag are multiple areas.

The tag starting `<SharePoint:AspMenu id="QuickLaunchMenu"` *is contained within a tag* `<SharePoint:UIVersionedContent UIVersion="3" runat="server">` *and hence doesn't apply in SharePoint 2010 (version 4) — so don't get confused when it doesn't change anything on your page.*

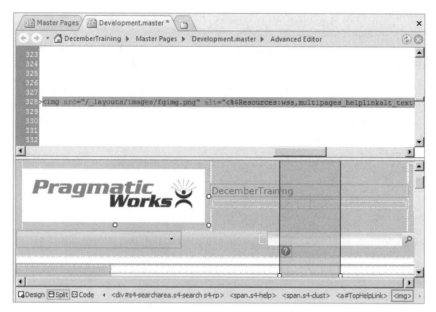

FIGURE 23-8

FIGURE 23-9

Looking a little further down, a tag starting with `<SharePoint:AspMenu id="V4QuickLaunchMenu"` is contained in a tag `<SharePoint:UIVersionedContent UIVersion="4" runat="server">` and therefore applies to SharePoint 2010. This versioning is used when functionality has changed substantially between SharePoint 2007 and SharePoint 2010.

One of the possible changes we can make to this navigation involves changing the orientation to horizontal, the static display levels to 1, and the dynamic display levels to 1. This will make the navigation behave like the top nav, that is, be laid out horizontally and have flyouts for the lower levels. Obviously, the design will need to be adjusted to suit the new layout, or the navigation will end up distorted, as shown in Figure 23-10.

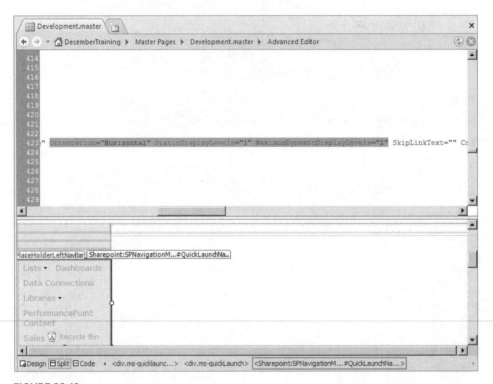

FIGURE 23-10

The final tag of interest is `<asp:ContentPlaceHolder id="PlaceHolderQuickLaunchBottom" runat="server">`. The contents of this tag contain the Recycle Bin and All Site Content links. As long as the content within the tags starting with `<Sharepoint` are unchanged, the items within this placeholder can be moved around as desired.

CSS IN MASTER PAGES

The CSS link that SharePoint uses in the master page is `<SharePoint:CssLink runat="server" Version="4"/>`. When the page is rendered, this will be replaced with CSS links similar to the following:

```
<link rel="stylesheet" type="text/css"
href="/_layouts/1033/styles/portal.css?rev=0gSit0FmDdWuMu7kF0JZ9g%3D%3D"
/>
<link rel="stylesheet" type="text/css"
 href="/_catalogs/theme/Themed/EC8F5A82/search-7E1AFF02.css?ctag=4"
/>
<link rel="stylesheet" type="text/css"
href="/_catalogs/theme/Themed/EC8F5A82/wiki-ECF524AA.css?ctag=4"
/>
<link rel="stylesheet" type="text/css"
href="/_catalogs/theme/Themed/EC8F5A82/corev4-8A0ABD2F.css?ctag=4"
/>
```

A key point to note here is that CSS changes that are theme specific would need to go into the CSS files associated with that theme. For styling that works for all pages using this master page, you insert a new CSS link. Start by copying your CSS file to `%Program Files%\Common Files\ Microsoft Shared\Web Server Extensions\14\TEMPLATE\LAYOUTS\1033\styles` (1033 being the standard locale — if you are using a non-standard locale, use the appropriate folder instead).

Then add a line directly below the tag to point to your CSS file, similar to the following two lines:

```
<SharePoint:CssLink runat="server" Version="4"/>
<link rel="stylesheet" type="text/css"
href="/_layouts/1033/styles/development.css"
/>
```

> *Adding JavaScript to the Master Page functions exactly the same way as adding a reference to a CSS file, except that it goes directly in the* `%Program Files%\Common Files\Microsoft Shared\Web Server Extensions\14\ TEMPLATE\LAYOUTS\1033\` *folder rather than the styles subfolder.*

A good way to start customizing the styles is to copy the existing styles, rename and modify them, and put them in your new style sheet.

To copy the existing styles when you're not on the SharePoint machine, right-click a SharePoint page and view the source. Copy the contents of the `href` attribute, and paste them at the end of the site URL. For example, `href="/_catalogs/theme/Themed/EC8F5A82/corev4-8A0ABD2F`.

css?ctag=4"/> for the site http://bi.sharepoint.com will become http://bi.sharepoint
.com/_catalogs/theme/Themed/EC8F5A82/corev4-8A0ABD2F.css?ctag=4. Save this file to
your local machine to have a separate copy of the file. You can then upload this style sheet to a
SharePoint library to use instead of using the folder structure on the server.

For instance, if you wanted to change the styling of the title, start by browsing to the title placeholder — <asp:ContentPlaceHolder id="PlaceHolderSiteName" runat="server">. In this
case, the style is held in the tag containing the placeholder, as shown in Figure 23-11.

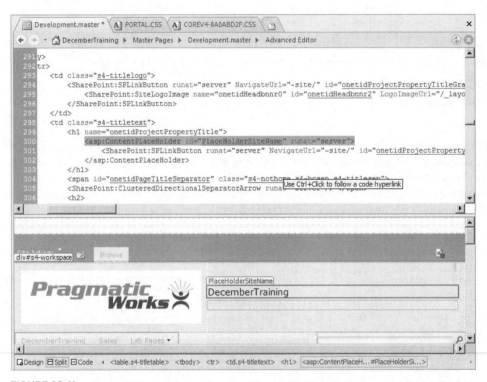

FIGURE 23-11

The CSS class is s4-titletext. Hold down the Ctrl key, and click s4-titletext to jump to the
class definition. As shown in Figure 23-12, the appropriate style sheet from the current theme will
be opened.

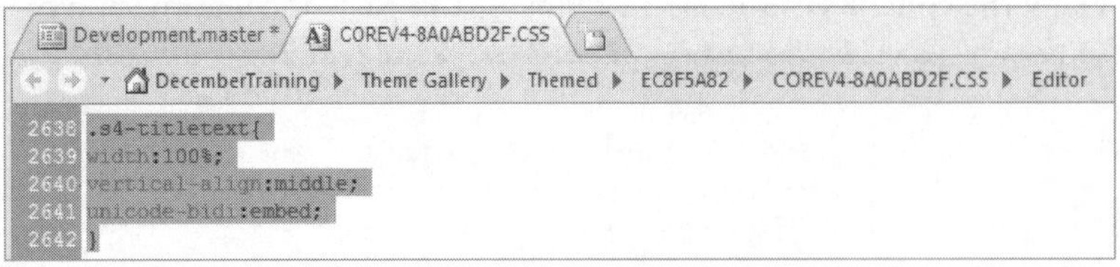

FIGURE 23-12

Editing the style sheet here will apply to this theme only. Often, this will be a good approach during development and testing. When moving to a production system, it is a good idea to do a new style sheet file to remove any irrelevant styles.

However, these are cascading style sheets, so multiple styles may apply. Do a search for `s4-titletext` to find any other styles that will be applied, as shown in Figure 23-13.

FIGURE 23-13

In this instance, only the first style will apply, because the subsequent styles require that the other classes are also applied. That is, for the second style to be applied, the class would have to be "s4-titletext ms-titlewpTitleArea".

Copy the entire style into your new CSS file, and rename `s4-titletext` to `dev-titletext`, to give the code below as the sole contents of your `development.css` file. Add an additional line to align the text to the center.

The contents of Development.css should be the following:

```
.dev-titletext{
width:100%;
vertical-align:middle;
unicode-bidi:embed;

align:center;
}
```

The final step is to change the reference in the class name, to look like this : `<td class="dev-titletext">`.

This stepwise editing of existing styles is a good way to learn how CSS works — for a complete restyle, it is better to create a new set of styles and build them into the Master Page.

TRY IT

In this Try It, you copy the master page and customize it to have a new, more minimal look.

Lesson Requirements

Copy the `v4.master` file in the Master Pages library to `dev-minimal.master`, and create a `dev-minimal.css` to store your style changes. Delete the search box and help icon, and move the left-hand nav to sit in their place. Remove the Recycle Bin and All Site Content menu items. Make this navigation bar horizontal, with flyouts for the second menu rather than static menu items.

Hints

➤ Reuse the styles of the `<div>` around the search box to position the left-hand navigation correctly in its new position.

➤ If you need to go back and edit changes to your CSS, you will need to restart IIS. Do this by going Start ➪ Run and typing **IISReset**, then hitting Enter.

➤ When searching for tags, search for the ID if the whole value isn't found, to allow for whitespace differences.

The final contents of your `dev-minimal.css file` should look like the code below:

```
.dev-spacer{
padding:0px !important;
}
.dev-rp{
float:right;
padding:2px 10px 2px 5px;
}
.dev-rp div,.dev-lpi div{
display:inline;
}

.dev-ca{
 background:#fff;
margin-left:0px;
margin-right:0px;
min-height:324px;
}
```

Step-by-Step

1. Create an empty `dev-minimal.css` in `%Program Files%\Common Files\Microsoft Shared\Web Server Extensions\14\TEMPLATE\LAYOUTS\1033\styles`. Add this line to include a reference to the original CSS file: `@import "corev4.ss";`

2. Copy `v4.master` to `dev-minimal.master` by copying, pasting, and renaming the new file. Click Yes when asked about changing attached pages.

3. Edit `dev-minimal.master` by right-clicking and selecting Edit File in Advanced Mode.

4. Click Yes when SharePoint Designer asks if you want to check the file out.

5. Search for `<div id="s4-searcharea" class="s4-search s4-rp">`.

6. Delete `<SharePoint:DelegateControl runat="server" ControlId="SmallSearchInputBox" Version="4"/>` to remove the search box.

7. Delete all content between and including the `<span class="s4-help">` and `</span>` tags to remove the help box.

8. Ctrl-click `s4-search`, and copy the highlighted text to your new CSS file. Rename `s4-search` to `dev-spacer`.

9. Return to the Master Page and Ctrl-click `s4-rp`, and copy the highlighted text to your new CSS file. Rename the CSS class `s4-rp` to `dev-rp`.

Also copy:

```
.s4-rp div,.s4-lpi div{
display:inline;
}
```

This code sits directly below the previous piece of code, and we are copying it because, as a style applying to `s4-rp`, we need to include the style changes it applies.

10 Change the `s4` in the text you just copied to `dev`.

11. Change the two class references to the new names, and rename the `div` to `dev-rightpanel`:

```
<div id="dev-rightpanel" class="dev-spacer dev-rp">
```

12. Cut all the code inside the `<div id="s4-leftpanel-content">` and `</div>` closing tags. The easiest way to do this is to highlight this tag by clicking in the design surface, or by right-clicking on the tag and clicking Select Tag, then cutting all of it, pasting it into Notepad, and deleting the open and close tags before copying again. See Figure 23-14 for the highlighted text. This is just some of the appropriate text; it is a large section.

13. Look for all instances of `StaticDisplayLevels="2"` within the code you pasted and change them to `StaticDisplayLevels="1"`.

14. Look for all instances of `DynamicDisplayLevels="0"` within the code you pasted and change them to `DynamicDisplayLevels="1"`.

15. Look for all instances of `Orientation="Vertical"` within the code you pasted and change them to `Orientation="Horizontal"`. See Figure 23-15 for an example.

16. Paste this code between the `<div id="dev-rightpanel" class="dev-spacer dev-rp">` and `</div>` tags. Put it directly after the opening tag, and before any other content in this tag.

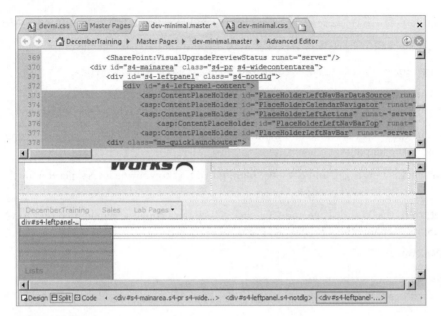

FIGURE 23-14

```
382
383 lse" Orientation="Horizontal" StaticDisplayLevels="1" MaximumDynamicDisplayLevels="1" SkipLinkText="" Css
```

FIGURE 23-15

The full code after making the changes is included on the website at www.wrox.com.

17. Find the tag `<asp:ContentPlaceHolder id="PlaceHolderQuickLaunchBottom" runat="server">` and delete it, and everything until the next closing `</asp:ContentPlaceHolder>` tag. Make sure to keep these opening and closing tags and only delete the content. Select the tag, copy to Notepad, and paste it back once you've deleted the content inside.

18. Find the tag starting `<SharePoint:AspMenu ID="TopNavigationMenuV4"` (remember to search for the TopNavigationMenuV4 to find this tag), and copy its CSS class value — s4-tn. This is the top navigation menu, and all you need is this class name.

19. Search for the tag starting with `<SharePoint:AspMenu id="V4QuickLaunchMenu"`. This is the left navigation menu. Replace the current CSS class value (s4-ql) with the value copied in the previous step—s4-tn. This will give the new navigation the same formatting as the old one.

20. Search for the tag `<div class="s4-ca s4-ca-dlgNoRibbon" id="MSO_ContentTable" style="left: 0px; top: 0px">` — this is the tag containing the main content on the page.

21. Ctrl-click s4-ca.

22. Copy the content into dev-minimal.css, changing the name to dev-ca.

23. Change the left margin to be 0, as in the following code:

```
.dev-ca{
background:#fff;
margin-left:0px;
margin-right:0px;
min-height:324px;
}
```

24. Change the class reference in the master page to be `dev-ca` instead of `s4-ca`, as shown in Figure 23-16. Change back to the master page tab where you did the Ctrl-Click in order to do this.

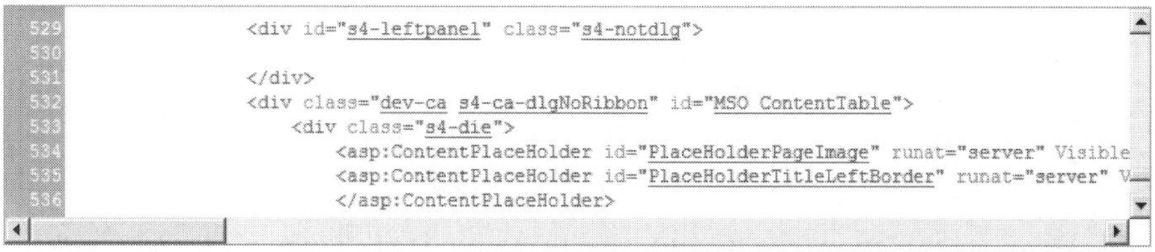

```
529        <div id="s4-leftpanel" class="s4-notdlg">
530
531        </div>
532        <div class="dev-ca s4-ca-dlgNoRibbon" id="MSO_ContentTable">
533            <div class="s4-die">
534                <asp:ContentPlaceHolder id="PlaceHolderPageImage" runat="server" Visible
535                <asp:ContentPlaceHolder id="PlaceHolderTitleLeftBorder" runat="server" V
536                </asp:ContentPlaceHolder>
```

FIGURE 23-16

25. Save the css file.

26. Save the master page. Click Yes when the message box asking about customizing the page from the site definition comes up.

27. Click Master Pages on the left menu.

28. Right-click `dev-minimal` and choose Check-in.

29. Select Publish a Major Version.

30. Click Yes to approve the document.

31. On the page that opens, scroll over `dev-minimal`, and choose Approve/Reject from the drop-down menu.

32. Select Approved and click OK.

33. Click Site Actions ➪ Site Settings.

34. Click on Manage Site Features under Site Actions.

35. If the SharePoint Server Publishing feature is not active, click on Activate.

36. Click on Site Settings in the breadcrumb.

37. Click Master Pages under Look and Feel.

38. Select `dev-minimal` in both drop-downs, and set the CSS file to be used to

```
/_Layouts/1033/styles/dev-minimal.css
```

as shown in Figure 23-17.

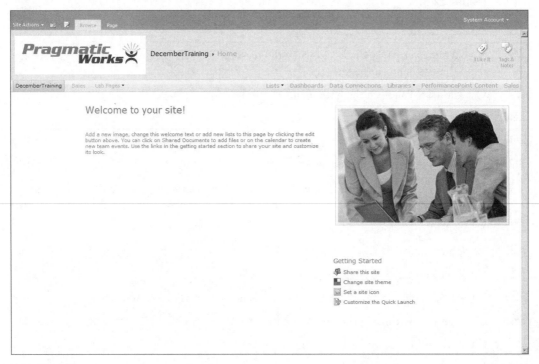

Site Master Page

The site master page will be used by all publishing pages. Select the first option to inherit the site master page of the parent site. Select the second option to select a unique master page. Check the box to apply this setting to all subsites.

- ○ Inherit site master page from parent of this site
- ● Specify a master page to be used by this site and all sites that inherit from it:

  `dev_minimal.master ▾`

- ☐ Reset all subsites to inherit this site master page setting

System Master Page

Use the system master page for all forms and view pages in this site. Select the first option to inherit the system master page of the parent site. Select the second option to select a unique master page. Check the box to apply this setting to all subsites.

- ○ Inherit system master page from parent of this site
- ● Specify a system master page for this site and all sites that inherit from it:

  `dev_minimal.master ▾`

  Specify a system master page for this site and all sites inherit from it:

- ☐ Reset all subsites to inherit this system master page setting

FIGURE 23-17

39. Click OK.

40. Click the site title to see the master page being used, as shown in Figure 23-18.

FIGURE 23-18

Please select Lesson 23 on the DVD to view the video that accompanies this lesson.

24

Controlling Your Reporting with Versioning, Auditing, and Content Expiration

Now that your reports are developed and deployed to your SharePoint site, you must ensure that the site can consistently provide a stable environment in which your users can work. To do this, certain policies and principles should be put in place that govern how and when items are developed and implemented. This should guarantee that things such as navigation, look and feel, and menus are common across the entire site. If the menus on one Business Intelligence site differ from that of another common site, imagine how much confusion would have to be resolved among the end users. In this lesson you will learn how to implement strategies that will assist you in applying governance policies and procedures in regard to your SharePoint design and deployment methodologies.

SHAREPOINT GOVERNANCE AS APPLIED TO BUSINESS INTELLIGENCE

As mentioned, when designing your SharePoint Business Intelligence solution and the corresponding objects, you and your team should adhere to a certain set of predefined policies and procedures. These policies and procedures are also known as *governance*. This governance is the driving force behind your design standards, version control, and auditing. When creating your PowerPivot Workbooks, SQL Reports, and PerformancePoint Dashboards, you should follow any design principles that have been defined as part of your governance.

Often the most difficult part of SharePoint governance is getting started. Typically the starting point is creating a governance committee, which should consist of individuals from the entire company. As a team, this group should be able to define the policies and procedures and meet the needs of the entire organization. In addition, this group creates a process that reviews, in this case, all the Business Intelligence initiatives and structure that support all end user questions, concerns, and issues. One of the final, but probably most significant products of this teamwork is a framework lifecycle, which will be used to develop all Business Intelligence content. There may be multiple frameworks, which will depend on the type of content that will be developed and deployed.

REPORTING LIFECYCLE FOR SELF-SERVICE BI ENVIRONMENT

As mentioned in the previous section, it is important to develop a lifecycle framework for your BI SharePoint environment. This lifecycle should ensure that each step in the report definition, creation, deployment, and management is identical for all reports. The framework will also enforce use of the governance that has already been put in place. A typical report lifecycle resembles Figure 24-1.

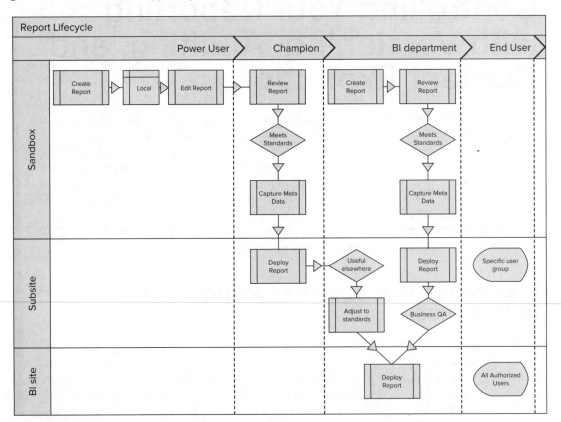

FIGURE 24-1

The first step is the creation of the report by a power user. This typically occurs on their local machine or in a sandbox environment. The sandbox is not a development or production environment. Once the user is satisfied with the report, he or she may decide that the report should be deployed. Prior to deployment, a member of the governance team reviews the report and ensures that it meets all the policies, procedures, and standards. In addition, documentation will be created for the report and its content. Finally, the report is deployed. In some environments there is a subsite, which may be a location specific for individual users, groups, or departments. If this is the case, the report will be deployed there. If not, the report will go the BI department.

The BI department may simply deploy the report to a site for Quality Assurance or they may determine that it could be useful in other areas. If the latter is the case, the report will undergo another round of standards review. Once the review is complete, the report will be deployed to the BI site. At this point those authorized users will have access to view the report.

USING ANALYTICS AND CONTENT EXPIRATION

Now that you have implemented a Self-Service BI Environment lifecycle framework, how are you going to manage all the reports that your end users create and deploy into SharePoint? Fortunately for you, SharePoint 2010 provides a centralized way to manage, maintain, and monitor this type of environment. For example, using the PowerPivot Management Dashboard, which is part of the Central Administration console, you can view various metrics about all the PowerPivot workbooks that have been created and deployed.

To access the dashboard, open the Central Administration console, click General Application Settings, and click Management Dashboard under the PowerPivot heading. The first graph, as shown in Figure 24-2, displays overall server health.

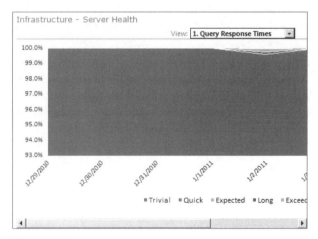

FIGURE 24-2

By default the graph shows Query Response Time. You can change the view of the graph by changing the selected value in the drop-down list labeled View, which is located directly above the graph.

Below the Server Health graph is the Workbook Activity chart, as shown in Figure 24-3. In this chart you see a time-series visualization that shows you PowerPivot workbook activity over time.

The size of each circle represents the size of each workbook. If you hover over a circle on the chart, it displays a tooltip that provides detailed information about a certain workbook. You can actually play the timeline to see changes in how workbooks are being used and how many users are using them. To play the timeline, click the slide and drag it back to the beginning of the chart. Then click the green play button, which is located below the chart.

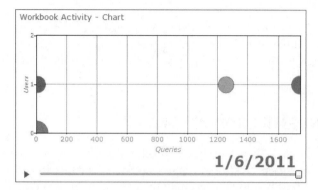

FIGURE 24-3

Now that your users are creating and deploying reports, you will need to know how to manage all this new content. Because the reports are all stored in a somewhat centralized repository, the process of managing the content should not be too difficult. As with most administrative items, SharePoint 2010 contains features that assist the IT staff in accomplishing this task. Typically when end users are given the ability to create reports, the end result is an enormous amount of unused or out-of-date items. In an effort to proactively mitigate this problem, Microsoft includes the concept of *policies*. Four types of polices can be created: Expiration, Auditing, Labels, and Barcodes. This book focuses on the Expiration policy.

The Expiration policy should help organizations delete or remove out-of-date content from their sites in a manner that is consistent and that can be tracked. To configure an Expiration policy, browse to your main BI site. Locate Site Actions in the top-left corner and click the drop-down arrow to the right. Select Site Settings from the list of available choices. You will be presented with several choices on the Site Settings page. Under the Site Collection Administration category click Site Collection Policies. On the Policies page, as shown in Figure 24-4, click Create.

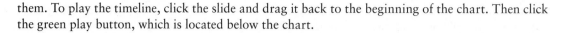

FIGURE 24-4

You will be directed to the Edit Policy page, as shown in Figure 24-5.

FIGURE 24-5

On this page, as mentioned earlier, you can specify policies for retention (expiration) auditing, labels, and barcodes. However, before specifying either you need to name your policy and specify an Administrative Description and a Policy Statement. The Administrative Description is what list managers will see. The Policy Statement will be seen by end users when they open items that are subject to that policy. Next you should check the box labeled Enable Retention. Doing this will allows you to schedule how the content is managed and disposed. Then click Add a Retention Stage, which appears after Enable Retention is checked. You will then be presented with the Stage Properties Webpage Dialog box, which is shown in Figure 24-6.

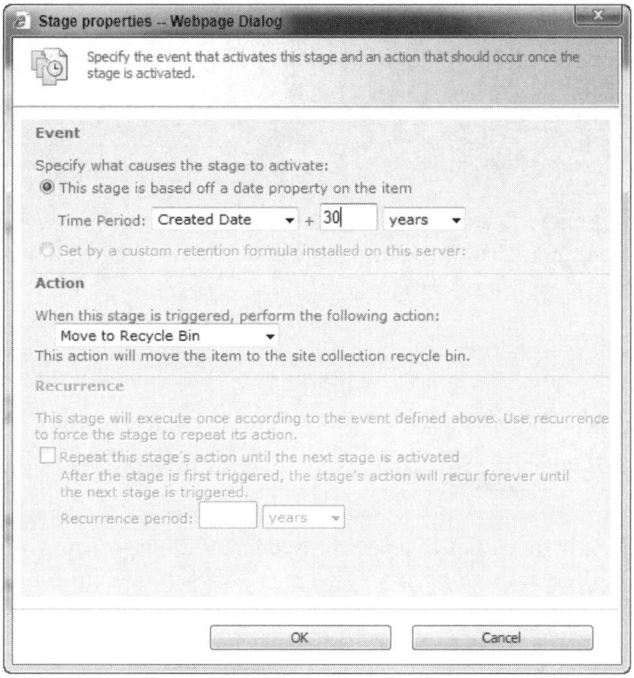

FIGURE 24-6

On this page you must first select the date that will determine the retention period and how many years, days, or months to add to that date. For example, if you want content to be deleted 30 days after it was created in a specific library, type 30 in the text box after the plus sign and select Days from the drop-down list. Finally, in the Action section you must specify what to do with the content if it meets the Expiration policy. You have several choices to choose from. In this case, select Move to Recycle Bin.

Once the policy is created, you must apply it to a list or library. To do this, locate a content library, and on the ribbon locate the Library Tools tab and select Library. On the Library ribbon select Library Settings. In the Permissions and Manage section click Information Management Policy Settings. Select Document or Folder from the Content Type column. For this example, we selected Document. On the right side of the Document page, shown in Figure 24-7, you can specify a policy by defining a new one or using a site collection policy.

FIGURE 24-7

Because you have already created one, select the radio button next to Use a Site Collection Policy. Select the name of the policy that was created earlier and click OK.

TRY IT

In this Try It you first create a site collection policy and then apply the policy to a document library.

Lesson Requirements

In this lesson, you create a site collection policy. The policy will delete the content that exists in a document library 30 days after its creation. In addition, you apply the policy to an existing document library.

Hints

➤ Use the Site Actions button on your main Business Intelligence site.

➤ The site collection policy is located under the Site Collection Administration section of the Site Settings page.

➤ Use the Library Settings item to apply the policy to a specific document library.

Step-by-Step

1. Navigate to your main Business Intelligence site.

2. Locate the Site Actions button on the top-left corner of the page.

3. Click the drop-down arrow located to the right of the work Site Actions box.

4. Click Site Settings, which is the last item in the list, as shown in Figure 24-8.

5. Under the Site Collection Administration section, locate and click Site Collection Policies as shown in Figure 24-9.

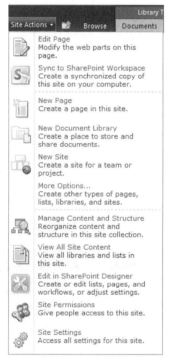

FIGURE 24-8

FIGURE 24-9

6. Click the button labeled Create on the Policies page.

7. In the text box labeled Name, which is located on the right side of the page, enter **30 Day Deletion**.

8. In the text box labeled Administrative Description enter **This policy will delete content 30 days after the creation date.**

9. In the text box labeled Policy Statement enter **This policy will delete content 30 days after you create it.**

10. Check the box labeled Enable Retention. Once done, Add a Retention Stage will appear as shown in Figure 24-10.

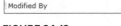

11. Click Add a Retention Stage and the Stage Properties dialog box will appear.

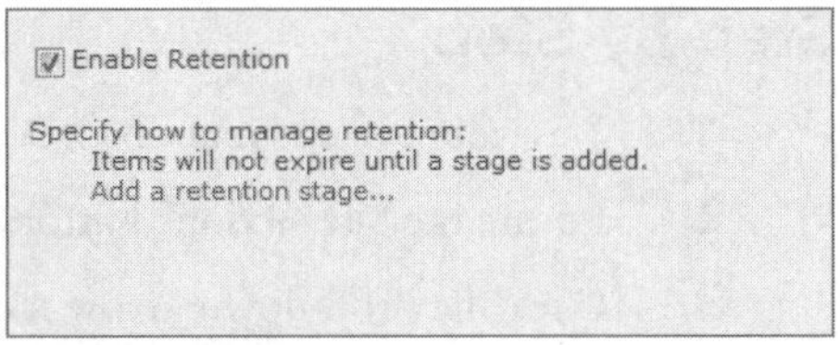

12. In the drop-down list labeled Time Period select Create Date and enter 30 in the next text box. Finally, select Days from the drop-down list that currently contains Years.

FIGURE 24-10

13. In the Action section select Move to Recycle Bin in the drop-down list labeled "When this stage is triggered, perform the following action."

14. Click OK to close the Stage properties dialog box.

15. Click OK to close the Edit Policy Page.

16. On the left side of the Policies page click the item labeled All Site Content, as shown in Figure 24-11.

17. Click the document library named Documents.

18. On the top ribbon under the Library Tools tab select Library.

19. Click the item labeled Library Settings, as shown in Figure 24-12.

FIGURE 24-11

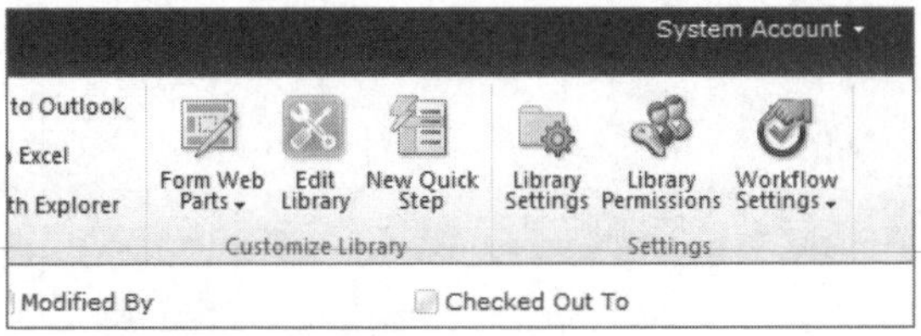

FIGURE 24-12

20. Under the Permissions and Management section click Information Management Policy Settings.

21. In the list on the Policy Setting page click Document.

22. On this page, select the radio button labeled Use a Site Collection Policy, which is located in the right section of the page, as shown in Figure 24-13, and select the 30 Day Deletion policy you just created.

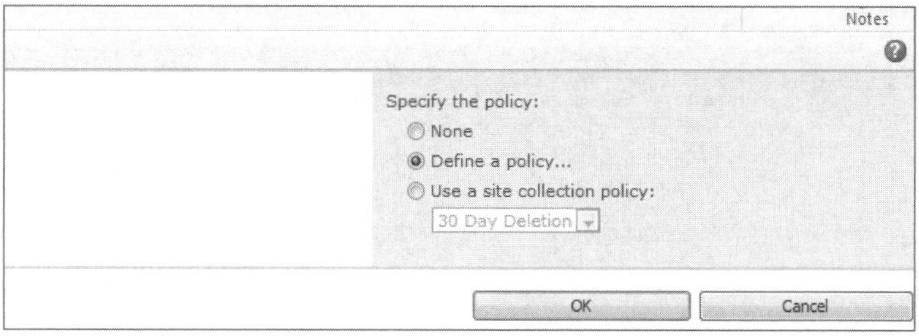

Specify the policy:

- ○ None
- ⦿ Define a policy...
- ○ Use a site collection policy:
  30 Day Deletion ▾

Notes

OK   Cancel

FIGURE 24-13

23.   Click OK.

 Please select Lesson 24 on the DVD to view the video that accompanies this lesson.

25

Managing Report Approval with SharePoint Workflow

In SharePoint workflow, it is important that the Require Content Approval option in the Library Settings be set to Yes. Otherwise, content will be published automatically. You can find this option under Versioning Settings on the Library Settings page. Also be sure to set the Draft Item Security options on the same page so only approvers and the person who published the document can view it before it is approved.

In this lesson, you will learn how your organization can benefit from using SharePoint workflow. You will also learn how to enable and implement this useful feature.

INTRODUCTION TO SHAREPOINT WORKFLOW

Workflows in SharePoint are a great way to automate business processes. This may be a very simple task such as managing a set of values on a SharePoint list. For instance, there may be a list of products and a price associated with each. If this list is supposed to contain only items that are proposed new products that have a price tag of under $1000, a workflow could automate that process. Rather than having an employee monitor the list and remove items that have a value listed in the price column of $1000 or more, a combination of approval and workflows can take care of this. Simply tell the list that all items must be approved before being shown, and create a workflow that will look at all new list entries and automatically switch them to Rejected if the price is $1000 or greater. Even a very simple example such as this can save considerable time and money in the long term.

Some places where workflows can help your business may include:

➤ Escalating tasks that have gone past their due date

➤ Report approval

➤ Travel reimbursement approval

➤ Human Resources tasks

➤ Task tracking through a team of developers

Not all business processes are going to be that cut and dry. More often than not they are much more complicated. Someone will inevitably have to review a portion of the work or item uploaded, especially in the case of dashboard content, Excel workbooks, and Word files. Workflows can still assist in this process to help alleviate some of the communication breakdowns that can prove to be very costly.

The process of approving a report can be quite cumbersome in certain situations; for instance, if a report needs to have the approval of all members of a team before being approved. An e-mail may be sent out from the report writer to your management staff of five people. Three of those five see that the report meets their portion of the requirements and approve it. However, the other two staff members do not see all of their requirements being met. To fix this, a series of e-mails and phone calls may take place and the staff members who were satisfied may be left out of the loop by accident. Fortunately, a workflow could be customized and created for purposes such as this.

The goal of a workflow shouldn't necessarily be to automate the entire process, because that could be an unrealistic goal in many cases. Workflows should, however, help automate the collaboration and communication process between individuals. As a result, you will notice a streamlined process, which will raise your organization's efficiency and ultimately lower downtime and mishaps.

In the preceding example of the team approving an item, the process was not fully automated. A workflow could have allowed each member of the team to make comments on the pending report, approve or reject accordingly, and have the report sent back to the person who authored it. Everyone would have known that the report was ultimately rejected and would be waiting to review it again as soon as the changes were made, eliminating confusion around why the report had not yet been made live.

Many organizations struggle to build and maintain standards. Oftentimes a standard is designed and documented but difficult to implement or track. Workflows help maintain the standards necessary to keep certain processes running at an efficient level. If all contracts for an organization are required to go to the legal department before being signed by anyone in upper management, a workflow could help keep that standard in place. Without it, a contract could inadvertently be passed to the president and get signed without being reviewed by the legal department. However, a workflow set up to monitor new documents being added to a Contracts document library could notify legal for approval before notifying the president. Not only does this help keep the process going in the correct order, but it also helps ensure that the right people are involved each step of the way.

Seven templates are included in SharePoint 2010 to help get you started:

➤ Approval

➤ Collect Feedback

➤ Collect Signatures

➤ Disposition Approval

➤ Issue Tracking

➤ Three-State

➤ Translation Management

Each of these has its own unique advantage. Later, this lesson focuses on a derivative of the Approval template.

You have several options for creating and customizing workflows: SharePoint Designer 2010, Visio 2010, and Visual Studio 2010. Each has its own learning curve and advantages.

Workflows can be created and used in association with a list, library, or content type. If a workflow is added directly to a list, it can only be used there. Conversely, if you create a global workflow, it can be assigned to multiple lists or libraries.

This lesson focuses on workflows being used for report approvals.

BUILDING SIMPLE WORKFLOWS FOR REPORT APPROVAL

The easiest way to build workflows in SharePoint 2010 is by using the SharePoint Designer 2010 available for download free from Microsoft. Once the SharePoint Designer is installed, you can access it from the Start menu or from the Site Actions menu, as shown in Figure 25-1. If you are opening the site from inside SharePoint Designer, simply enter the URL of your site and all your site information will be loaded.

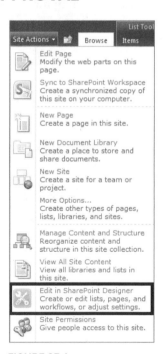

FIGURE 25-1

Once your site is open for editing in the designer, click the Workflows icon on the left side of the screen, as shown in Figure 25-2. Several pre-made workflows will be shown in the window: Approval, Collect Feedback, Collect Signatures, and Publishing Approval. If you are not a site administrator and you click any of the predefined workflows, a message will appear for you to edit a copy. Either way, it is generally a good idea to create a copy of any workflow you want to change so that if anything breaks, you have a safety net to fall back on.

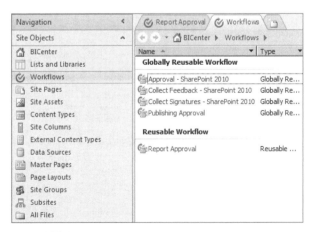

FIGURE 25-2

You can build your own workflows by clicking Reusable Workflow or selecting a list from the drop-down. Another option, which for simple tasks is a great choice, is to edit one of the existing work-flows. As mentioned before, it is a good idea to make a copy before making changes. To create a copy of an existing workflow, right-click it then select Copy and Modify. Change the name to some-thing unique that identifies the workflow's function and click OK. The copy of the workflow will open automatically. Click the Save button and close the newly created workflow. This will bring you back to the Workflows tab that was previously open where you will see the copy has been added to the list. If you click the Approval workflow that is already in place and then click the Edit Workflow button in the center of the page, you will notice there is only one step in the workflow. This step will run the Approval process. Click Approval, which is underlined, to open the options for this process.

Under the Customization section there is an option to Change the Behavior of a Single Task. This will allow you to edit the individual tasks that make up the process. You can edit any of these items such as logging and notifications, customize e-mails, and add or remove steps you don't want to include. Click the link for Change the Completion Conditions for This Task Process. The screen shown in Figure 25-3 will appear and you will be able to change options such as number of users who have to approve the item before it is shown as approved in the library. You can change this to a lower number or even a percentage of approvers.

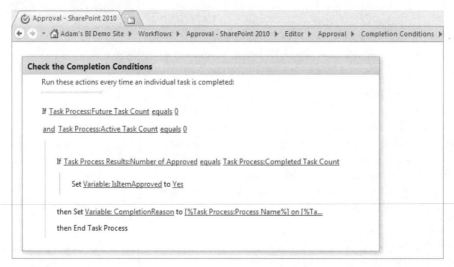

FIGURE 25-3

Click the Workflow Settings icon on the ribbon to return to the workflow editor. There are several important options to take into consideration when customizing this workflow. They are Disable Automatic Start on Item Creation and Disable Automatic Start on Item Change, as shown in Figure 25-4. Checking these prevents those options from being used and thus prevents the workflow from being run accidentally.

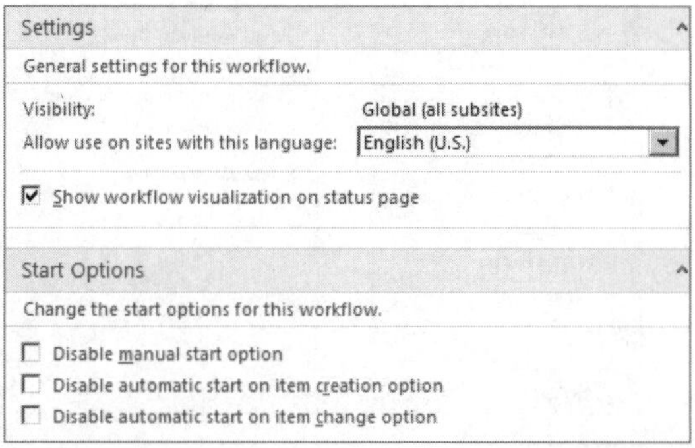

FIGURE 25-4

While still on the workflow editor screen, the link for Initiation Form Parameters on the ribbon will allow you to customize the form used when setting up and starting the workflow. Here you can change the fields that are available to the users and add new fields as well.

Once all your options are set up the way you want, this workflow is ready to be used in conjunction with your SharePoint library. Just click the Save button and then Publish from the ribbon. The workflow will be validated and if there are no errors, it will be deployed and ready to use. Change as many settings as you would like or change no settings at all. Either way, this is a very easy way to get an approval workflow created complete with notifications and a simple set of parameters.

USING VISIO TO BUILD WORKFLOWS

One of your options for creating workflows for SharePoint is Visio 2010. Workflows can be created and imported into the SharePoint Designer for deployment to your site. To create a workflow in Visio 2010, click New and select the Flowchart category from the template selection screen. Then select the Microsoft SharePoint Workflow template, as shown in Figure 25-5. Click the Create button on the far right side of the screen to open the blank document.

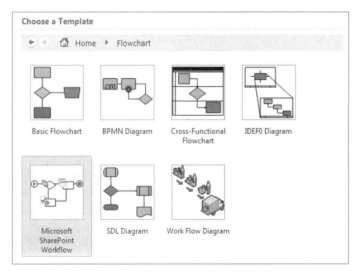

FIGURE 25-5

The left side of the screen, as shown in Figure 25-6, shows the toolbox that contains all the items necessary to create a workflow. These items include the Start and Stop functionality listed under the SharePoint Workflow Terminators as well as all the actions, such as sending e-mail, under the SharePoint Workflow Actions. Simply drag and drop the items you want to be a part of your workflow. Be sure to always start the workflow with the Start icon and always end it with the Terminate icon.

Once you have your workflow created, save it someplace on your local system. When saving locally, you will save the file as a standard Visio diagram. This will enable you to make changes at a later date if necessary. Then click the Process tab at the top of the ribbon and choose Export. The workflow will be validated and require you to resolve any issues. You will then be prompted to save the export to your machine; this will be in the form of a Visio Workflow Interchange (.vwi file). In the

SharePoint Designer go back to the main Workflow page. On the ribbon at the top select Import from Visio and locate the `.vwi` file on your machine. Select whether the workflow is to be reusable or assigned to an existing SharePoint object and click Finish. Finally, the workflow will be opened; make any modifications necessary then save and publish. A sample of what the workflow will look like in Visio is shown in Figure 25-7.

FIGURE 25-6

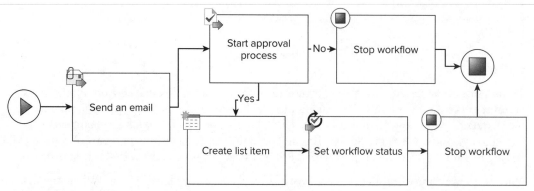

FIGURE 25-7

TRY IT

In this Try It, you create a workflow to allow users to approve or deny reports that are deployed to a SharePoint library.

Lesson Requirements

Create a workflow that will change the status of an uploaded Excel workbook to Approved or Rejected based on the end users' feedback. It should be set up so that if 80 percent of the users accept it, the status will be set to Approved. You will need to use an already existing Excel library.

Hints

- ➤ Use SharePoint Designer 2010.
- ➤ Modify the preexisting Approval workflow.
- ➤ You will need to change the completion condition in the Approval process.
- ➤ The workflow should run automatically anytime a new Excel sheet is uploaded.
- ➤ Enable content approval on your library.

Step-by-Step

1. Open Internet Explorer and enter the URL to your SharePoint site.
2. Navigate to the library called Excel Reports.
3. Under Library Tools on the ribbon click Library.
4. Select Library Settings on the right side of the ribbon.
5. Click the Versioning Settings link.
6. Change the Content Approval option to Yes and Draft Item Security to Only Users Who Can Approve Items (and the author of the item).
7. Click OK.
8. Open SharePoint Designer 2010.
9. Click Open Site, enter the URL for your site, and click Open.
10. Under Site Objects select Workflows.

11. Right-click the item labeled Approval – SharePoint 2010 and select Copy and Modify.

12. In the Name field enter **Excel Reports**. The screen should look like Figure 25-8. Click OK.

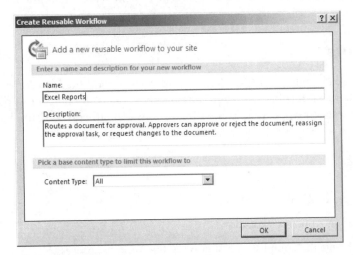

FIGURE 25-8

13. The workflow editor will appear. Click the link between the words "Start" and "process" to open that process.

14. Click the link for Change the Completion Conditions for This Task Process under the Customization section.

15. Locate the second IF statement.

16. Click the text Task Process Requests Number of Approved.

17. Change the Field From Source value to Percentage of Approved.

18. Click the word "equals" to open the drop-down menu.

19. Change the option to Is Greater Than or Equal To.

20. Click the blue link labeled Value and enter the number 80.

21. When your screen looks like Figure 25-9, click Save on the ribbon and then click Publish.

22. Go back to your SharePoint site (it should still be open).

23. If the Library Settings page is not still open, navigate back to it.

24. Select the option for Workflow Settings under the Permissions And Management section.

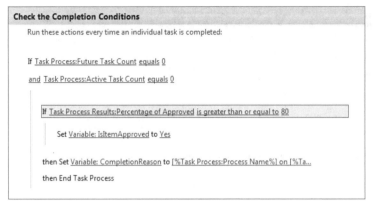

Check the Completion Conditions

Run these actions every time an individual task is completed:

If Task Process:Future Task Count equals 0

and Task Process:Active Task Count equals 0

> If Task Process Results:Percentage of Approved is greater than or equal to 80
>
> Set Variable: IsItemApproved to Yes
>
> then Set Variable: CompletionReason to [%Task Process:Process Name%] on [%Ta...
>
> then End Task Process

FIGURE 25-9

25. In the Workflow section highlight Excel Reports, the workflow you just created and published.

26. In the Name box type **Excel Report Approval**.

27. Make note of the list that is shown next to the Task List option because you will need to navigate to this list later.

28. Check the box next to Start the Workflow When a New Item Is Created. This allows the workflow to start automatically, as was mentioned in the requirements.

29. Click Next and enter all the users who will be doing report approval. In this case enter only your account.

30. In the Request box enter a note for the recipient. For instance, **A new report has been published, please review**.

31. Click Save.

32. Navigate back to your Excel library and upload any Excel workbook. Give it just a moment and then refresh the page. The last column should be labeled Excel Report Approval and say In Progress next to your Excel workbook. The Approval Status should read Pending.

33. Navigate to the task list that you made note of previously in step 28.

34. In this list click the title for the workbook you just uploaded. It will read Not Started in the Status column.

35. A box will appear for you to enter comments and choose to approve, reject, request changes, or reassign approval to someone else. Click Approve. The screen will look like Figure 25-10.

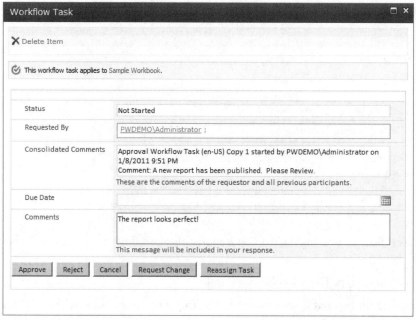

FIGURE 25-10

Congratulations, you have just created and used your first workflow. Workflow creation can get complicated, so be sure to test each thoroughly. Also, don't forget that custom code can be added when creating workflows in Visual Studio 2010. That is, however, outside the scope of this book.

 Please select Lesson 25 on the DVD to view the video that accompanies this lesson.

26

Setting Up SharePoint Search to Catalog Analytics and Reports

This lesson covers the basics of search in SharePoint 2010. Search is important in the context of Business Intelligence because once you create all those great reports and store them in SharePoint, you need a great way to quickly find what you're looking for without manually clicking your way through different team sites, document libraries, and attached file servers.

This lesson goes through the basics of search, the different types of search offered in SharePoint, and how to configure basic search in SharePoint to begin seeing value in quickly accessing your Business Intelligence reports.

WHY DO YOU NEED SEARCH?

With the advent of improved search functionality in every aspect of our lives, we've come to expect this functionality from every piece of technology. Our computers have Windows search, our phones have search for both the phone's files and the Internet, and the rise in tablet computers is only driving this further.

Internet search is optimized for following a large number of links throughout the Web, and cataloging the "map" of websites, the sites they link to, and the content in those sites. Internet search has a fatal flaw, though, because it can't reach into the confines of your corporate network and index your files. It certainly can't handle complex situations like Lotus Notes, Domino, or UNIX filesystems.

Many firms have tried the new "all in one" Internet search appliances that are "plug and play" in your environment, but many leave this strategy disappointed. SharePoint search comes to the rescue. With the new architecture improvements and scale out technology allowing over a million items in SharePoint Search and up to a billion items to be indexed with the new FAST Server technology, organizations are now investing significant time and resources into testing and deploying this new technology. New improvements also include wildcard searches, refinement management, and a new AJAX-driven search screen with more real estate.

SharePoint Search Options

The different versions of search include:

➤ SharePoint Foundation Search

➤ SharePoint Server and Search Server

➤ FAST Search Server 2010 for SharePoint and FAST Search Server 2010 for Internet Sites

SharePoint Foundation Search

SharePoint Foundation Search is what this lesson focuses on demonstrating. It is the most basic search functionality, but provides a lot of bang-for-the-buck where BI search is concerned. More functionality for this area is covered later in this lesson. Your search needs may extend beyond this, however, so before we jump into the Search configuration and setup, let's explore the other search options in SharePoint 2010.

Search Server

Some of you may have used Search Server 2008 and will be really impressed by the new improvements in Search Server 2010. This new version is basically an upgrade and includes some exciting new features. These include:

➤ Boolean query support

➤ Wildcard prefixes in your search (*.txt)

➤ Query suggestions

➤ Suggestions for query variations

➤ Refinement panels for users to refine search results

➤ Improvements in relevance of results

➤ Ranking and relevance based on inferred metadata

➤ PowerShell support

➤ Query federation

SharePoint Search 2010

The new SharePoint Search is part of a core shift in enterprise Search technology. This diverges from previous versions of search in SharePoint and other Microsoft Search products. This version is more heavily explored in other texts and online at `Microsoft.com`. It has even stronger features, including:

➤ Social Search

    ➤ Search by location, skills, projects, and expertise

    ➤ Ranking by names, position, or social tags

    ➤ Personal search and improved restrictions on search

- ➤ User Experience Improvements
  - ➤ Best Bets
  - ➤ Query federation
  - ➤ Improved query language with wildcard support, "did you mean," and improved complex Boolean operations
  - ➤ Phonetic Search (in some languages)
  - ➤ Taxonomy Integration
- ➤ Administration
  - ➤ PowerShell scriptable deployments and operation
  - ➤ GUI administration
  - ➤ Systems Center Operations Management Pack
  - ➤ Health Monitoring
  - ➤ PowerShell Configuration Cmdlets
  - ➤ Usage Reporting

Fast Search Server 2010 for SharePoint and FAST Search Server 2010 for Internet Sites

Fast Search is a new technology that was acquired and integrated by Microsoft into a new top-tier enterprise search offering. FAST is beyond the scope of this book, but it's important to know some of the features and improvements that you will get by exploring this technology:

- ➤ Updated, one-stop search center to find items quickly
- ➤ Deep refiners, allowing quick visual exploration or results
- ➤ Additional web parts for improved out-of-the-box user experience and flexibility
- ➤ Visual cues through presentation of visual Best Bets, document previews, and document thumbnails
- ➤ Contextual search to meet the needs of different groups
- ➤ Customizable ranking models
- ➤ Easy to configure end user experiences
- ➤ Advanced query capabilities

SharePoint Foundation Search

Now that you've explored all the options, let's discuss the one you're going to focus on in this lesson. The benefit of Foundation Search is that there is very little to configure or maintain, but it provides some great functionality that users will expect as a minimum in a new solution that is based on the new SharePoint 2010 platform. Let's walk through that setup now.

Configuring Foundation Search in SharePoint 2010

First go to Central Administration and review the services running on the server by going to Manage Services on Server in the upper left. See this list in Figure 26-1.

FIGURE 26-1

Next locate SharePoint Foundation Search in the list of services and click Start. You are presented with an options screen as shown in Figure 26-2.

From here you will configure a few key settings:

➤ **Search Service Account** — Make sure this account is dedicated to this service. You've seen this recommended practice in other services in this book, and it's a good one.

➤ **Content Access Account** — Because this is Foundation Search, you need one account that allows access to all the content you'd like to index on this site. You will use administrator but you should have an account for content access to help control security and account proliferation.

➤ **Search Database** — You can change the location and name of the database for storing search results and configuration. The default should be fine unless you need it on a different server for scalability.

➤ **Specify a failover server** — If you're running this farm and SQL backend in a clustered scenario.

➤ **Configure your index schedule** — Configure indexing to match your needs. Remember to match your need for frequent updates with the performance of your system. Starting with a default of hourly updates is a good place to baseline and then increase frequency based on user feedback or needs.

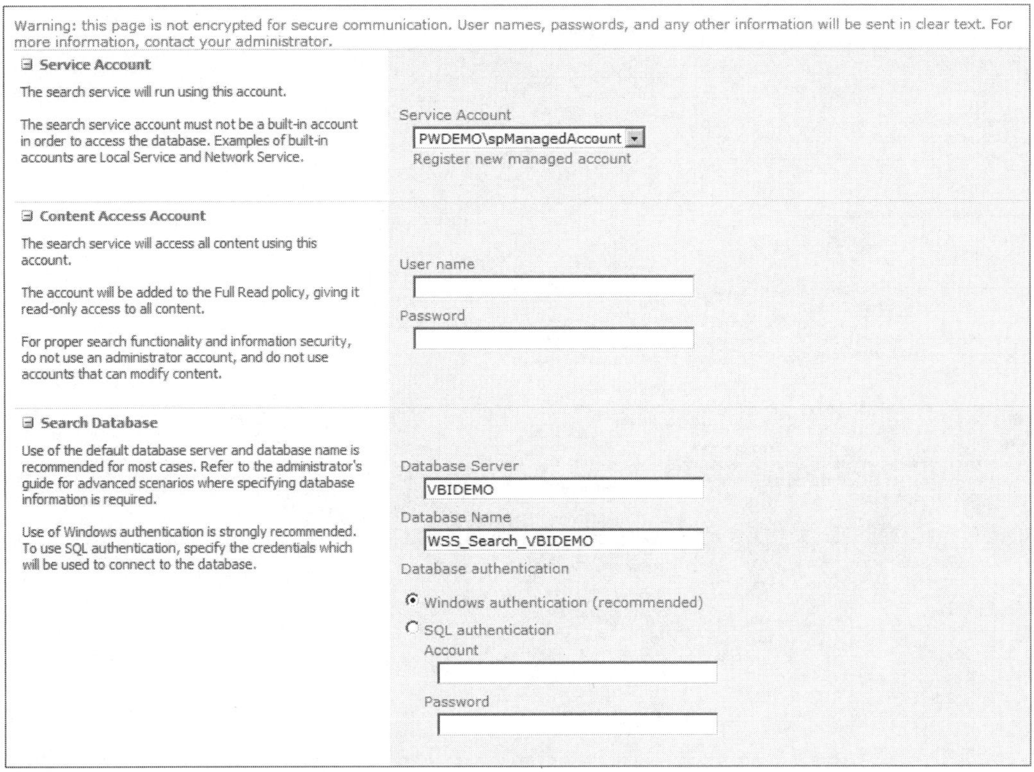

Warning: this page is not encrypted for secure communication. User names, passwords, and any other information will be sent in clear text. For more information, contact your administrator.

Service Account

The search service will run using this account.

The search service account must not be a built-in account in order to access the database. Examples of built-in accounts are Local Service and Network Service.

Service Account

PWDEMO\spManagedAccount

Register new managed account

Content Access Account

The search service will access all content using this account.

The account will be added to the Full Read policy, giving it read-only access to all content.

For proper search functionality and information security, do not use an administrator account, and do not use accounts that can modify content.

User name

Password

Search Database

Use of the default database server and database name is recommended for most cases. Refer to the administrator's guide for advanced scenarios where specifying database information is required.

Use of Windows authentication is strongly recommended. To use SQL authentication, specify the credentials which will be used to connect to the database.

Database Server

VBIDEMO

Database Name

WSS_Search_VBIDEMO

Database authentication

⦿ Windows authentication (recommended)

◯ SQL authentication

Account

Password

FIGURE 26-2

A fully populated configuration is shown in Figures 26-3 and 26-4.

Once you click Start, you will be brought back to the Manage Services Screen, and you need to assign this server as an indexer to each content database.

Under Application Management \ Manage Content Databases, select the name of your content database and select the correct index server. See details in Figure 26-5.

Once that is selected, the next time the indexer runs, a crawl will collect information about your content and process it for searching. If you are impatient you can run an STSadm.exe command to force a full process immediately. The command can be executed from a command prompt as shown in Figure 26-6.

It's important to remember that you either need to be in the SharePoint root directory and then \bin to run this command, or you could open the SharePoint Management Shell because it handles the stsadm.exe portion for you. The message Operation Completed Successfully will return quickly. This does not mean the index is finished, only that the start command was given and accepted by the service. If you want to know when it's finished you can monitor Event Viewer on the computer and look for Event 85: "A master merge has completed for catalog Search." See an example of this in Figure 26-7.

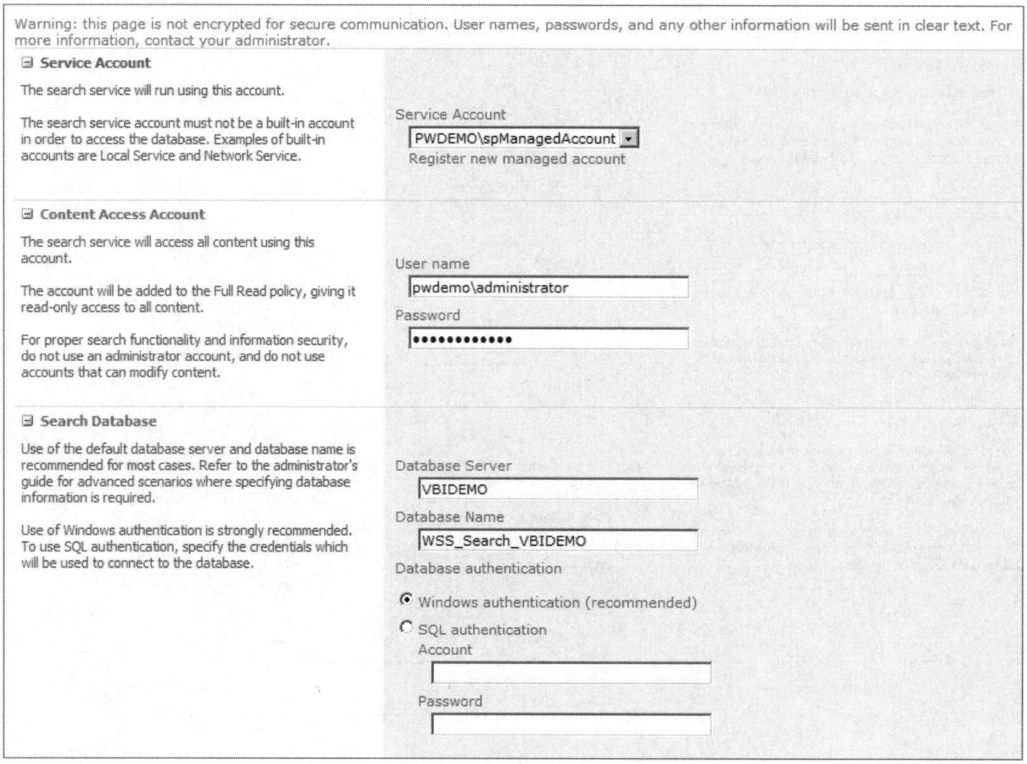

Warning: this page is not encrypted for secure communication. User names, passwords, and any other information will be sent in clear text. For more information, contact your administrator.

⊟ **Service Account**

The search service will run using this account.

The search service account must not be a built-in account in order to access the database. Examples of built-in accounts are Local Service and Network Service.

Service Account

PWDEMO\spManagedAccount ▾

Register new managed account

⊟ **Content Access Account**

The search service will access all content using this account.

The account will be added to the Full Read policy, giving it read-only access to all content.

For proper search functionality and information security, do not use an administrator account, and do not use accounts that can modify content.

User name

pwdemo\administrator

Password

••••••••••••

⊟ **Search Database**

Use of the default database server and database name is recommended for most cases. Refer to the administrator's guide for advanced scenarios where specifying database information is required.

Use of Windows authentication is strongly recommended. To use SQL authentication, specify the credentials which will be used to connect to the database.

Database Server

VBIDEMO

Database Name

WSS_Search_VBIDEMO

Database authentication

⦿ Windows authentication (recommended)

○ SQL authentication

Account

Password

FIGURE 26-3

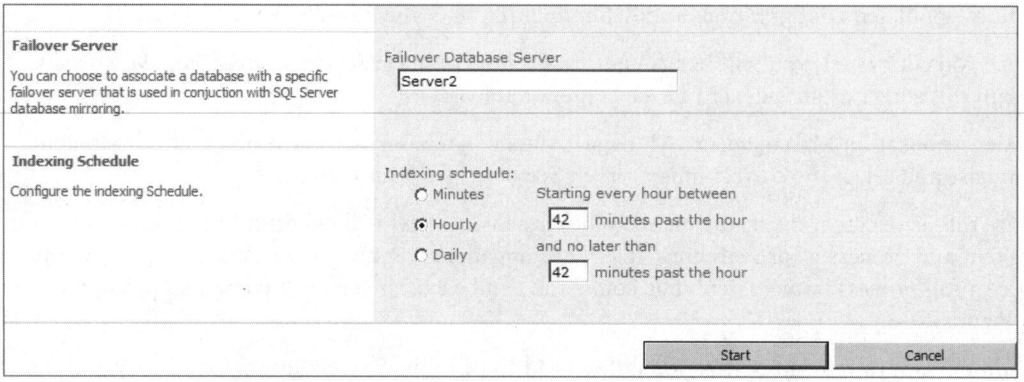

Failover Server

You can choose to associate a database with a specific failover server that is used in conjuction with SQL Server database mirroring.

Failover Database Server

Server2

Indexing Schedule

Configure the indexing Schedule.

Indexing schedule:

○ Minutes

⦿ Hourly

○ Daily

Starting every hour between

42 minutes past the hour

and no later than

42 minutes past the hour

| Start | Cancel |

FIGURE 26-4

Warning: this page is not encrypted for secure communication. User names, passwords, and any other information will be sent in clear text. For more information, contact your administrator.

Database Information

Specify database connection settings for this content database. Use the **Database status** options to control whether or not new Site Collections can be created in the database. When the database status is set to **Ready**, the database is available for hosting new Site Collections. When the database status is set to **Offline**, no new Site Collections can be created.

Database server
VBIDEMO

SQL Server database name
WSS_Content_04a25125aef4410e9ae434ee899bc0e4

Database status
Ready ▾

Database Read-Only
No

Database authentication
Windows authentication

Database Versioning and Upgrade

Use this section to check the version and upgrade status of this database. If the Current SharePoint Database Schema Version is less than the Maximum SharePoint Database Schema Version, the database should be upgraded as soon as possible.

Database Schema Versions
Microsoft.SharePoint.Upgrade.SPContentDatabaseSequence
Current Schema Version: 4.0.145.0, Maximum Schema
Version: 4.0.145.0
Microsoft.SharePoint.Upgrade.SPContentDatabaseSequence2
Current Schema Version: 4.0.8.0, Maximum Schema
Version: 4.0.8.0
Microsoft.SharePoint.Administration.SPContentDatabase
Current Schema Version: 14.0.4762.1000, Maximum
Schema Version: 14.0.4762.1000

Failover Server

You can choose to associate a database with a specific failover server that is used in conjuction with SQL Server database mirroring.

Failover Database Server

Database Capacity Settings

Specify capacity settings for this database.

Number of sites before a warning event is generated
9000

Maximum number of sites that can be created in this database
15000

Search Server

You can choose to associate a content database with a specific server that is running the Microsoft SharePoint Foundation search service.

Select Microsoft SharePoint Foundation search server
VBIDEMO ▾

FIGURE 26-5

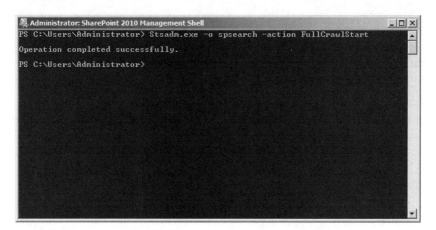

FIGURE 26-6

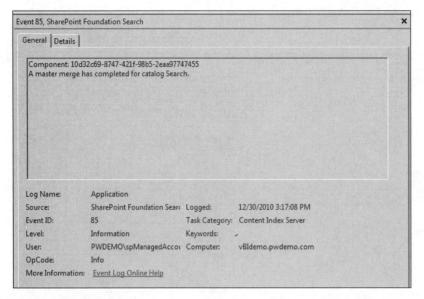

FIGURE 26-7

Basic Search Administration

Administering search in SharePoint 2010 is a big topic, but this section focuses on the basics to get you up-and-running. Search can be a daunting technology but the next few sections cover some important concepts to give you the confidence to explore more complicated areas if your organization requires.

Security Trimming

Security trimming is an important concept to think about when implementing and then running searches in your enterprise. SharePoint will only return results for content that you have access to and for which SharePoint understands the security. For example, when you include a Windows file share in the index, SharePoint can match your AD permissions to the access control list governing that file share and return the appropriate files.

If SharePoint is set up to index an external source with a cookie or anonymous login, SharePoint cannot understand those permissions and will show you all the results from that source. This is an important security concept and why we mention it right at the beginning of this section. If you need security trimming or external sources, you will need to develop your own. That topic is out of scope in this text.

Site Search Administration

There is great news in this section. When dealing with Foundation Search, there is virtually no administration to speak of. When you go to the Search Settings page under Site Settings, the only options are Search and Offline Availability. This allows you to control whether or not the current web application is included in the search results and how to handle any ASPX page use. That's it! Very straightforward.

Extending Your Search Configuration

Extending your search configuration can provide some much needed functionality. This section discusses some common ways to extend your search capabilities and put that new functionality to good use.

What Do You Need from Search?

If you have higher volume needs from search beyond departmental or prototyping efforts, you will want to explore the expanded offerings and tests that cover those offerings in depth. There is significant potential for corporate benefit from employing these new search tools.

TRY IT

In this Try It you configure the Search Service and then force a crawl to populate the index.

Lesson Requirements

This lesson's Try It section will require you to set up search functionality on a site where you have reports and other Business Intelligence items stored. You are going to use the Central Administration and site settings to configure SharePoint Search, force a crawl of the site, and then view your search results.

Hints

- ➤ Don't forget to set the indexer on your content database.
- ➤ Make sure you run the `stsadm` command to force a crawl or you'll be waiting a while for your results to show up.

Step-by-Step

1. Open Central Administration from the Start menu.
2. Select Manage Services on this Server.
3. Find SharePoint Foundation Search Service and click Start to start the service.
4. Fill in the information for a service account, content access account, and index scheduler based on explanations in this lesson (see Figure 26-3) and your needs for your application.
5. Click Submit at the bottom of the page.
6. Next, go back to Central Administration and select Manage Content Databases under the Application Management heading.

7. Select the content database you're using and you will be presented with the options screen for that database. See Figure 26-5 for suggestions on filling this out.

8. Select your new server name in the drop-down for the indexer and click Submit.

9. Now you're configured, so you need to force a crawl.

10. Open the SharePoint Management Shell on the server from the Start menu.

11. Type in **Stsadm.exe -o spsearch -action fullcrawlstart**.

 Please select Lesson 26 on the DVD to view the video that accompanies this lesson.

SECTION VI
Scaling SharePoint 2010 Business Intelligence

▶ **LESSON 27:** Managing and Optimizing SharePoint SQL Server Databases

▶ **LESSON 28:** Tuning and Scaling SharePoint Service Applications

27

Managing and Optimizing SharePoint SQL Server Databases

When you install SharePoint Server 2010 Enterprise Edition, you will start with several SQL Server databases. Most of the databases will be suffixed with a system-generated GUID. These names can be changed, but that is a book within itself. This lesson provides an overview of the different databases, a brief explanation of what is stored in most of the databases, and provides a few techniques that can be used to optimize each database type.

OVERVIEW OF SHAREPOINT 2010 DATABASES

As mentioned earlier, when SharePoint is installed several databases are created. Each database contains data that is specific to a certain area of SharePoint 2010. In some cases there will be more than one of the same type of database, but it will be suffixed with a different GUID. Figure 27-1 lists the databases that will be created after a default farm install.

The database model in SharePoint 2010 has been modified significantly. Instead of storing all content in a few large tables, the data is stored in different tables. This change allows several people to work on large projects without creating contention on the SQL Server.

SharePoint 2010 also introduced a few new databases. Whenever you configure a new service, a new database is created. For example, when you configure the Secure Store Service and PerformancePoint Service Application, two corresponding databases are created, as shown in Figure 27-2.

FIGURE 27-1

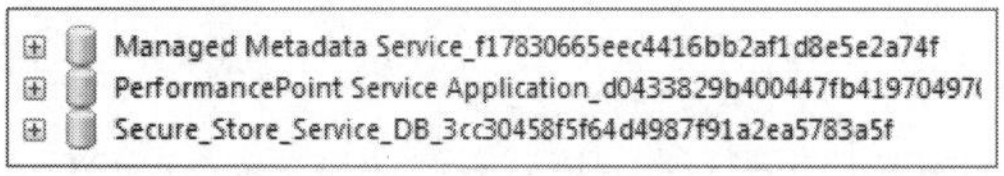

FIGURE 27-2

In addition, User Profiles requires three databases: Synchronization, Profiles, and Social Tagging, as shown in Figure 27-3.

User Profile Service Application_ProfileDB_bfdabfbc946745a6b0b1dt
User Profile Service Application_SocialDB_4c322b5a472f469aa85f7b8
User Profile Service Application_SyncDB_9c9b1b8f0b684dc6abbe8dc!

FIGURE 27-3

This is not an exhaustive list of all the changes, but it provides you with some insight into how Microsoft has changed the structure to accommodate large-scale deployments of SharePoint 2010.

TYPES OF CONTENT IN THE SHAREPOINT 2010 DATABASES

SharePoint 2010 databases contain five basic types of information: Logging, Configuration, Content, Service Application, and Search. The Search type could be grouped with the Service Application content, however, we separated it because it serves a different purpose.

Each database serves a specific purpose; therefore they each store data that is specific to that purpose. Careful consideration should be taken when designing your server architecture and disk layout for these databases. A few tips are given in the next section in regard to these topics. This section focuses on the data that is stored inside of these databases.

The first content type is Logging. The only database under this category is the WSS_ UsageApplication database or the Usage and Health Data Collection Database. This is the only database whose schema can be modified and its data queried. It stores health monitoring and usage that can be used for reporting. The data in this database is temporary and is removed based on schedules that are configurable in the Central Administration console. In the list of databases it is prefixed with WSS_UsageApplication.

The next type is Configuration. Two databases fall into this category: the Configuration database, whose name will appear as SharePoint_Config on the SQL Server, and the Central Administration database, whose name will appear as SharePoint_AdminContent. The Configuration database stores information about SharePoint databases such as Web Part packages, web application and farm settings, web applications, and websites. These are read-intensive databases because most of the configuration information is needed as regularly as the site is accessed. This database also coordinates all deployment administration, which includes managing load-balancing and directing appropriate database requests. For example, when a web server receives a request, a call is made to the Configuration database to determine which content database contains the data for the requested site. The Central Administration database stores all site content. When you upload documents to your document libraries, that content is stored in this database. In addition, Web Part properties and Central Administration user names and site collections rights are also stored in this database. Finally, if you install PowerPivot, the workbooks and the corresponding data are stored in this database.

In addition to Configuration databases are Content databases. These databases contain data specific to site collections. Note that a content database can be associated to more than one site collection. In addition to the site collection, content databases contain Office Web Application caches. Each content database is suffixed with a GUID. Your installation of SharePoint

FIGURE 27-4

may have several content databases, and they will all be prefixed with WSS_Content, as shown in Figure 27-4.

The next type is the Service Application content. As mentioned earlier, each service application produces a new database and each database will contain information about that service application. For example, in the Business Data Connectivity Database, which is prefixed with Bdc_Service_DB_, data regarding external content types and related objects are stored. When you create a connection to an external data source, the metadata about that connection is stored in this database. There is also a PerformancePoint database that stores temporary objects, persisted filters, and user comments. This is all information specific and pertinent to the content that is relevant to your scorecards and dashboards. The State database is another service application database. It stores temporary state information for Visio Services and chart Web Parts.

The user experience is a major part of SharePoint 2010. Therefore, Microsoft scaled the storing of user information to three databases. The Profile database, User Profile Service Application_ProfileDB_, stores information about each user and their associated information. The Synchronization database, User Profile Service Application_SyncDB_, contains staged data that has been synchronized with a directory service like Active Directory. Lastly, the Social database, User Profile Service Application_SocialDB_, stores all the notes and tags created by users.

The final type is Search content data. There are three Search service application databases similar to the User Profile databases. There is an Administrative, Crawl, and Property database. The Administrative database, Search_Services_Application_DB, is accessed for every user administrator and user action. It stores the access control list (ACL) and the search service application configuration data. The Crawl database stores the crawl history and the state of the crawled data. For example, it stores information about items and hosts that are pending processing or already indexed. The final search service application database is the Property database. This database stores properties, queues, and history that is associated with the crawl data. The Crawl and Property databases work together to assist in SharePoint Search capabilities.

This is not an exhaustive list of all the databases that may be part of your SharePoint configuration. However, this section includes most databases that are part of your default installation and a few that are required to finalize your Business Intelligence deployment.

OPTIMIZATION TECHNIQUES FOR EACH CONTENT TYPE

As with any SQL Server, certain configurations must be done on the databases to ensure that they are optimized. In addition, steps must be taken to guarantee that the data is available in the event of a catastrophe or some type of unforeseen failure. This section provides a few techniques that will assist you in improving the performance of your SharePoint SQL Server deployment and a few methods that will assist in making sure that your data is available at all times.

We start the discussion with the configuration databases. These databases are very important to the SharePoint deployment because they contain information that is accessed more frequently than most of the data. They both are read-intensive databases. As a result, you must take precautions to ensure that the data retrieval is fast and that the databases are always online. Generally, the two configuration databases are small. However, if you are using PowerPivot, the Central Administration database may grow over time. Coupling this with the fact that there is only one of these types of databases per farm requires that you implement a strategy that allows the database to scale up. The database recovery models for these databases will be different. For the configuration database, if you do not plan to use Database Mirroring, we recommend that you change the recovery model to Simple. This will help limit the growth of the transaction log. For the Central Administration configuration database you should set the recovery model to Full. Because you may store user data (PowerPivot) in the database, there may be a need to restore to a point in time. By setting the recovery model to Full, you can back up the transaction log and quickly restore to a specific date and time if needed.

The databases that contain the content data can be both read- and write-intensive. The nature of the IO will depend on the purpose of the site. If you are using it for document management, it will be read-intensive. However, if you are using it for collaboration, it will be write-intensive. Regardless, we recommend that you plan for both. Therefore, the databases should be able to grow as large as needed while at the same time support as many users as needed. Capacity planning and SQL Server configuration is a little beyond the scope of the book. However, if you anticipate that your content databases are going to grow in excess of a terabyte, you should plan for at least 32 gigabytes of memory. In addition, you should ensure that you create multiple database files for your content databases and distribute those files across separate dedicated disks.

The Logging database will be a very active database in regard to IO. Therefore, we recommend that the database is placed on its own set of dedicated disks. Also, just as with aforementioned databases, you should have plans in place that will allow this database to scale up. This is because it will be the only database of its type in the farm and it will grow larger. The size of the database will depend solely on how the retention factor is configured and the number of items that have been enabled for logging. There are certainly other factors, but these will contribute most of the data. Because this database can easily be re-created in the event of a failure, the recovery model should be set to Simple.

In regard to the Service Application databases, it is really challenging to provide specific methods and techniques because they all store different types and amounts of data. They also have very different IO patterns, thus making the challenge of defining optimizations more difficult. The fact is that when architecting your database design strategy for this content type, you should take a holistic view of all the service applications you are going to configure and devise a scheme that accommodates the database that will require the most read- and write-intensive scenarios. For example, let's assume that you configure the Secure Store Service and PerformancePoint Services. The Secure Store Service database is read- and write-intensive, whereas the PerformancePoint database's read and write patterns are variable. As a result, you could decide to locate the two databases on separate disks, which would help limit the contention on the disk. On the other hand, you could configure the disks in such a manner that they can handle both read-and write-intensive operations via RAID configuration. Either approach should yield a highly performing set of databases.

In regard to your backup strategy, we recommend that you specify the recovery models based on the content that is stored within the database. For example, if you have configured PerformancePoint, some user annotations are persisted and may increase as the number of users increase. Therefore, we recommend that you set the recovery model to Full to ensure the availability of the data. On the other hand, this strategy could be changed for those service applications that contain data that is not changed very often. Additionally, the backup and optimization techniques that have been outlined for the service application content type apply to the search content type also.

TRY IT

In this Try It you create a spreadsheet that will be used to architect your SharePoint SQL Server database configurations.

Lesson Requirements

Create spreadsheet in which you will define three characteristics about each SharePoint database. These characteristics will help the database administrator properly configure the database. The characteristics are Read/Write Intensive, Stores User Data, and Size. You will need to download the Lesson27_Workbook from www.wrox.com.

Hints

➤   Databases that are accessed frequently are read-intensive.

➤   Databases that receive a lot of user data are write-intensive.

Step-by-Step

1. Open the `Lesson27_Workbook.xlxs`.

2. On the row that contains SharePoint_Config as the database name, click in the column labeled Read/Write Intensive. A drop-down arrow will appear, as shown in Figure 27-5.

3. Click the drop-down arrow and select Read.

4. Click in the column labeled Stores User Date and a drop-down arrow will appear.

5. Click the drop-down arrow and select No.

6. Click in the column labeled Size and a drop-down arrow will appear.

7. Click the drop-down arrow and select Small.

8. Repeat the steps for the WSS_Content database and select Both from the Read/Write Column, Yes from the Stores User Data column, and Large from the Size column.

9. Repeat the steps for the PerformancePoint Service Application database, selecting Both from the Read/Write Column, Yes from the Stores User Data column, and Small from the Size column.

10. Repeat the steps for the WSS_Logging database, selecting Write from the Read/Write Column, No from the Stores User Data column, and Large from the Size column.

11. Repeat the steps for the SharePoint_Admin_Content database, selecting Write from the Both Column, Yes from the Stores User Data column, and Small from the Size column.

    Your spreadsheet should resemble Figure 27-5.

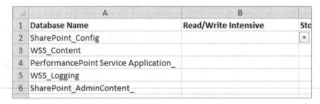

	A	B	
1	Database Name	Read/Write Intensive	Sto
2	SharePoint_Config		▾
3	WSS_Content		
4	PerformancePoint Service Application_		
5	WSS_Logging		
6	SharePoint_AdminContent_		

FIGURE 27-5

 Please select Lesson 27 on the DVD to view the video that accompanies this lesson.

28

Tuning and Scaling SharePoint Service Applications

SharePoint 2010 introduced more flexible services that can be shared between farms. These applications are called SharePoint Service Applications (SSAs). SSAs are applications that are installed on a server farm and perform some specific function or functions. The unique thing about the SSAs is that they can be configured for a specific farm. SharePoint 2010 offers a plethora of service applications, as shown in Figure 28-1.

Name	Type
Access Services	Access Services Web Service Application
Access Services	Access Services Web Service Application Proxy
Application Discovery and Load Balancer Service Application	Application Discovery and Load Balancer Service Application
Application Discovery and Load Balancer Service Application Proxy_a675d7ef-8753-4772-830e-9b238f0b230f	Application Discovery and Load Balancer Service Application Proxy
Application Registry Service	Application Registry Service
Application Registry Service	Application Registry Proxy
Business Data Connectivity Service	Business Data Connectivity Service Application
Business Data Connectivity Service	Business Data Connectivity Service Application Proxy
Excel Services Application	Excel Services Application Web Service Application
Excel Services Application	Excel Services Application Web Service Application Proxy
Managed Metadata Service	Managed Metadata Service
Managed Metadata Service	Managed Metadata Service Connection
Performance Point Application Service 2	PerformancePoint Service Application
Performance Point Application Service 2	PerformancePoint Service Application Proxy
PerformancePoint Service Application	PerformancePoint Service Application
PerformancePoint Service Application	PerformancePoint Service Application Proxy
Secure Store Service	Secure Store Service Application
Secure Store Service	Secure Store Service Application Proxy
Security Token Service Application	Security Token Service Application
State Service	State Service
State Service	State Service Proxy

FIGURE 28-1

As a result, they assist in scaling your farm and handling larger loads. They are also flexible and offer richer development features. This lesson focuses on three main Business Intelligence SSAs: PerformancePoint, Excel Services, and PowerPivot Services. We explain how the concept of SSAs allows each to scale across and on server farms to assist in improving the performance of your SharePoint installation.

TUNING AND SCALING PERFORMANCEPOINT

As you create and implement more Business Intelligence, it is likely that your end users will continue to request and/or create more PerformancePoint content. As a result, you may notice some degradation in the performance of your BI sites. To mitigate this problem, all you need to do is create another PerformancePoint Service Application. Once the application is created, you can associate your various BI sites to a specific PerformancePoint Service Application.

To create a custom PerformancePoint Service Application, open the Central Administration console. On the Central Administration homepage click Manage Service Applications under the Application Management section. On the Service Applications page click the drop-down arrow under New and select PerformancePoint Service Application, as shown in Figure 28-2.

FIGURE 28-2

When you click New, the New PerformancePoint Service Application page opens, as shown in Figure 28-3.

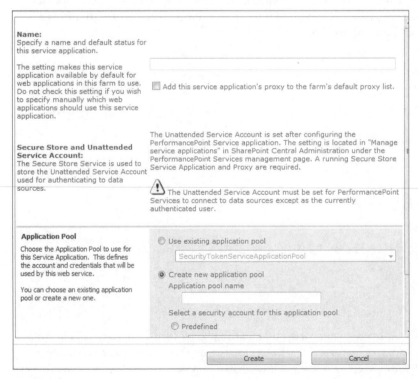

FIGURE 28-3

On this page you must provide a name for the new application service, use an existing application pool or create a new one, and finally, select a security account for the application pool. Once all these items have been provided, click OK and the new application service will be created.

Now that you have created the custom PerformancePoint Service Application, all you need to do is associate it to a specific BI site. To do that, go back to the Central Administration homepage. Select Manage Web Applications under the Application Management category. Click a web application in the list of available web applications. When you select the web application several items become enabled in the ribbon. Click Service Connections on the ribbon. On the Configure Service Application Associations page select the custom PerformancePoint Service Application that you want your BI site to use and click OK.

When the new service application is created, a new database is created on your SQL Server, as shown in Figure 28-4.

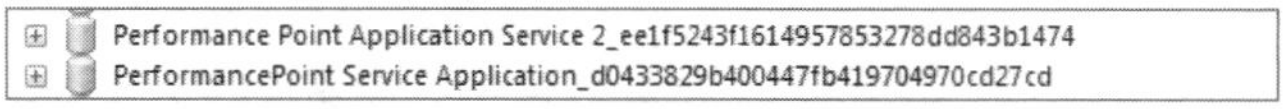

FIGURE 28-4

This database will act as the backend for the new PerformancePoint Service Application. To scale the service even further and possibly improve the performance, you could locate the data files for this database on a dedicated set of disks or on a different SQL Server. Either method should yield positive results in regard to the performance of the application.

TUNING AND SCALING EXCEL SERVICES

Several factors will affect the performance of your Excel Service Applications. The two main factors are the size and makeup of what is stored in the Excel workbooks that are hosted by your service. The size of the workbooks and the complexity of the calculations inside the workbooks contribute directly to how the application performs. As a result, you may need to scale your Excel Service Application deployment.

The techniques that you will use to scale Excel Services are similar to those used to scale PerformancePoint. As with PerformancePoint, you can scale out the application by creating a custom one and you can also scale the SQL Server deployment. Another approach that may be considered is adding more memory to the SQL Servers that host your existing PerformancePoint databases. As with any SQL Server, memory is a key hardware requirement. Because your workbooks are kept in memory, adding additional memory could improve the overall throughput on your SQL Server.

TUNING AND SCALING POWERPIVOT

The techniques used to tune and scale PowerPivot are a little different than the methods that were used in the previous sections. Similar to Excel and PowerPivot, you can create a custom PowerPivot application and create a custom association list for a specific web application. The primary difference is that to scale PowerPivot you must install it on each application server that you want to perform query processing. When a query request for PowerPivot is issued, data allocation is distributed to any PowerPivot for SharePoint server that is available. When you have a farm SharePoint installation, the default allocation methodology is round-robin. In other words, when a query is issued, the data processing is allocated to any PowerPivot server that is available; the availability is determined by the aforementioned methodology. A scaled-out deployment of PowerPivot resembles Figure 28-5.

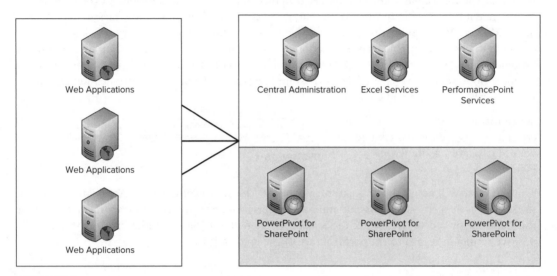

FIGURE 28-5

When you add more PowerPivot servers to the farm, you essentially add more query processing for all deployed web applications that are dependent upon or use the service. The negative to this is that you cannot scale PowerPivot data allocation processing for some web applications. However, similar to Excel and PerformancePoint Service Applications, you can create a custom association list that excludes the service application. This should guarantee that those web applications with the custom associations will not send query requests to the PowerPivot servers. In addition, you can also scale and improve the performance of PowerPivot Service Applications by creating custom PowerPivot Service Applications.

TRY IT

In this Try It, you create a custom PerformancePoint Service Application and a custom association list for a specific web application.

Lesson Requirements

In this lesson, you create a custom PerformancePoint Service Application that will be used in a custom association list. You then modify the association list for a specific web application so that it uses the newly created PerformancePoint Service Application.

Hints

➤ Use the Central Administration console to create the new service application.

➤ To create a custom association list, in the Central Administration console choose Manage Web Applications and select the Services Connections button that is enabled when you choose a web application.

Step-by-Step

1. Open the Central Administration console.

2. Click Manage Service Applications under the Application Management section.

3. Click the drop-down arrow under the button labeled New on the Service Application window to see the list of service applications, as shown in Figure 28-6.

4. Select PerformancePoint Service Application from the drop-down list.

5. In the first textbox labeled Name, enter **PerformancePoint Custom Service Application**.

6. Select the radio button labeled Use Existing Application Pool. Your screen should resemble Figure 28-7.

Access Services
Business Data Connectivity Service
Excel Services Application
Managed Metadata Service
PerformancePoint Service Application
Secure Store Service
User Profile Service Application
Visio Graphics Service
Web Analytics Service Application
Word Automation Services

FIGURE 28-6

Name:
Specify a name and default status for this service application.

The setting makes this service application available by default by web applications in this farm to use. Do not check this setting if you wish to specify manually which web applications should use this service application.

PerformancePoint Custom Service Application

☐ Add this service application's proxy to the farm's default proxy list.

The Unattended Service Account is set after configuring the PerformancePoint Service application. The setting is located in "Manage service applications" in SharePoint Central Administration under the PerformancePoint Services management page. A running Secure Store Service Application and Proxy are required.

⚠ The Unattended Service Account must be set for PerformancePoint Services to connect to data sources except as the currently authenticated user.

Secure Store and Unattended Service Account:
The Secure Store Service is used to store the Unattended Service Account used for authenticating to data sources.

Application Pool
Choose the Application Pool to use for this Service Application. This defines the account and credentials that will be used by this web service.

You can choose an existing application pool or create a new one.

◉ Use existing application pool
SecurityTokenServiceApplicationPool ▼

○ Create new application pool
Application pool name

Select a security account for this application pool
○ Predefined
Network Service ▼

◉ Configurable
Patrick\LP\Patrick ▼
Register new managed account

[Create]   [Cancel]

FIGURE 28-7

7. Click the button labeled Create.

8. Click OK on the new PerformancePoint Service Application screen.

9. In the left navigation pane click Central Administration.

10. Click Manage Web Applications under the Application Management section.

11. Select the 24 Hour SharePoint web application.

12. Click the button labeled Service Connections in the ribbon.

13. On the Configure Service Application Associations window select [custom] from the drop-down list labeled Edit the Following Group of connections, as shown in Figure 28-8.

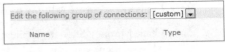

FIGURE 28-8

14. Check all the boxes next to the service applications that you want to associate to the web application. Ensure that you select only the PerformancePoint Service Application Proxy labeled PerformancePoint Custom Service Application. Your screen should resemble Figure 28-9.

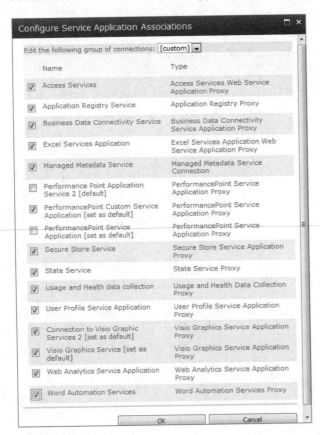

FIGURE 28-9

15. Click OK.

 Please select Lesson 28 on the DVD to view the video that accompanies this lesson.

SECTION VII
Implementing SharePoint Business Intelligence in Your Organization

▶ **LESSON 29:** Planning Your SharePoint Business Intelligence Project

▶ **LESSON 30:** Preparing Your Business Intelligence Implementation

▶ **LESSON 31:** Creating Your SharePoint Project Checklist and Kickoff Plan

29

Planning Your SharePoint Business Intelligence Project

Now that you have worked with the clay that makes up the SharePoint BI offerings, it's time to plan for an initiative in your environment. This initiative will be focused on getting a prototype SharePoint solution up-and-running for your organization. This lesson covers the major focus areas for that effort. They include priority drivers, necessary information, and planning processes that have been successful in the authors' experience.

PRIORITY DRIVERS

Priority drivers are the things that are pushing your organization towards the types of solutions SharePoint 2010 can provide. Perhaps it's too many reports, or too few with problems accessing the data. There are a number of factors that could be driving this new initiative. This section discusses those.

Why Are You Doing This?

One of the first things you need is to identify the organizational drivers behind this new effort. Some major drivers for a SharePoint initiative include:

➤ **Executive request** — Did your boss go to a conference and come home and demand SharePoint? This is happening more and more as Microsoft continues to show its leadership in this technology. Nothing's perfect, but SharePoint is by far the most mature and extensible collaboration and enterprise management platform on the market.

➤ **Problems aligning data in your enterprise** — Many organizations have a wealth of data that data services, reporting, and BI teams struggle to align because they come from very disparate systems and processes. Microsoft BI provides a tremendous platform to help accomplish this, but even without centralized warehouse capabilities, PerformancePoint and SharePoint BI allow you to begin to tie data together in ways you didn't know you could.

➤ **Trying to stay ahead of the technology curve** — Many organizations have time and budget set aside to make sure that they are not caught by surprise when the next major technology shift happens. With the advent of SharePoint, Office Online, and many Microsoft core products becoming deeply integrated with SharePoint, more companies are putting this effort into understanding and applying SharePoint in their environment.

➤ **Need an environment to train the team for internal development** — It's great that you're reading this book, but unless it's a team reading assignment (and it should be), your peers or team will need some hands on time with the tools. This will require some type of base environment. This could be virtual servers as long as you pay attention to the system requirements.

➤ **The authors recommend a minimum of 4 cores and 8GB of RAM from a performance perspective.** Storage will be dependent on your application, but ensure you're meeting minimum requirements because they have been increased for this version of SharePoint. Also remember that you need 64-bit operating systems for this version to work.

End Users Are Important

Many SharePoint projects are put in peril because up-front analysis on getting adoption, stakeholder buy in, and implementation is not properly analyzed. This section provides some guidance on important things to consider. Many times this effort is driven by technical folks without a lot of exposure to the ins and outs of management and budget topics.

Getting Stakeholder Buy In

Who your primary or first customer will be is critically important to how you will approach this task. Your customers may be internal, external, or even partners. This will drive your focus. Perhaps you need better access to reports, more intuitive data drive analysis, or even just to be able to present the data to them that they have to get themselves right now.

Talk to your customers and see what their priorities are. Don't assume you know because this can result in mixed communication and less than ideal results. Find out what they feel are shortcomings in the current system, and where they would like to see it improved. They will likely mention things like seeing more information aligned together, being able to quickly drill down, or being able to get that data into and out of Excel or a database easily. These are some of the most common requests of data consumers who are feeling challenged in their current environment. As you know from this text, these are all things SharePoint does quite well.

Where Is Your Data?

Keep in mind your data may be spread over the enterprise in multiple systems. See Figure 29-1 for some examples. This may require some ETL to centralize it for the type of analysis you want to do, but in many cases this is not necessary. You'll notice this task is placed after talking to the customers. Many organizations do these in reverse. You don't need to spend time mapping all your data until you know what you need to go get and align. Your data quality will be very important as well. Make sure to check this and get feedback on it from your customers, because poor data quality will seriously impact your ability to design a useful BI solution in SharePoint. The most common data sources for SharePoint BI are:

➤ SQL Server databases

➤ Analysis Services databases

➤ SharePoint Lists

➤ PowerPivot workbooks

➤ ODATA Streams (through PowerPivot workbooks)

➤ OLE DB Compatible Data Sources

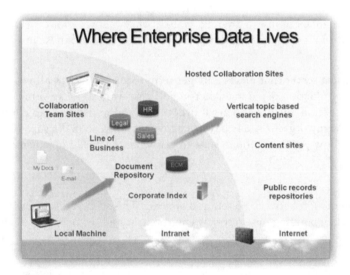

FIGURE 29-1

Like many organizations you likely have many if not all of these in your environment. Make sure you evaluate the limitations and benefits that each data source will bring. Some, like PowerPivot, will require additional configuration in your SharePoint environment to support their new functionality. Don't shy away from this thought because the configuration is straightforward and well documented (and included in this text for basic implementations).

What Is Your Budget?

Not every organization is going to go out and purchase a large amount of server hardware to get this initiative going, and you don't need to. Make sure you know what your budget is and what you have to work with. Once you have this information, begin focusing on a prototype (more on this later). Make sure when you are building your prototype that you focus not only on the development pieces, but also on the infrastructure impact. This information will be important to management to help them plan for future expansion and budgetary needs.

Many organizations do annual budgeting for capital expenses, so you will want to get an environment where you get some prototypes working and get the business excited, and then use that as your use case to get additional resources allocated in the budget based on business need. Your use case is typically a business need that is supplied with a proposal to management to help them see why this new prototype is needed. Many times the support of the business driven from those prototypes can provide a needed boost when budget time comes around.

When Do You Need It Online?

Maybe you're in an executive pressure cooker situation where they need something for a board meeting, or your boss needs something for an annual management retreat to show off to his/her peers. This will necessitate a faster prototyping and delivery approach. It would be better to attempt to prototype and deliver on existing hardware potentially than to wait for an order of a new server. There is a full set of instructions on MSDN to install SharePoint 2010 on Windows 7 for development only if you want to install and run it on a beefy desktop or laptop. You can find those instructions here: `http://msdn.microsoft.com/en-us/library/ee554869.aspx`.

Otherwise you may want to procure a server that meets a longer term requirement and allows for multiple prototypes and potential production deployments. You will also want to make sure you gather the information in the next section quickly and get it over to your administrators to configure security, accounts, and so on. Many organizations have a change window, so make sure you're familiar with these procedures to allow yourself enough time to get what you need implemented.

Systems and People

Technology has always been an interaction between people and systems. This section discusses the systems you will need to plan for when building out your new environment and the people you will need to partner with.

Security

Many security requirements exist when implementing SharePoint BI. The required ones were addressed in other lessons in the book, but some of the important things to consider for information gathering are:

➤ Who will need access to the data?

➤ Should there be a data access proxy account? (Most likely)

➤ What service applications will the organization be running?

➤ What external data sources will be required?

➤ Will you be transporting data and need to access other systems or partner systems?

➤ Have you identified which SharePoint Farm accounts will be needed to run the farm?

➤ Do you know who the developers and administrators are who will need access?

➤ Do you understand your organization's security policies and how to request these items?

Some of this will require you to help plan with your administrators who and what systems will need to talk to each other. Make sure to take time and plan this correctly because you will not be able to proceed in some phases of installation and configuration without the appropriate security in place.

Requirements

Requirements are a critical phase of any project. The number one complaint the author team hears in the field from technical personnel is "they didn't give us any requirements and then said it was wrong." We are not taking sides because we've been on both sides of that debate, but if you are asked to paint a house and someone will not tell you a color, you will likely not do it or paint a small area and then say "do you like this?" "Lighter or darker?" and so on. If you cannot get clear requirements, take a look at anything existing and create a portion of a mockup. Most customers will appreciate the initiative and be eager to give feedback. If you've never thought through a requirements process before, Figure 29-2 will give you some pointers on where to focus.

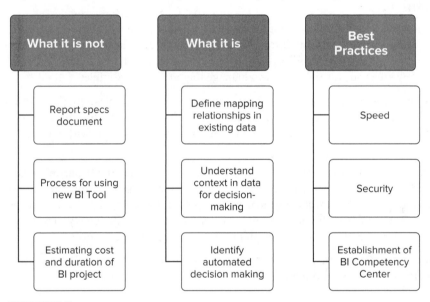

FIGURE 29-2

Now you're on your way to a good set of requirements. Then go ahead and write them yourself so you can give them to the next set of customers and say "This was what Suzie in finance was looking for, maybe this can be a good starting point for you." Often with new technology, you will need to help lead the business until they understand some of the capabilities.

Stakeholders

A successful BI effort will rely heavily on the investment and adoption by stakeholders. These could be anyone in the organization with the drive and budgetary power to help you succeed in getting resources to begin building your solutions. These folks are important in helping you navigate the following obstacles that are common in many projects, especially Business Intelligence and SharePoint projects:

➤ Helping the business understand the value

➤ Gathering information to help you deliver value early in the process

➤ Promoting the project before it begins to build buzz

➤ Lining up viewers for demos and other internal marketing events to promote the effort

➤ Planning the budgetary impact with you to help ensure you can deliver value for an introductory cost factor

Your stakeholders can be anyone in your management chain or a parallel chain such as a business unit. Make sure, however, that your management team is supportive of exploring this topic before you go off and try lining up stakeholders. The most important stakeholders will be your personal management team because they are effectively vouching for you and your ability to make this happen. Make your stakeholders the priority.

Hosting and Infrastructure

Does your firm host its own servers, or does it source this to a provider? This will play a large part in the speed and availability of hardware and infrastructure configuration. The best approach here assumes that you're not the person who handles these items day-to-day. It will help get the ball rolling if you proceed with a few scenarios for the folks who manage that area. For example:

➤ **Introductory needs** — This is a package of servers and licenses for development only that meet or slightly exceed the minimum requirements, but are only for prototyping. This provides a very cost-effective way to get into the technology and show it off without breaking the bank.

➤ **Departmental implementation** — This is a package that will ensure that a department can get rolled out and provides some growth allowance. This may include some scaling out of web front-end servers, but perhaps still consolidating the content database servers with the application servers. This will provide some additional capacity while still allowing you to keep the application and data together to help save on the largest servers in the group.

➤ **Divisional rollout** — This is the point where your organization will begin scaling out all levels of the infrastructure. This would typically include all or some combination of:

➤ Multiple web front-end servers

➤ Dedicated application servers

➤ Search and index/crawl servers

➤ SQL Server to host content and metadata databases

This will enable each area to scale individually based on the growth rate and level of adoption from the division or enterprise.

Integrated Systems

Make sure to compile a list of integrated systems that will be working with the SharePoint environment. This may include:

➤ **Corporate or partner e-mail systems** — E-mail is critical to any enterprise and SharePoint has lots of capabilities around e-mail. Submitting documents to SharePoint libraries, automating workflows and approvals, and other great functionality should be explored for implementation.

➤ **Enterprise applications (CRM, ERP, etc.)** — Many organizations have centralized data sources for much of their important customer or marketing data. These could be a CRM, ERP, or other manufacturing or sales management systems. SharePoint can work with many of these data sources through BCS, so make sure you know what type of platform they run on and have read-level credentials to experiment with value-added solutions in SharePoint.

➤ **Change control systems** — SharePoint's benefit is in consolidating access to and working on systems and web-based applications. If you have a change control system, you will want to integrate it into a workflow process in SharePoint to help with deployments. This can work well with both SharePoint and non-SharePoint deliverables from a tracking perspective.

➤ **Ticket tracking systems** — Tracking deployments, bugs, and help desk tickets can be integrated right into your Business Intelligence so you can monitor internal performance of different departments. They too can also be built into workflow.

➤ **Partner data sources and systems** — As your business grew, you likely developed relationships and data sharing as part of your operations. The good news is that much of this data is usually accessible once you have the firewall rules, IP addresses, and logins. Make sure to include this in your discussions with stakeholders because many of them may not think about bringing in data from partners to provide increased context to your analysis.

TRY IT

In this Try It you create a spreadsheet with headers and items that are important for discussions with stakeholders.

Lesson Requirements

This lesson assumes you're familiar with the concepts of Excel and have some experience using it as a planning tool. In this lesson you will make a list of systems and people that you will need to work with to ensure a successful deployment of your prototype.

Hints

➤ Make sure to think about technical and non-technical requirements.

➤ Remember to focus on a department, team, or data set that is already out there.

Step-by-Step

1. Create a new empty worksheet in Excel and save it as **SharePoint Planning.xlsx**.

2. Across the top, list the major areas for planning from this lesson.

3. Down the side, begin to list possible data sources. This will help you select the combination of data sources that are already the best fit for prototyping.

4. Create a Word document with the topics in this chapter that will serve as a roadmap for working through these questions with stakeholders.

5. You can then fill in your spreadsheet with the answers you receive and then begin to research for your prototype.

 Please select Lesson 29 on the DVD to view the video that accompanies this lesson.

30

Preparing Your Business Intelligence Implementation

This lesson introduces the common planning steps and hopefully helps you avoid the missteps many organizations face when launching their first forays into SharePoint. It covers infrastructure, licensing, planning, and other concerns. This lesson will help you when you reach the final lesson and begin working through your SharePoint Project checklists.

INFRASTRUCTURE CONCERNS

Infrastructure is obviously a major concern for those implementing SharePoint. It used to be that you could implement MOSS 2003 or 2007 on a small server and leave it alone. The challenge now is that SharePoint has become a broader, more complicated product, as shown in Figure 30-1.

These new areas make infrastructure a more complicated decision. You've already learned about how prototyping will drive your initial infrastructure, but now we're talking about the real production implementation. You have several areas to consider:

➤ **Web Applications** — These web applications are the websites that the users will log in to. This is the first layer of scale out that you will typically implement. This will enable you to scale out web servers to handle different web applications, such as Finance Dashboard and Reports, Marketing Analysis, and so on. These web applications will get a lot of traffic and do a lot of work rendering pages, but they don't do the application heavy lifting. This is done by the service applications. A well-balanced group of web front-ends is important, but too many on any level can overload the lower tiers, as shown in Figure 30-2.

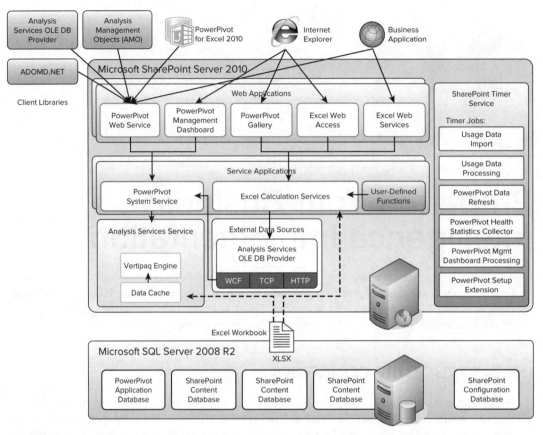

FIGURE 30-1

➤ **Service Applications** — Service applications do the heavy lifting for whatever their purpose is. The web front-ends pass the data to the service applications to process and either gets and delivers the dashboard, Excel Services document, Visio strategy map, or other service-related data. These applications handle the data access, document retrieval, storage, and so on. Some services are single server and others are cross farm, as shown in Figure 30-3.

➤ **SharePoint Timer Services** — This set of services runs checks and handles kicking off things like data refresh. They're typically not heavy hitters from a performance perspective but should be all enabled because if they don't run, data fresh and other automated tasks may not happen that will impact other users downstream.

➤ **Analysis Services Service (PowerPivot)** — This is an instance of Analysis Services running inside a `.dll` file that does the heavy lifting. Once the PowerPivot Service Application has retrieved the data from Analysis Services, the in-memory analysis is taking place right inside this service. You can see where it fits in, as shown in Figure 30-4. If PowerPivot is a big part of your deployment, you will want to scale this service out to handle to load. Remember that this service can quickly become more widely used so it's important to monitor the PowerPivot management dashboard to see when usage is increasing so you can manage it properly. An example of the dashboard from Central Administration is included in Figure 30-5.

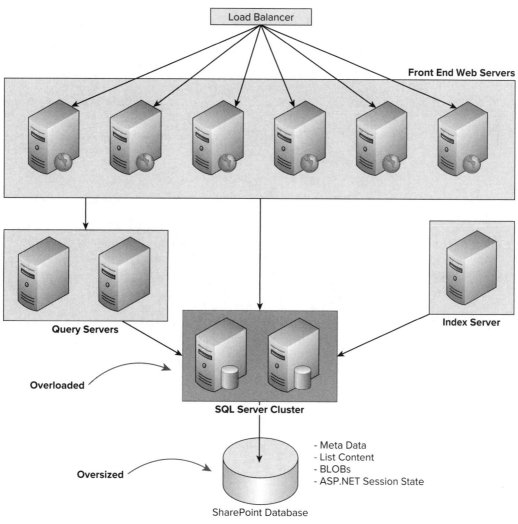

FIGURE 30-2

➤ **External Data Sources** — External data is a critical driver to the success of the types of intelligence you'll be creating, collaborating, and making decisions with in your new SharePoint environment. Make sure that your external data systems can handle the extra load this new set of users will place on it. In many cases this data should be coming from OLAP environments via a proxy user, so perhaps use a combination of Resource Governor or Windows Resource Manager to help govern that user's activity to ensure the system does not overload. You can get a sense for all the directions data will come from in Figure 30-6.

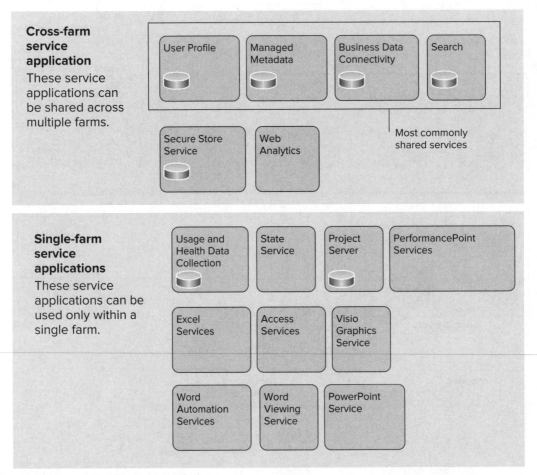

FIGURE 30-3

➤ **Exchange or Mail System** — Notification, workflow, and other messages are all generated through the SharePoint environment. Many of these outgoing messages work through SMTP but will be arriving in your regular inbox like that nagging note from the boss, so make sure you test to confirm that you or your servers won't get overloaded.

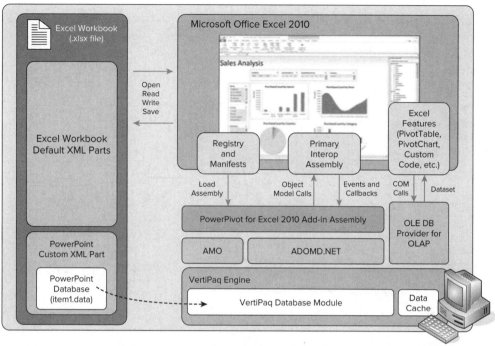

FIGURE 30-4

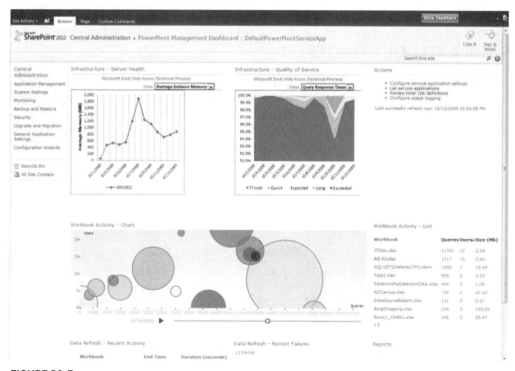

FIGURE 30-5

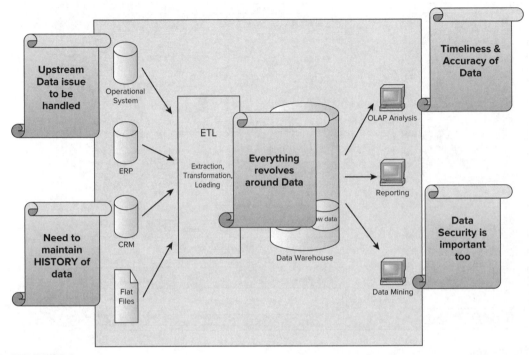

FIGURE 30-6

STORAGE AND SQL CONCERNS

These new servers and created artifacts are going to need to be stored somewhere. That somewhere is the SharePoint content databases. Other lessons have covered the SharePoint databases and what is stored in them, but we are highlighting it here to make sure you plan for growth in those areas. Server capacity is critical not only from a storage perspective but from a processing perspective as well. SQL Servers holding SharePoint databases should not really be shared with any other important applications in case their processing overhead begins to impact the other applications in that instance or any other instances on that server.

Some items to review before sizing these databases would include:

➤ File servers currently housing data that would normally reside in SharePoint

➤ E-mailed reports and documents sitting on your Exchange server

➤ Reports spread throughout report servers

➤ Access databases that may be served up via Access services in SharePoint

➤ Excel documents commonly spread and managed by teams who will want to put them on SharePoint

These areas and more will have hidden storage requirements that you should pay attention to when beginning to build out your SharePoint environment. Make sure you review carefully with your stakeholders and do your best to predefine the areas where increased data requirements will come at you from left field.

LICENSING CONCERNS

As you can see in Figure 30-7, several editions of SharePoint are available and what editions you're running determine the level of features you will have available. Many of the BI features require SharePoint Enterprise in 2011. A license is required for SQL Server, SharePoint, and Office in conjunction with your licensing agreements, but remember many times this does not play into a decision around development.

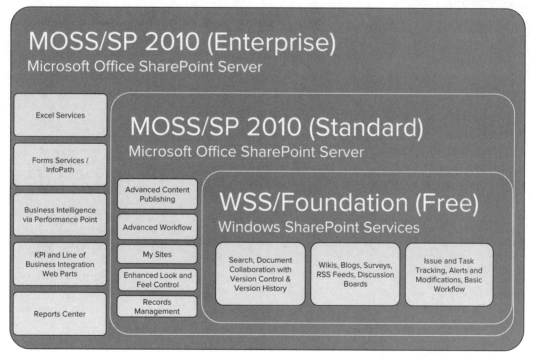

FIGURE 30-7

END-USER TECHNOLOGY

A lot of end-user technology is in play with the new version of SharePoint. The major items are highlighted in Figure 30-8.

As you can see, these programs and tools are critical to a strong end-user experience. You will want to make sure that workstations and deployments for different user groups take these new tools into account and that the users have the tools installed so they can begin experimenting with and using this new technology. Following are the user groups and some suggested programs for each role.

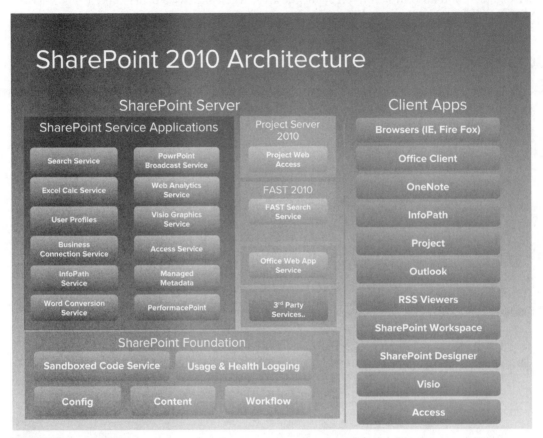

FIGURE 30-8

- ➤ Developer
  - ➤ Browser
  - ➤ Office Clients
  - ➤ SharePoint Designer
  - ➤ PerformancePoint Dashboard Designer
- ➤ Analyst
  - ➤ Browser
  - ➤ Office Clients

- ➤ SharePoint Designer
- ➤ PerformancePoint Dashboard Designer
- ➤ Executive
  - ➤ Browser
  - ➤ Office Clients
  - ➤ Visio Viewer
- ➤ Project Manager
  - ➤ Browser
  - ➤ Office Clients
  - ➤ Project
  - ➤ OneNote
- ➤ Server Administrator
  - ➤ Browser
  - ➤ Office Clients
  - ➤ SharePoint Designer
  - ➤ PerformancePoint Dashboard Designer

These breakdowns should serve as guidelines for working up deployment manifests and plans for additional licensing requirements for the client-side or end-user technology.

TRY IT

In this Try It, you make a preliminary plan for the rollout that you will use in the next lesson as you build your checklist for deployment.

Lesson Requirements

In this Try It, you build a spreadsheet to help you begin planning your rollout plan. This spreadsheet will help you identify key people and processes that you should be considering based on the information in the chapter.

Hints

- ➤ Remember to review each section and think through service applications you will be deploying.
- ➤ Remember to include a list of the types of user roles and the number of them so you can take licensing into account.

Step-by-Step

1. Create a new spreadsheet and list the service applications down the left.

2. Across the top, create headers for user count and other important categories for service applications.

3. Fill in the matrix with the data for your organization.

4. Create another worksheet in the same document and do the same for end users and their roles.

5. The final worksheet should step through the server and infrastructure roles and servers you think you will need.

6. Play with the formatting and see what will work for you. There are some examples on the DVD of the author creating some common layouts to help get you started.

 Please select Lesson 30 on the DVD to view the video that accompanies this lesson.

31

Creating Your SharePoint Project Checklist and Kickoff Plan

As with any good effort, the first thing you need to do is prioritize what you're going to do. Checklists are a great way to make sure you're able to prioritize and then adjust those priorities once you get more information. This lesson walks you through the most appropriate first steps. These include:

➤ **Rounding up the troops** — You need to have the right technical and business resources lined up for this project. This section outlines who they are and how to do that.

➤ **Planning your schedule** — You need to plan your schedule because this will be the only thing you're working on right? Sure it is. This section talks about how to balance your regular job with this new venture of rolling out a new generation of Business Intelligence.

➤ **Creating your first checklist** — Many people work from a "to do" list but few ever work from a checklist. Learn what the difference is and how you can make sure you don't miss deliverables as they come up.

➤ **Putting things in motion** — Now that you're ready, you can get the ball moving forward.

ROUND UP THE TROOPS

Your team is the most important part of your project. It's important to have the following skills and knowledge sets on your team to make the most of your project:

➤ **SQL Server DBA** — Many content databases were discussed previously. These need to be cared for and configured correctly.

➤ **SharePoint Server Administrator** — This person is responsible for making sure SharePoint is installed correctly and that security is configured as required for your efforts.

➤ **Business Intelligence Developer** — This person is going to use the skills developed in this book and others to build the types of solutions discussed in all the previous lessons.

➤ **Business Liaison** — This person should understand the area of business that you're working with and its data needs. He or she will help you drive the requirements process by being able to answer many questions.

➤ **Business Sponsor** — This person could come from any area of the business but should be at a level where he or she can direct you through the budget and project approvals as well as help guide adoption efforts.

This core team will position you with the right resources to begin moving forward. At other times you'll potentially need to scale these folks depending on the level of your implementation efforts. This is the core skill set and group that you should begin thinking about now.

PLAN THE SCHEDULE

With all that you have going on you'll now be juggling a SharePoint BI project as well. Make sure to follow the approach in Lesson 30 that recommends an agile approach. Start by figuring out what you need to do to show value to the business and begin breaking that into deliverable chunks. A deliverable chunk means functionality that is:

➤ Usable

➤ Verified

➤ Tested

➤ Adopted

This will enable you to work with your team and break the requested deliverables into the work required to deliver them. Then these sections of work can be broken down into sprints that can be delivered in an iterative approach, delivering value each step of the way. See an example of an agile process in Figure 31-1.

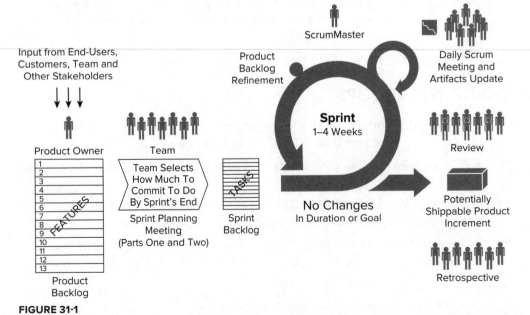

FIGURE 31-1

CHECKLIST CREATION 101

Working from a checklist means that watch items have a couple of statuses that need to be "checked" off. A sample checklist will include items for your requirements phase and then move to additional items for development as shown in the following table.

ITEM	ASSIGNED TO	DATE CLEARED	DATE APPROVED
Document Requirements for Marketing Dashboard	Business Liaison and BI Developer	1/25/2011	1/26/2010
Prototype Dashboard and Report	BI Developer	1/27/2010	1/29/2010
Review Prototype with Business Customers		1/31/2010	2/3/2010
Adjust and Tune Performance of Solution	BI Developer, Business Liaison	2/6/2010	2/8/2010
Deploy Solution	BI Developer, DBA	2/13/2010	2/16/2010

Make sure to put together your own sample checklists. Working from a written list keeps everyone accountable and gets rid of the "I don't remember that" syndrome common to so many projects.

PUTTING THINGS IN MOTION

To get things moving you'll need to get the team together. Doing this in phases will prevent you from springing the project on your team and in the meantime let them begin thinking about their roles.

➤ 30 days ahead:

  ➤ Have a quick meeting with the team, letting them know the project is approaching and what role you're looking for them to play. If they need to substitute a peer for the effort, this will allow them time to do so.

  ➤ Make sure hardware is on the way and the infrastructure teams will be able to install it in time.

  ➤ Address any last-minute training issues or skill gaps.

➤ 2 weeks ahead:

  ➤ Ensure all the hardware is being configured and installed.

  ➤ Make sure any week 1 meetings for your team are booked on their calendars.

  ➤ Line up any client tool installation for members of the team.

  ➤ Meet with team members individually to discuss their roles and key responsibilities for sprint 1.

➤ 1 week before:

  ➤ Log in and verify security on all hardware.

  ➤ Begin collecting requirements as they become available from the business.

Run your project in a series of sprints, where you're adding value in a short period of time, typically 3–6 weeks. That way you're giving the business something even if you need to work on other projects in between the sprints. The following is a sample overview of a 4-week sprint you can use to get kicked off.

➤ Week 1:

    ➤ Begin development and requirement prototyping.

    ➤ Deliver the week 1 demo on Friday to get feedback from the business.

➤ Week 2:

    ➤ Review feedback from the Friday demo and incorporate it into this week's deliverables for the new Friday demo.

    ➤ Add scope to include new functionality and reporting for the week 2 Friday demo with the business liaison.

➤ Week 3:

    ➤ Keep up your pattern of reviewing feedback. This week should include some additional constructive feedback from the business.

    ➤ This week's demo should include others from the department you're building for so that this feedback can be incorporated during week 4.

➤ Week 4:

    ➤ This week is it! Time to deliver this to production.

    ➤ Your code should be complete to give your team time to deploy it and test performance and security. Have the business begin acceptance testing mid-week as soon as it's available in production.

    ➤ Deploy and accept those pats on the back for the great work you and the team have done!

I hope this lesson has helped you see how you can get prepared, and ensure a strong kickoff to your project and pull together the right team. Next, in the Try It section you put those skills to good use.

TRY IT

In this Try It you will create a project kickoff checklist for your SharePoint BI project. You will use the techniques you have learned in this lesson along with the new technical skills from the other lessons in this book.

Lesson Requirements

In this Try It you will be responsible for:

➤ Creating your checklist for getting your project going and moving through your first four sprint weeks

➤ Outlining pre-project tasks and assigning time frames to them based on your organization

Hints

➤ Remember to think about change control processes, and other important policies that will impact your timeline.

Step-by-Step

1. Create a new empty worksheet.

2. Make two tabs, one for Pre-Project Checklist and one for Sprint Schedule.

3. Make a list of items, breaking them down into these categories:

   ➤ Pre 30-day before project Activities

   ➤ 16–30-day before project Activities

   ➤ 8–15-day before project Activities

   ➤ 1–7-day before project Activities

4. Then take your requirements and break them down into a set of weekly deliverables that build on each other to make sure you will accomplish what is reasonable during your 4-week sprint schedule. More details on how to build this are available on the DVD or on www.wrox.com under Lesson Downloads.

 Please select Lesson 31 on the DVD to view the video that accompanies this lesson.

APPENDIX

What's on the DVD?

This appendix provides you with information on the contents of the DVD that accompanies this book. For the latest and greatest information, please refer to the ReadMe file located at the root of the DVD. Here is what you will find in this appendix:

- ➤ System Requirements
- ➤ Using the DVD
- ➤ What's on the DVD
- ➤ Troubleshooting

SYSTEM REQUIREMENTS

Most reasonably up-to-date computers with a DVD drive should be able to play the screencasts that are included on the DVD. You may also find an Internet connection helpful for downloading updates to this book.

If your computer doesn't meet the following requirements, then you may have some problems using the software:

- ➤ PC running Windows XP, Windows Vista, Windows 7, or later
- ➤ A processor running at 1.6GHz or faster
- ➤ An Internet connection
- ➤ At least 1GB of RAM
- ➤ At least 3GB of available hard disk space
- ➤ A DVD-ROM drive

USING THE DVD

To access the content from the DVD, follow these steps:

1. Insert the DVD into your computer's DVD-ROM drive. The license agreement appears.

 The interface won't launch if you have autorun disabled. In that case, click Start ⇨ Run (for Windows 7, click Start ⇨ All Programs ⇨ Accessories ⇨ Run). In the dialog box that appears, type **D:\Start.exe**. *(Replace D with the proper letter if your DVD drive uses a different letter. If you don't know the letter, check how your DVD drive is listed under My Computer.) Click OK.*

2. Read through the license agreement, and then click the Accept button if you want to use the DVD.

    The DVD interface appears. Simply select the lesson number for the video you want to view.

WHAT'S ON THE DVD

Each of this book's lessons contains a Try It section that enables you to practice the concepts covered by that lesson. The Try It includes a high-level overview, requirements, and step-by-step instructions explaining how to build the example program.

This DVD contains video screencasts showing how to work through key pieces of the Try Its from each lesson. The audio explains what is happening step-by-step so you can see how the techniques described in the lesson translate into actions.

We recommend using the following steps when reading a lesson:

1. Read the lesson's text.

2. Read the Try It's overview, requirements, and hints.

3. Try to write a program that satisfies the requirements.

4. Read the step-by-step instructions. If the program you wrote doesn't satisfy all the requirements, use these instructions to improve it. Also look for places where my solution differs from yours. In programming there's always more than one way to solve a problem, and it's good to know about several different approaches.

5. Watch the screencast to see how we handle the key issues.

Sometimes a screencast mentions useful techniques and shortcuts that didn't fit in the book, so you may want to watch the screencast even if you feel completely confident about your solution.

You can also download all of the book's examples and solutions to the Try Its at the book's website.

Finally, if you're stuck and don't know what to do next, you can visit the p2p forums (p2p.wrox .com), locate the forum for the book, and leave a post.

TROUBLESHOOTING

If you have difficulty installing or using any of the materials on the companion DVD, try the following solutions:

➤ **Reboot if necessary.** As with many troubleshooting situations, it may make sense to reboot your machine to reset any faults in your environment.

➤ **Turn off any anti-virus software that you may have running.** Installers sometimes mimic virus activity and can make your computer incorrectly believe that it is being infected by a virus. (Be sure to turn the anti-virus software back on later.)

➤ **Close all running programs.** The more programs you're running, the less memory is available to other programs. Installers also typically update files and programs; if you keep other programs running, installation may not work properly.

➤ **Reference the ReadMe.** Please refer to the ReadMe file located at the root of the DVD for the latest product information at the time of publication.

CUSTOMER CARE

If you have trouble with the DVD, please call the Wiley Product Technical Support phone number at (800) 762-2974. Outside the United States, call 00+1(317) 572-3994. You can also contact Wiley Product Technical Support at `http://support.wiley.com`. John Wiley & Sons will provide technical support only for installation and other general quality control items. For technical support on the applications themselves, consult the program's vendor or author.

To place additional orders or to request information about other Wiley products, please call (877) 762-2974.

INDEX

INDEX

A

accounts
    Managed Accounts, 29–31
    unattended service account, 31
Active Directory, OU
  (Organizational Unit), 13
actuals, 189
ADFS (Active Directory Federated
  Services 2.0), 18
administration, PowerShell, 20
Administrative database, 333
Administrative Description, 303
AdventureWorks2008R2 database, 35
AJAX-driven search screen, 319
analysis features, 6
Analysis Services (PowerPivot), 7, 356–357
  Dashboard Designer, 180
  Excel and, 8
  Excel workbooks, 133–137
  reports, scorecard link, 213–221
  scorecard creation, 197–203
Analysis Services KPIs, 190
analysts, suggested programs, 362–363
analytic charts (PerformancePoint), 177
analytic grid (PerformancePoint), 177
Application Management section (CA), 24
  Site Collections, 26
application servers, 14
application structure
  Service Application, 17
  Service Application Connections, 17
  Service Application Database, 18
  Service Application Group, 16–17
  Service Application Services, 18
  Web Application, 16
applications
  Central Administration, 20–21
  Excel Services, creating, 41–42, 47–50
  PerformancePoint Services, 340–343
  service, 356
  SharePoint Timer Services, 356
  Target Application Type, 54–55
  Visio Services, 61–62
  web, 355
Approval template, 310
Approval workflow, 311
approving reports, 310
architecture, new features, 10
associations, 114–123
  custom list, 340–343
Auditing policy, 302
authentication
  claims based, 18–19
  classic mode, 19
  Excel Services, 43–45
  per-user, 53
  PerformancePoint Services,
    configuration, 52–55
  PowerPivot, 74–76
  Single Sign On, 33
  Visio Services, 63–64
  Windows Authentication, 32–33
Automatically Link feature (Visio), 156

B

Barcodes policy, 302
BCS (Business Connectivity Services)
 configuration, 108–111
 CRUD (Create/Read/Update/Delete),
  107
 description, 107
 design principles, 108
 installation, 108–111
 list, new, 111–114
BDC (Business Data Catalog), 107
BDC (Business Data Connectivity)
 Server, 25
BIDS (Business Intelligence Development
 Studio)
 reports, 252–256
  deployment to SharePoint, 257
 SharePoint deployment, 256–257
breadcrumbs, master pages, 284
budget, 349–350
business intelligence
 Analysis Services Service, 356–357
 exchange system, 358
 external data sources, 358
 focus of, 3
 governance, 299–300
 infrastructure, 355–360
 libraries, 92–93
 mail system, 358
 prototype, 4–6
 reporting lifecycle, 300–301
 service applications, 356
 SharePoint and, 3
 SharePoint Timer Services, 356
 sites, 92–93
 web applications, 355
Business Intelligence Center
 Excel workbook upload, 133–137
 template, 93
Business Intelligence Developer, 365

Business Intelligence Site Collection,
 building, 26–28
business liason, 366
business sponsor, 366

C

caching
 Excel Services, 46
 PerformancePoint Services, 55–56
 Visio Services, 64–65
Calculated Columns, 143–144
Calculated Measures, 144–145
 DAX and, 148–151
CBA (Claims Based Authentication), 18–19
Central Administration, 15–16
 accessing, 23
 applications, 20–21
 Applications Management section, 24
  Site Collections, 26
 BDC (Business Data Connectivity)
  Server, 25
 database, 333
 database, site content, 333
 Excel Services, 25
 PPS (PerformancePoint Services), 25
 Secure Store Service, 25
 Security, 29
 services, 20–21
 site management, 25–26
 tasks, categories, 23, 24
 Visio Graphic Services, 25
change control systems, 353
chart reports
 decomposition tree, 186–188
charts, PerformancePoint, 7
checklist, 368–369. *See* project checklist
Classic Mode Authentication, 94
CMA (Classic Mode Authentication), 19
collaboration, MS Office, 31–34
Collect Feedback template, 310

Collect Feedback workflow, 311
Collect Signatures template, 310
Collect Signatures workflow, 311
color, themes, 265–266
comparison filters, 113
concatenation, Calculated Columns, 143
configuration
    databases, optimization, 334
    Secure Store Target Application,
      testing, 76–78
Configuration database, 333
Configuration type (databases), 332, 333
connections
    embedded, 127–128
    linked, 127–128
Content type (databases), 332, 333
content types, external, 114–123
cores, requirements, 13
cost analysis report, 186–188
Crawl database, 333
crawls, populating indexes, 327–328
Create Site Collections link, 27
credentials, data refreshs, 171
CRUD (Create/Read/Update/Delete), 107
CSS (Cascading Style Sheets), master
  pages, 291–293
Custom MDX filter, 230–231
customization, 9

D

Dashboard Designer, data source, 180
dashboards
    parameters, 206
    PerformancePoint, 190
      building, 205–209
      filters, 224
      interactivity, 209–213
    scorecards, 213–221
    web part pages comparison, 205
    zones, 206

data, displaying, 130
    graphically, 131–132
    PivotTables, 130–131
    tables, 130
Data Connection Library, 130
    SQL Server Analysis Services
      filter and, 232
data connectivity, diagrams and, 153–156
data refreshes
    Excel Services, 168
    failure monitoring, 172
    PowerPivot, 170–172, 173–176
data sources
    creating, 128–130
    Excel Services, reporting, 127–130
    external, 358
Database Mirroring, 334
databases
    AdventureWorks2008R2, 35
    configuration, optimization, 334
    content, types, 332–334
    double hop, 52
    optimization
      configuration, 334
      Logging, 334–335
      Service Application, 335
    overview, 331–332
    read-intensive, 334–335
    spreadsheet architect, 335–336
    Web Part packages, 333
    write-intensive, 334–335
DAX (Data Analysis Expressions), 143–145
    Calculated Columns, 143–144
    Calculated Measures, 144–145,
      148–151
    functions, 143
decomposition tree (PerformancePoint),
  178, 186–188
deployment
    BIDS SharePoint deployment,
      256–257

deployment *(continued)*
  diagrams (Visio), 157–158
  reports, 300–301
    BIDS to SharePoint, 257
    Excel Services, 132–133
    to library, 258–262
  strategy maps, 244, 245–249
developers, suggested programs, 362
diagrams
  data connectivity and, 153–156
  Visio
    deploying, 157–158
    interactive, 156–157
Disposition Approval
  template, 310
document library, site collection
  policy, 304–307
double hop, 52
drill-through capabilities, 7
drivers, priority drivers, 347–350
  hosting, 352
  infrastructure, 352
  integrated systems,
    352–353
  requirements, 351
  security, 350–351
  stakeholders, 351–352
DVD accompanying book
  accessing content, 372
  contents, 372
  customer care, 373
  system requirements, 371
  troubleshooting, 373

E

e-mail, servers, 14
embedded connections, 127–128
encryption
  Farm PassPhrase, 13
  proxy accounts, 10
end-user technology, 361–363
end users, stakeholders, 348
enterprise applications, 353
Enterprise Features, enabling, 51
environment, sandbox, 300
Event Viewer, master merge, 323
Excel
  Analysis Services and, 8
  workbooks
    Analysis Services cube,
      133–137
    best practices, 34–35
    importing/exporting, 31–32
    sharing, 133
Excel Services, 25
  applications, creating, 41–42,
    47–50
  authentication, configuration,
    43–45
  caching, 46
  data refreshes, implementing,
    168–170
  enabling, 42–43
  libraries, trusted connection, 44
  reporting, 46
    data sources, 127–130
    deploying reports, 132–133
    PerformancePoint, 179–180
  security, configuration, 43–45
  workbooks, storage, 44
Excel Services Applications
  options, 20–21
  scaling, 339
  tuning, 339
exchange system, 358
executives, suggested programs, 363
Expiration policy, 302
extending search configuration, 326–327
external content types, 114–123
external data sources, 358
external lists, 114–123

F

Farm Configuration Wizard,
  PerformancePoint Services, 51
Farm PassPhrase, 13
farm server requirements, 14
FAST Search, servers, 14
FAST Search Server 2010 for Internet Sites,
  320, 321
FAST Search Server 2010 for SharePoint,
  320, 321
FAST Server, 319
filters
    comparison filters, 113
    Custom MDX, 230–231
    KPIs, 192–193
    Member Selection, 228–230
    Named Set, 230
    PerformancePoint, 190, 223
    PerformancePoint Dashboards, 7
    Product Category, 234–240
    Query String, 232
    SharePoint, 223
    SQL Server Analysis Services, 232–234
    TI (Time Intelligence), 192–193,
      225–228, 234–240
financial data, business intelligence
  and, 4–5
fonts, themes, 265–266
formatting, scorecards, 194–197
From Other Sources Wizard, 130

G

galleries (PowerPivot), reports, 145–147
Geneva framework, 18
Geneva Server, 18
Global Navigation, 270
governance, 299–300
government data, business intelligence and, 6
GPO (Group Policy Objects), 13
graphic display of data, 131–132

H

hard disk requirements, 13
healthcare data, business intelligence
  and, 5–6
hosting, priority drivers, 352

I

identity, tokens, 18
images, themes, 268
indexes, populating, 327–328
infrastructure
    business intelligence,
      355–360
    priority drivers, 352
installation
    BCS, 108–111
    Farm PassPhrase, 13
    PerformancePoint Services,
      56–59
    Secure Store Services, 56–59
    SharePoint, requirements, 69
    SQL Server
      requirements, 69
      standalone, 70
    SQL Server PowerPivot for
      SharePoint, 70–71
    standalone, 78–85
Installation Rule dialog, 81
integrated mode, Reporting Services,
  99–101
integrated systems, 352–353
interactive diagrams (Visio),
  156–157
interfaces, Touch-Screen, 270
Internet search, 319–320
Issue Tracking template, 310

J

joins, Calculated Columns, 144

K

Kerberos, 53–55
KPA (Key Performance Area), 189
KPIs (Key Performance Indicators), 25, 189
    Analysis Services KPIs, 190
    creating, 190–192
    details reports (PerformancePoint), 180
    filtering, 192–193

L

Labels policy, 302
LDAP (Lightweight Directory Access
    Protocol), ADFS and, 18
liason, business, 366
libraries
    business intelligence, 92–93
    creating, 93–97
    Data Connection, 130
    document site collection policy, 304–307
    Report, 93
    report deployment to, 258–262
    trusted connection, 44, 128
licensing, 361
limit parameters, 113
linked connections, 127–128
lists, external, 114–123
LOB (Line of Business), 107
Logging type (databases), 332
    optimization, 334–335

M

mail system, 358
Managed Accounts, configuration, 29–31
manufacturing data, business intelligence
    and, 5
many-to-one relationships, Calculated
    Columns, 144
master pages
    CSS, 291–293

    customizing, 293–298
    placeholders, 281–282
    SharePoint Designer, 280,
      282–290
      placeholders, 283–285
    zones, 281
Matrix reports, 254
Maximum Unused Object Age value, 46
MDX, members, 274
Member Selection filters, 228–230
Memory Cache Threshold, 46
metrics, 189
    viewing, 301–304
MS Office, collaboration, 31–34

N

Named Set filter, 230
navigation
    editing, 270
    Global Navigation, 270
    master pages, 284
New Visio Graphics Service Application
    wizard, 62
Note Boards, 211

O

objectives, 189
ODC (Office Data Connection), files, 169
Office
    integration, 7–9
    Ribbon, 15–16
Office Data Connection, files, 127
operations, BCS, 108
optimization
    configuration databases, 334
    databases
      Logging, 334–335
      Service Application, 335
OU (Organizational Unit), 13

P

parameters
  connections, 206
  dashboards, 206
  limit parameters, 113
  URLs, 274
partner data sources and systems, 353
passwords, Farm PassPhrase, 13
per-user authentication, 53
PerformancePoint
  actuals, 189
  dashboard, 190
    building, 205–209
    filters, 7, 224
    interactivity, 209
  filters, 190, 223
    dashboard, 224
  KPAs (Key Performance Area), 189
  KPIs (Key Performance Indicators), 189
  metrics, 189
  objectives, 189
  reports, 190
    analytic charts, 177
    analytic grid, 177
    creating, 180–183
    decomposition tree, 178
    Excel Services, 179–180
    extending, 183–186
    KPI details, 180
    ProClarity Analytics Server
      Page, 180
    Reporting Services, 180
    show details, 178–179
    strategy maps, 180
    web page, 180
  scorecards, 190
    formatting, 194–197
    sources, 193–194
  strategy maps, 241–242
  targets, 189

PerformancePoint Dashboard Designer,
  strategy maps, 242
PerformancePoint Services, 7
  applications, custom, 340–343
  authentication, 52–55
  caching, 55–56
  configuration, 56–59
  enabling, 51–52
  installation, 56–59
  reporting, 55–56
  security, 52–55
  unattended service account, 35–38
PerformancePoint SSA, tuning, 338–339
phases of schedule, 367–368
PivotDiagrams, 154, 155
  customer demographics and, 159–164
  PivotDiagram wizard, 154
PivotTables, 130–131
placeholders, master pages, 281–282
  SharePoint Designer, 283–285
planning schedule, 366
  rollout, 363–364
policies, 302
  Administrative Description, 303
  Policy Statement, 303
  site collection, 304–307
populating indexes, 327–328
PowerPivot
  authentication, 74–76
  data refreshes, 173–176
    scheduling, 170–172
  reports, 140–142, 148–151
    deploying, 145–147
  scaling, 339–340
  service applications, creating, 72–73
  SharePoint sites, 73–74
  tuning, 339–340
  workbooks
    deploying to gallery, 78–85
PowerPivot for Excel, 139
PowerPivot for SharePoint, 139

PowerPivot Management Dashboard
   data refresh, failures, 172
   viewing, 172
PowerPivot Solution, deploying, to
  SharePoint, 72
PowerPoint themes, creating, 265–270
PowerShell administration, 20
PPS (PerformancePoint Services), 25
priority drivers, 347–350
   people
      security, 350–351
      stakeholders, 351–352
   system
      hosting, 352
      infrastructure, 352
      integrated, 352–353
   systems
      requirements, 351
      security, 350–351
ProClarity Analytics Server Page
  (PerformancePoint), 180
Product Category filter, 234–240
Profile database, 333
project checklist, 368–369
   knowledge base, 365–366
   sample, 367
   schedule phases, 367–368
   schedule planning, 366
   skill set, 365–366
project managers, suggested programs, 363
Property database, 334
proxy accounts, encrypted data, 10
Publishing Approval workflow, 311

Q

Query Builder, 254
Query Response Time, 301
Query String filters, 232
Quick Launch menu, master pages, 283

R

RAM requirements, 13
read-intensive databases, 333–335
Report Builder, 251–252
   opening, 252
Report library, 93
Report Server
   native mode to SharePoint integration,
     103–106
Report Server Database Configuration
  Wizard, 100
Report Wizard, 253
reporting
   Excel Services, 46
      data sources, 127–130
      deploying reports, 132–133
   lifecycle, 300–301
   PerformancePoint, 7
   PerformancePoint Services, 55–56
   PowerPivot, deploying reports, 145–147
   Visio Services, 64–65
Reporting Services, 180
   add-in, configuration, 102
   configuration, 99
      testing, 103
   integrated mode, 99–101
   reports
      creating, 251–256
      deployment to SharePoint library,
       258–262
Reporting Services add-in for Microsoft
  SharePoint Technologies 2010, 104
reports
   Analysis Services scorecard link,
     213–221
   approval, 310
      workflow building, 311–313,
       315–318
   BIDS (Business Intelligence Development
     Studio), 252–256

cost analysis, 186–188
deploying, 300–301
    BIDS to SharePoint, 257
    to SharePoint library, 258–262
Matrix, 254
Note Boards, 211
PerformancePoint, 190
    analytic charts, 177
    analytic grid, 177
    creating, 180–183
    decomposition tree, 178
    Excel Services, 179–180
    extending, 183
    KPI details, 180
    ProClarity Analytics Server Page, 180
    Reporting Services, 180
    show details, 178–179
    strategy maps, 180
    web pages, 180
PowerPivot, 140–142, 148–151
Query Builder, 254
Solution Explorer, 253
Tabular, 254
uploading, 132
Require Content Approval option, 309
Resource Governor, 358
retail data, business intelligence and, 5
Ribbon, 15–16, 20–21
    SharePoint Designer, 279, 286
rollout planning, 363–364

S

sandbox environment, 300
scaling, 337
    Excel Services Applications, 339
    PowerPivot, 339–340
schedule phases, 367–368
schedule planning, 366
scorecards, 190
    creating, 197–203

dashboards, 213–221
formatting, 194–197
sources, 193–194
Search Server, 320
    configuration, 327–328
Search type (databases), 332
    Administrative database, 333
    Crawl database, 333
    Property database, 333
searches. *See also* Internet search; SharePoint
Search
    AJAX-driven screen, 319
    configuration, extending, 326–327
    FAST Search Server 2010 for Internet
      Sites, 320, 321
    FAST Search Server 2010 for SharePoint,
      320, 321
    master pages, 284
    Search Server, 320
    security trimming, 326
    SharePoint Foundation Search, 320,
      321–324
    SharePoint Search 2010, 320–321
      administration, 321
      improvements, 321
      Social Search, 320–321
    SharePoint Server, 320
    site search administration, 326–327
Secure Store Service, 10, 25, 63
    configuration, 56–59
    installation, 56–59
Secure Store Target Application,
  configuration, 76–78
security
    authentication
      claims based, 18–19
      classic mode, 19
    Central Administration, 29
    Excel Services, 43–45
    Farm PassPhrase, 13

security *(continued)*
    Managed Accounts, 29–31
    PerformancePoint Services,
      configuration, 52–55
    priority drivers, 350–351
    Visio Services, 63–64
security trimming (searches), 326
server administrator, suggested
  programs, 363
servers
    application, 14
    e-mail, 14–15
    Farm PassPhrase, 13
    FAST Search, 14
    requirements, 14
    SQL, 14
    Web front-end, 14
Service Application, 17
Service Application Connections, 17
Service Application Database, 18
Service Application Group, 16–17
Service Application Services, 18
Service Application type (databases), 332, 333
    optimization, 335
service applications, 356
Shared Service Provider, 10
SharePoint
    BIDS (Business Intelligence Development
      Studio), deployment, 256–257
    filters, 223
    installation, requirements, 69
    reports, deployment from BIDS, 257
SharePoint Designer
    design surface, 279
    master pages, 280, 282–290
      placeholders, 283–285
    ribbon, 279, 286
SharePoint Foundation Search, 320, 321–324
    configuration, 322–324
SharePoint Products Configuration
  Wizard, 79

SharePoint Search 2010, 320–321
    administration, 321
    improvements, 321
    Social Search, 320–321
SharePoint Search versions, 320
SharePoint Server, 320
SharePoint Server Administrator, 365
SharePoint Timer Services, 356
SharePoint_AdminContent, 333
SharePoint_Config, 333
sharing Excel workbooks, 133
show details (PerformancePoint), 178–179
Single Sign On, 33
site collection policy, 304–307
Site Collections, 26, 87–89
    creating, 93–97
site management, 25–26
site search administration, 326–327
sites, 87–89
    business intelligence, 92–93
    creating, 89–91, 93–97
    navigating, 270–274
    templates, 91–92
    title, master pages, 283
sizing concerns, 360–361
Social Database, 333
Social Search, 320–321
Solution Explorer, reports, 253
sponsor, business, 366
spreadsheets
    SharePoint SQL Server database,
      335–336
    stakeholder discussions, 353–354
SQL (Structured Query Language),
  servers, 14
SQL Server, installation
    requirements, 69
    standalone, 70
SQL Server Analysis Services, 139.
  See Analysis Services
    filter, 232–234

SQL Server DBA, 365
SQL Server PowerPivot for SharePoint, 70–71
SQL Server Reporting Services, report storage, 93
SQL Server Views for Visio, 155
SSAs (SharePoint Service Applications)
    Excel Services Applications
        scaling, 339
        tuning, 339
    PerformancePoint, tuning, 338–339
    PowerPivot
        scaling, 339–340
        tuning, 339–340
    scaling, 337
SSP (Shared Service Providers), 16–18
SSS (Single Sign On), 33
stakeholders, 348, 351–352
    spreadsheet for discussions, 353–354
standalone installation, 70, 78–85
storage, sizing concerns, 360–361
STP (Simple Time Protocol), 192–193
    reference sheet, 226
strategy maps, 180
    creating, 242–244
    deploying, 244
    reasons for, 241–242
    testing, 244
    Visio, 241–243
        deployment to site, 245–249
Synchronization database, 333
system requirements
    32-bit version, 13
    DVD accompanying book, 371

T

tables
    data display, 130
    PivotTables, 130–131
Tabular reports, 254

Target Application Type, 54–55
targets, 189
templates, 310–311
    Business Intelligence Center, 93
    sites, 91–92
testing, strategy maps, 244
Theme Gallery, 267–268
    uploading themes, 274–278
themes
    creating, 265–270
    images, 268
    overview, 265
    previewing, 268
    uploading to Theme Gallery, 274–278
Three-State template, 311
TI (Time Intelligence) filter, 192–193, 225–228
ticket tracking systems, 353
Time Intelligence
    filter, 234–240
    formulas, 199
time-series visualization of workbook activity, 301
tokens, identity, 18
Touch-Screen interfaces, enabling, 270
Translation Management template, 311
trusted connection libraries, 44
tuning
    Excel Services Applications, 339
    PerformancePoint SSA, 338–339
    PowerPivot, 339–340

U

Unattended Service Account, 10, 31, 35–38, 55–56, 63
    mapping, 66
uploading, reports, 132
    Theme Gallery, 274–278
URLEncoding, 274

URLs (Uniform Resource Locators)
    parameters, 274
    Query String Filters, 232
Usage and Health Data Collection
    database, 332
user experience, databases, 333
User Profile Service
    Application_ProfileDB_, 333
User Profile Service
    Application_SocialDB_, 333
User Profile Service
    Application_SyncDB_, 333
users
    analyst, 362
    developer, 362
    executives, 363
    project managers, 363
    server administrator, 363

V

Visio
    diagrams
        deploying, 157–158
        interactive, 156–157
    PivotDiagram, 155
    SQL Server Views for Visio, 155
    strategy maps and, 241–243
        deployment to site, 245–249
    workflows, building, 313–314
Visio Access Web part, 61
Visio Graphic Services, 25
Visio Services, 8, 153
    applications, creating,
      61–62, 65–68
    authentication, configuration,
      63–64
    caching, 64–65
    diagrams, data connectivity and,
      153–156
    enabling, 62–63

reporting, 64–65
    security, configuration, 63–64
Visio Web Drawings, 61

W

Web Application, 16
web applications, 87–89, 355
    creating, 93–97
Web front-end servers, 14
web pages (PerformancePoint), 180
Web Part packages, 333
Web Parts, 93
web parts pages, dashboards
    comparison, 205
WIF (Windows Identity Foundation), 18
Windows Authentication, 32–33, 63
Windows CardSpace 2.0, 18
Windows Resource Manager, 358
wizards
    Farm Configuration, 51
    New Visio Graphics Service
      Application, 62
    From Other Sources, 130
    Report Server Database
      Configuration, 100
    Report Wizard, 253
    SharePoint Products Configuration
      Wizard, 79
workbooks
    Excel
      activity, 301
      Analysis Services cube, 133–137
      sharing, 133
      storage, 44
    PowerPivot, deploying to gallery,
      78–85
workflow
    benefits, 309–310
    global, 311
    goals, 310

pre-made, 311
report approval, building, 311–313, 315–318
Require Content Approval option, 309
Visio, building, 313–314
write-intensive databases, 334–335
WSS_UsageApplication database, 332

Z

zones
dashboards, 206
master pages, 281

WILEY PUBLISHING, INC.
END-USER LICENSE AGREEMENT

READ THIS. You should carefully read these terms and conditions before opening the software packet(s) included with this book "Book". This is a license agreement "Agreement" between you and Wiley Publishing, Inc. "WPI". By opening the accompanying software packet(s), you acknowledge that you have read and accept the following terms and conditions. If you do not agree and do not want to be bound by such terms and conditions, promptly return the Book and the unopened software packet(s) to the place you obtained them for a full refund.

1. **License Grant.** WPI grants to you (either an individual or entity) a nonexclusive license to use one copy of the enclosed software program(s) (collectively, the "Software") solely for your own personal or business purposes on a single computer (whether a standard computer or a workstation component of a multi-user network). The Software is in use on a computer when it is loaded into temporary memory (RAM) or installed into permanent memory (hard disk, CD-ROM, or other storage device). WPI reserves all rights not expressly granted herein.

2. **Ownership.** WPI is the owner of all right, title, and interest, including copyright, in and to the compilation of the Software recorded on the physical packet included with this Book "Software Media". Copyright to the individual programs recorded on the Software Media is owned by the author or other authorized copyright owner of each program. Ownership of the Software and all proprietary rights relating thereto remain with WPI and its licensers.

3. **Restrictions on Use and Transfer.**

   (a) You may only (i) make one copy of the Software for backup or archival purposes, or (ii) transfer the Software to a single hard disk, provided that you keep the original for backup or archival purposes. You may not (i) rent or lease the Software, (ii) copy or reproduce the Software through a LAN or other network system or through any computer subscriber system or bulletin-board system, or (iii) modify, adapt, or create derivative works based on the Software.

   (b) You may not reverse engineer, decompile, or disassemble the Software. You may transfer the Software and user documentation on a permanent basis, provided that the transferee agrees to accept the terms and conditions of this Agreement and you retain no copies. If the Software is an update or has been updated, any transfer must include the most recent update and all prior versions.

4. **Restrictions on Use of Individual Programs.** You must follow the individual requirements and restrictions detailed for each individual program in the "About the CD" appendix of this Book or on the Software Media. These limitations are also contained in the individual license agreements recorded on the Software Media. These limitations may include a requirement that after using the program for a specified period of time, the user must pay a registration fee or discontinue use. By opening the Software packet(s), you agree to abide by the licenses and restrictions for these individual programs that are detailed in the "About the CD" appendix and/or on the Software Media. None of the material on this Software Media or listed in this Book may ever be redistributed, in original or modified form, for commercial purposes.